:ABHARLANNA CHONTAE FHINE G/

FINGAL COUNTY LIBRARIES~~BALDOY~~

STORE ~~LIBRAF~~
~~Ph. 890~~

~~ıld be~~   ~~r b~~ ~~the~~
~~s may~~   ~~y~~
~~ND: SP/~~   ~~Text, Time~~

IRELAND:
SPACE, TEXT, TIME

Edited by
Liam Harte, Yvonne Whelan and *Patrick Crotty*

The Liffey Press

Published by
The Liffey Press
Ashbrook House
10 Main Street, Raheny,
Dublin 5, Ireland
www.theliffeypress.com

A catalogue record of this book is
available from the British Library.

ISBN 1-904148-83-2

Special Acknowledgement

This publication was grant aided by the
Academy for Irish Cultural Heritages, University of Ulster

Printed in Ireland by ColourBooks Ltd.

Contents

3. Negotiating Migrant and Diaspora Spaces

Contributors

Ruth Barton, O'Kane Senior Research Fellow, Centre for Film Studies, University College Dublin

Richard Danson Brown, Lecturer in English, Literature Department, The Open University

Thomas Byrne, Department of History, National University of Ireland, Maynooth

Patrick Crotty, Professor of Irish and Scottish Literary History, School of Languages and Literature, University of Aberdeen

Terry Eagleton, Professor of Cultural Theory and John Rylands Fellow, School of Arts, Histories and Cultures, University of Manchester

Borbála Faragó, Department of English, University College Dublin

Liam Harte, Lecturer in Irish and Modern Literature, School of Arts, Histories and Cultures, University of Manchester

Róisín Higgins, Postdoctoral Scholar, Humanities Research Institute, University College Dublin

Seán Kennedy, Department of English, National University of Ireland, Galway

Brian Lambkin, Director, Centre for Migration Studies at the Ulster-American Folk Park, Omagh

Elizabeth Malcolm, Gerry Higgins Chair of Irish Studies, Department of History, University of Melbourne

Aidan McQuillan, Associate Professor of Geography, Department of Geography, University of Toronto

Tony Murray, Deputy Director, Irish Studies Centre, London Metropolitan University

Máirín Ní Cheallaigh, Department of Archaeology, University College Dublin

Loredana Salis, School of Languages and Literature, University of Ulster at Coleraine

Julie Anne Stevens, Lecturer in English, Department of English, St. Patrick's College, Dublin

Catherine Switzer, Academy for Irish Cultural Heritages, University of Ulster

Charles Travis, Department of Geography, Trinity College Dublin

Derval Tubridy, Lecturer in English, Department of English and Comparative Literature, Goldsmith's College, University of London

Bronwen Walter, Professor of Irish Diaspora Studies, Department of Geography, Anglia Polytechnic University

James Ward, School of English, University of Leeds

Yvonne Whelan, Lecturer in Human Geography, School of Geographical Sciences, University of Bristol

Introduction

Liam Harte

Ireland has long been a debatable land, both literally and meta-phorically, an anomalous space open to multiple readings and conflicting interpretations. Joep Leerssen's remark that the country has been seen since the Act of Union as "a mystery: something to be explained, an *explicandum*" (Leerssen, 1996: 38) is also applicable to much earlier periods. Indeed, some of the most provocative projections of Ireland's ambiguity are found in English commentaries from the Elizabethan era. While the most celebrated of these are textual – Shakespeare's *Henry V*, Spenser's *A View of the Present State of Ireland* – early modern cartographic engagements with Ireland's spatial otherness are no less remarkable for their portrayal of the island as a site of manifest savagery, shadowy sedition and connived-at subjugation. One of the most suggestive cartographic expressions of such prejudices is reproduced on the cover of this book. Baptista Boazio's *Irelande* marked a significant new departure in map-making when it was published in London in September 1599, being "the earliest English printed map of Ireland with any pretensions to detail" (Andrews, 1970: 29). But whereas cartographic historians have criticised both Boazio and his engraver, Renold Elstrack, for their geographical laxity and decorative excess, literary scholars have related these very same qualities to the characteristically anxious rhetoric of colonisation, seeing them as evidence of Ireland's destabilising impact on the cultural integrity of the Tudor state.

Two particular cartographic details bring these divergent readings into sharp focus. In the bottom right-hand corner of the map, positioned mid-way between Dunineny Castle and Rathlin Island, lies a tiny outcrop named "Baptistes rock". This imaginary protrusion has a geographical correlative at the north-western tip of Ulster, where "Elstrakes Ile" nestles among an island archipelago off the coast of Tyrconnell. To the geographer J.H. Andrews, these embellishments are "frivolities [...] of which the best that can be said is that they are one way of hinting at how little was known of the geography of northern Ulster at the time when Boazio's model was being put together" (Andrews, 1970: 32). The literary historian Bernhard Klein, conversely, reads them as spatial metaphors of Ireland's capriciousness in the English colonial mind, its oscillation between visibility and obscurity, fact and fiction: "Boazio's and Elstrack's names function as a kind of geographical signature, an eccentric gesture perhaps, but one that capitalizes on Ireland's status as the property of those that give it visual and verbal presence in maps and texts" (Klein, 2001: 117).

The subsequent history of literary and visual culture in Ireland may be understood as the elaborate working out of a struggle for representational mastery and control, one inflected at every turn by a complicated history of colonisation and resistance. As Boazio's sly cartographic interpolations suggest, the process of naming assumes profound political significance in such circumstances; space becomes place through a complex interaction of orality and textualisation over time. So intimately are language and power, history and geography interrelated, indeed, that "in some sense place *is* language, something in constant flux, a discourse in process" (Ashcroft *et al.*, 1998: 182, original emphasis). Identity, in this perspective, appears as adaptive and contestatory, continually reiterated, endlessly argued over.

No Irish place better embodies this discursive dynamic than Derry/Londonderry. Originally established as a sixth-century monastic site associated with St Columba, the small settlement of Derry was spectacularly transformed into a walled town during the Jacobean plantation of Ulster which commenced ten years after the publication of Boazio's map. When a British colony was established there as part of the plantation, "Derry" – itself an anglicised form of *doire*, meaning "oak wood" – was renamed "Londonderry" in 1613, in honour of the London merchant companies which funded the project, and so began the development of its "chronic dual personality" (McMahon, 2002: viii). Four centuries years later, the name of the city is still a matter of dispute, so that to live there is, in a sense, to dwell in contradiction, to be aware of "the coexistence of two places in the same space" (Smyth, 2001: 137). In Seamus Deane's view, such schizophrenia makes Derry an archetypal Irish space:

> Its two names – Derry/Londonderry; its two communities; its history of siege; its absorption of the effects of violence and economic demoralisation along with economic subsidy; the contrast between its beautiful setting and its ruined cityscape; and above all, its isolation, allow a visitor-native like myself to see it as a place small enough to be understood and big enough to be typical of others, as the North's, maybe the whole island's exemplary town. (Deane, 1983: 18)

What better location, then, in which to host a conference devoted to an exploration of the ways in which discourses of time, space and textuality have shaped understandings of issues of place and identity in Irish culture and society, past and present.

The "Ireland: Space, Text, Time" conference took place over three days in March 2004 at the Magee campus of the University of Ulster, under the auspices of the Academy for Irish Cultural Heritages. At a time when old allegiances of territory, community and class are being transformed by the effects of far-reaching political, social and economic changes, the Academy felt this to be an appropriate moment at which to assess the cultural and material manifestations of such transformations, both within and without the island of Ireland. The conference title acknowledged the prevalence of metaphors of space and time in literary, academic and popular discourses of identity, and invited papers on specific embodiments of these constructs, as well as on their conceptual potential and limitations. The conference's openness to diverse empirical and theoretical approaches was signalled by the choice of keynote speakers: the historians T.M. Devine and Elizabeth Malcolm, the cultural theorist Terry Eagleton, the writer John McGahern and the geographer Bronwen Walter. The response to our call for papers was hearteningly enthusiastic, enabling us to produce a programme that brought together young and established scholars to explore textual, spatial and temporal constructions of identity from a variety of disciplinary perspectives.

The conference itself began with a lively plenary session on the theory and practice of interdisciplinarity, with particular emphasis on its application within Irish historical and cultural studies. Endorsements of the creative possibilities opened up by a more flexible and self-reflexive attitude to disciplinary divisions were tempered by expressions of scepticism about the practical uses of interdisciplinarity as a methodological principle of teaching and research. To a large extent, this opening debate set the tone for the sessions that followed, the flavour of which this volume seeks to capture. In editing this selection of papers for publication, Patrick Crotty, Yvonne Whelan and I have tried to preserve the brevity, accessibility and freshness of the original presentations, while reconfiguring them into three broadly thematic clusters. This clustering emerged organically as we read and reflected upon the submitted papers, and even though we remain conscious of the many overlaps between the sectional boundaries we have set, we trust that readers will be stimulated as much by the book's critical and conceptual divergences as by its continuities and correspondences.

The papers in the opening section, "Landscape, Heritage, Memory", are generally concerned with the contested nature of history and memory in their material and textual manifestations. The section begins with a disquisition on the politics of forgetfulness by Terry Eagleton, in which he points up the need for nations to utilise rather than repudiate or repress the past. To move forward we must look back, he insists, but not to the extent that we become fossilised in an attitude of retrospection. This thesis provides a suggestive point of reference for several of the papers that follow, especially those dealing with Irish commemorative practices. Political and cultural contexts are, of course, crucial to any consideration of the nature and function of remembrance, as the papers by Máirín Ní Cheallaigh, Roisín Higgins and Catherine Switzer attest. All three are alert to the fact that acts of historical reclamation and public commemoration are seldom one-directional; while words and images can be set in stone, their meanings are much more difficult to stabilise. Thus, Higgins's assertion that nationalist memorials such as Dublin's Garden of Remembrance resist singular interpretation is echoed by Switzer's discussion of the interpretive openness of memorials to members of the security forces in Northern Ireland. Themes of fixity and flux are also central to Derval Tubridy's analysis of temporal and topographic tropes in the work of Thomas Kinsella and James Joyce. Paying close attention to intertextual lines of descent, she shows how both authors reconstitute Dublin as a vibrantly diachronic streetscape in which myth and history are interrogated in those moments when the shifting gaze of their peripatetic personae meets the fixed stare of statued figures.

Several of these thematic concerns resurface in the next section, "Geographies of Belonging", which opens with Elizabeth Malcolm's reflections on teaching Irish studies in different places and times. Using her own pedagogical odyssey as a navigational tool, she charts the subtle but significant ways in which location changes the angles of perception and response of student and teacher alike. This theme of the power of place to alter perspectives is obliquely recapitulated in the two papers on Samuel Beckett, a seemingly placeless writer whose abstract landscapes are in fact deeply coloured by his formative years in, and subsequent flight from, Ireland. Charles Travis explores Beckett's interrogation of the Cartesian spatial paradigm in his London-based novel *Murphy*, while Seán Kennedy uses the suggestive concept of a "topographical imaginary" as a lens through which to discuss Beckett's vexed relationship to his native place. The distinction Kennedy sketches between the playwright's astringent distaste for the culture of the Irish Free State and his residual affection for Irish landscapes is powerfully amplified in the work of that other great artist of exilic Protestant nostalgia, Louis MacNeice, whose critical and creative dialogue with W.B. Yeats is subtly explored by Richard Danson Brown. And in a further intertextual twist, Loredana Salis's use of "insularity discourse" to examine the trope of in-betweenness, as personified by Philoctetes, in works by Sydney Bernard Smith and Seamus Heaney, calls to mind Yeats and MacNeice's shared fascination for islands, both real and imagined, as enchanted spaces between myth and history.

The manifold personal and cultural implications of migration and displacement are explored further in the third section of the book, which focuses on the still emergent field of Irish diaspora studies. Bronwen Walters's skilful elaboration of the hybrid forms of Irishness embedded in the seemingly homogenous "diaspora space" of England makes effective use of all three of the conference's analytical categories. Her emphasis on the potential of mixed identities to disrupt essentialising narratives of Britishness resonates with Thomas Byrne's analysis of the trouble caused by the transgressive political affiliations of the eighteenth-century adventurer Nathaniel Hooke. However, as Aidan McQuillan's account of the violent tensions that characterised relations between Irish Catholics and Protestants in nineteenth-century Quebec reminds us, emigration can strengthen as well as soften inherited narratives of identity. Plural forms of identification are not an automatic consequence of leaving home, any more than staying put guarantees immunity from the depredations of displacement. That Irish diasporic culture is about routes as much as roots is amply borne out by Ruth Barton's analysis of the way films featuring songs of Irish migration helped foster a sense of commonality between audiences at home and abroad, and by Tony Murray's examination of use of the Cúchulainn myth as an emblem of masculinity in fictional accounts of Irish navvy culture in England.

Taken together, then, these essays comprise a diverse set of explorations of the many ways in which Irish identities have been shaped and contested at the multiple intersections of temporal, spatial and textual discourses. No book or conference on such a capacious theme can do more than offer a partial and fragmentary series of insights and analyses, in the hope of generating further discussion and research. Such, ultimately, is our modest ambition for this volume. To try to wring a consensus from the papers reproduced here would be futile, given the breadth of critical, theoretical and ideological perspectives they encompass. Nevertheless, just as Terry Eagleton's assertion that history is not a monolithic phenomenon supplies an appropriate prologue to the book, Elizabeth Malcolm's summative observation that "Ireland is an unstable entity and *what* it is depends very much on *who* you are, *where* you are and *when* you are" serves as its fitting conclusion.

Part 1

Landscape, Heritage, Memory

1

History, Remembrance and Oblivion

Terry Eagleton

The distinctiveness of the human species has been described in many different ways — we are the speaking animal, the laughing animal, the sartorial animal, the neurotic animal — but we might do worse in the end than call ourselves the amnesiac animal. It is one of the more disquieting claims of modernity that amnesia is essential to our make-up, that without a necessary self-oblivion we just would not be able to operate. And this is entirely different from the thinking of what we might risk calling pre-modern society, for which, broadly speaking, it is the past that makes you what you are. Becoming a person in pre-modern conditions means, roughly speaking, doing what your ancestors did (it is known as tradition), whereas assuming an identity in (post)modern conditions, means, roughly speaking, not doing what your ancestors did.

To this extent, modernity is a kind of adolescent rebellion, an Oedipal strike against the Fathers. For pre-modernity, what makes the present what it is is the fact that it is more or less in line with the past, so that revolutionary innovation would be unthinkable. God must surely have revealed all the most important truths to us from the outset, since he would not be so remiss as to neglect revealing doctrines essential for our salvation. In this sense, there can be strictly speaking no new truth, just as for the Muslim tradition all writing after the Koran is derivative and supplementary. By contrast, what makes the present what it is for modernity and postmodernity is the fact that it has broken with the past, crawled out from under it, shaken off the nightmare of history, burst audaciously through the symbolic order to come eyeball-to-eyeball with the Real. Everything up to ten minutes ago is relegated to tradition, to be discarded in the search for originality and self-invention. On this view, the past is just raw material for your self-fashioning.

Ironically, the idea that authenticity means breaking with history has a very long history. Even the word "modern" comes to us from classical antiquity. Few things are more venerable than the modern. One might even see history as a series of failed efforts to break with history. Such brashly avant-garde projects are bound to be self-defeating, since the act of trying to break with the past is itself an historical event, and so simply piles on more historical material to the very history you are trying to escape. We can indeed transform our situation; but the truth is that since the past is what we are made of, we can do so only by using the few poor compromised, contaminated instruments which it has handed down to us. Unlike the Irishman in the anti-Irish joke who is asked the best way to get to the railway station, we have to start from where we are.

Even in revolutionary situations, there is far more of the old than the new around. History is for the most part continuity even in turbulent times. This is not necessarily to be regretted, however, since only postmodernists and infantile ultra-leftists imagine that there is something sinister and uncool about continuity as such. They would thus presumably object vociferously to a century or so of unbroken peace and plenty. In any case, a total transformation would be logically unintelligible, since if it succeeded in transforming the past out of existence we would have no yardstick with which to measure its originality, or even to identify it *as* a change. Change, however radical, must imply a degree of continuity, otherwise we would be unable to say what exactly had changed. We would simply be stuck with a series of disconnected moments, as goldfish are (perhaps dubiously) said to be. (There is also what one might call the Goldfish Theory of History, for which history is a series of discontinuous presents.)

Philosophical modernism, however, holds that by far the best way to treat the past is to repress it. The way to shuck off the burden of history, which as Marx comments in *The 18th Brumaire of Louis Bonaparte* (1852) weighs like a nightmare on the brains of the living, is to "let the dead bury their dead" — to turn time around and "draw one's poetry from the future" rather than from the past. The socialist revolution, that is to say, must act as its own model, spring from its own head, rather than conform to existing paradigms. In other moods, Marx is rather less briskly avant-gardist about the whole affair: he recognises, for instance, that socialism must build upon the great traditions of the middle class (itself, of course, the most revolutionary class known to history) if it is to be authentic. But the modernist side of Marx is all about creative oblivion, spurning the past and fashioning your own models.

As, indeed, is that other great avatar of modernity Friedrich Nietzsche, for whom man is the amnesiac animal *par excellence*. It is those who have the enterprise and audacity to forget the blood-stained horror of history, lest they be overwhelmed by it, who win Nietzsche's patrician admiration. All of us can remember, but only a distinguished few of us are capable of this active, heroic forgetfulness. This rings oddly when one thinks of Sigmund Freud, yet another great doyen of philosophical modernism, since for Freud forgetfulness is our ordinary condition. For him, it is oblivion which comes naturally, not recollection. Indeed, remembrance for Freud is simply forgetting to forget. We are the self-repressive animal, and from this flows both our sickness and our glory. Our sickness, since for Freud an excess of forgetfulness makes us ill (the neurotic, as he famously remarks, is afflicted by reminiscences). Our glory, rather less obviously, since amnesia is necessary for us to function as coherent human subjects at all.

So the slogan of modernity is clear: repression is good for you. It is what makes us the unique human subjects we are. Unless you provisionally suppress the rules of grammar, you cannot speak. Unless you thrust the nightmare of history deep into the collective unconscious, you will never fashion a future for yourself. Unless the ego draws upon the anarchic forces of the id in order to repress it, it will never get round to constructing a civilisation. Or — in the terms of Louis Althusser — unless the human subject forgets the fact that he or she has no genuine autonomy, essential unity or ontological necessity, and comes instead to regard herself as a unified agent, the dominant social relations will not get reproduced.

For Althusser, this enabling forgetfulness is known as ideology. "Science" or "Theory" is aware that we are no more than the humble bearers of social functions and structures; but this Dionysian knowledge, were it insistently present to consciousness, would doubtless prevent us from ever getting out of bed, in which case social life would rapidly grind to a halt. Ideology thus intervenes here in Apollonian style, as the necessary fiction of feeling ourselves centred, integrated, recognised, interpellated, and thus capable sources of constructive social action. To put the point another way, knowledge is now structurally at odds with practice, or experience. It isn't quite that you can't chew gum and walk at the same time, as they used to claim about some of the more boneheaded American presidents, but that you cannot live and theorise at the same time. What you see is not what you get. Lived experience is fiction, not truth, because the truth would be too terrible to assimilate. So the Apollonian illusions of the ego, or of that set of shoddy fantasies known as everyday life, shield us mercifully from the horrors of the Dionysian, or in Lacanese, the Real. It is another grand motif of modernity.

The paradox, then, is clear: in order to become what we are, we need to repress an enormous amount that went into our making. The human subject is a subject only by virtue of this salutary repression. Forgetfulness is structural, not contingent. Even when we remember, it is in Freud's view only within the context of our

constitutive obliviousness. We touch here on another great modernist paradox: that for things to work, something has at all costs
to be excluded. It is this act of exclusion itself which sets things in
motion, just as it is the act of repression which brings the ego into
existence in the first place. We are dealing here, as Slavoj Žižek
(quoting Sam Goldwyn) puts it, with the garbled logic of "include
me out". A certain absence — an exclusion which is not once and
for all but which has to be constantly sustained in being by a for-
midable force of prohibition — lies at the source of human creativity. Misrecognition is the motor of human history, a theme familiar enough from Hegel. Only by our being absent from ourselves can history get off the ground.

This sobering consideration should give pause to all those ear-
nest, card-carrying liberal pluralists for whom "inclusivism" is
ipso facto a virtue. What is wrong with such inclusivism, among
several other things, is its assumption that the excluded can be
incorporated into the system as it stands. Whereas the truth is
that, since that system works precisely by excluding a certain element, driving it deeper into the political unconscious, incorporating that excluded element would involve a revolutionary transformation. This is clear enough for Marxism, for which the shat-
tering irony is that in class-society, it is actually the *majority* which
is excluded. (Postmodernism thinks of exclusion in terms of margins and minorities, but this is far too simple-minded). And you
cannot incorporate the majority without a change which cuts a lot
deeper than liberal pluralism.

For Marx, the working class is at once central and marginal,
hub and periphery, the source of the whole system yet banished
from power. It is the lynchpin or dynamic of the whole material
system, yet a peripheral presence within the state. It fashions a
structure within which it cannot itself be fully included. There is
thus something non-totalisable about the social structure to which
its labour gives birth, which is just the fact that this structure is
unable to comprehend its own ground. Rather as the eye is unable
to include itself in its field of vision (since it is the source of that
vision, not an object within it), so whatever is excluded is ban-

ished because it is the ground and quasi-transcendental precondi-
tion of the system as a whole.

The working class for Marx is thus the inherent contradictory
element, the joker in the pack, at once locatable and non-
locatable, particular and potentially universal — both a class and
not a class, and thus a formation that demands a certain decon-
structive or dialectical logic in order to be adequately grasped.
Not just excluded, then, but included out. Much the same goes
for psychoanalytic thought, for which the shunned and discarded, in the form of that which is thrust into oblivion because
it is making you ill, can indeed be retrieved, but only by an un-
natural and exhausting labour of remembrance, one which will
then radically reconstitute the psyche in a dramatic rewriting of
your individual history.

If there is one piece of your past in particular which, for modernity, you must forget at all costs, drive deep into the murky
depths of the political unconscious, it is the origins of the political
state. And this is because those origins are usually criminal and
illicit — a matter of violence, invasion, occupation, usurpation
and the like. It is certain, writes David Hume, that at the origin of
every nation we will find rebellion and usurpation; it is time alone
which reconciles men and women to an authority, and makes it
appear just and reasonable. This is an astonishingly candid con-
fession. Legitimacy is really longevity. The older a social system
grows, the more we come to forget about its violent, transgressive
beginnings. The sheer passage of time itself is enough to turn
bandits into bankers. And this saving oblivion must be carefully
nurtured by the state. Political legitimacy, then, is founded on fad-
ing memory, as crimes come to grow on us like old cronies. Blaise
Pascal puts the point with equally arresting candour in his *Pensées*
(1670), written on the very threshold of the modern age. Speaking
of the need to avoid "the ruin of those who are curious to examine
established customs", he advises:

> He must not be allowed to be aware of the truth about the
> usurpation. It was introduced once without reason and has

> since become unreasonable. He must be made to regard it
> as genuine and eternal, and its origins must be disguised if
> it is not to come to a swift end. (Pascal, 1995: 25)

Who said conspiracy theories were just for the paranoid?

Immanuel Kant, the pre-eminent philosopher of modernity and arguably the greatest philosopher of all time, makes just the same point, discouraging speculation on the origins of power, which he thought a menace to the stability of the state. The embarrassment is that the middle class is indeed a revolutionary class in the way it comes to power; but once it has scrambled into sovereignty it needs to eradicate its own disreputable origins, devoting itself instead to peace, sobriety, order, prudence and self-discipline in the cause of amassing as much profit as it can. It must shake off its discreditable Bohemian past like a hippie applying to law school, exchanging the epic drama of political revolution for the dull, decent prose of everyday life, Stendhal for Flaubert. As with Freud's so-called family romance, where the small child fantasises that its true parents are princes, bourgeois nations must dream up for themselves a more glamorous parentage than they actually have, tart themselves up (as Marx argues in the *Brumaire*) in the glamorous trappings of classical antiquity. Alternatively, they may fantasise that they were self-born, springing whole and entire from their own loins. This is one reason the bourgeoisie is so fascinated by art (its philosophers, at least, if not its notoriously philistine majority), since the work of art seems to be miraculously self-generating, self-originating, self-grounding and self-determining in just this way.

Then again, such social orders can dream that they were never born at all, but always were. After all, whatever was born can always die. States which find this transition from revolution to respectability hard to make because their origins are still too raw and recent — Israel, for example, or Northern Ireland — are likely to rank among the most unstable. Living down your turbulent genesis, dipping it in the waters of Lethe, is a politically astute move, since it means that you are then less likely to serve as a reminder to your political enemies that the world can be changed. If you could do it, so can they.

For the Irishman Edmund Burke, who being from Ireland knew a little about criminal powers and illicit occupations, the great blasphemy of the French revolutionaries was that they were unmasking this guilty secret of power, stripping authority of its decorous drapings and exposing the unlovely phallus of its power. There is something blasphemous or sexually indecent for Burke in this uncovering of the primal scene of power, this exposure of the father's phallus; and if he excoriates it so wholeheartedly, it is partly because he sees that exposing the criminal origins of power in this way is likely to bring all authority into discredit. The Jacobins have let the political cat out of the bag, pitilessly turning the searchlight of pure reason on the specious sources of power. Gazing into this glaring light will simply make you blind, disabling you for your duties as a citizen. As with Oedipus, finding out the monstrous truth of your origins puts out your eyes. The Jacobins' unforgivable sin in Burke's eyes is to put brazenly on show — to drag into the gaudy public theatre — what must at all costs be decorously veiled. Power for Burke is masculine, but to be effective it must sweeten its unlovely imperiousness, concealing its brutality with the seductive feminine garments of custom, sentiment, affection and consensus. The Law, in other words, is a cross-dresser. But there is always an ominous bulge in its garments. For Burke, women are beautiful and men are sublime — so that the Law, which is sublime because beyond representation, must deck itself out in the beauteous forms of consent (or hegemony, as we might call it today) if it is to prove effective. And this involves a great deal of merciful forgetfulness as to its true nature.

Yet forgetfulness is economic as well as political. Theodor Adorno remarks that the commodity is itself a form of oblivion — an oblivion, no doubt, to the processes which went into its production, which we are supposed to wipe from our minds as we encounter the commodity as an autonomous, self-born thing-in-itself, a veritable work of art (Adorno, 1997). The society of the commodity has also been the society of progress — and progress, too, is a sort of forgetfulness, since the present has no sooner arrived than it is instantly erased in the name of the future, which will itself also prove a mere empty gangplank to another future, and so on in what Hegel calls a "bad infinity". This is what Walter Benjamin meant by "homogeneous, empty time", a process of perpetual negating and disavowing (Benjamin, 1992: 252). It is the opposite of the idea of tradition, in which the present is pregnant not only with the future but also with the past. In pre-modern tradition, the present is authentic only if it constitutes a repetition of a past which is always somehow present; whereas in modernity the present authorises its own authenticity, leaps parentless from its own depths, and does so in part by eradicating the past lest it seems to be dependent on it. Modern freedom cannot have an origin, for then (being dependent on an anterior principle) it would not be freedom, any more than God would be God if he had received instruction in omniscience.

Mentioning Benjamin brings to mind his splendid observation that it is not dreams of liberated grandchildren which stir men and women to revolt, but memories of enslaved ancestors. This is what you might call revolutionary nostalgia — and only a mind as subtly dialectical and heterodox as Benjamin's could conjure a radical value even from nostalgia. Recollecting enslaved ancestors belongs to a Judaic ritual of remembrance, and the reason for recollecting them is to bring them to life once more at a moment of present crisis when we have urgent need of them. But since, for Benjamin, every historical moment is a state of emergency, this means that our need for them is always acute. For Benjamin, political transformation springs not from peering into the future — the Jews, as he reminds us, were forbidden to make images of the future — but rather, like his Angel of History, from turning one's horror-stricken face to that mounting pile of garbage which is the past. It is a matter, so to speak, of remembering the future, by recollecting those enslaved ancestors who can never in truth be resurrected and granted satisfaction for their injuries, but who can at least be given a new retroactive meaning, inscribed in a new political narrative, by what we accomplish in the present. We might at least strive to guarantee that the history of which they form part, and the struggles in which they engaged, do not end in utter catastrophe. It may even be that what happened the first time as tragedy may happen again, this time as comedy.

Whatever the ideologists of Progress may consider (and that there is progress, rather than Progress, is surely not in question), only by turning backward can we move forward — a lesson, incidentally, which revolutionary nationalism does not need to learn. Nationalism abides in this kind of time-warping, which is not the temporality of the metropolitan nation. Only by contemplating that devastated landscape which is class history can we be driven backwards into the future like the Angel of History, our eyes fixed mournfully on the past. What drives the revolution for Benjamin is thus less hope than melancholia — less the subjunctive mood of what the future *might* bring, than the indicative mood of how appalling the past has actually been. Only by this ritual of revolutionary remembrance can we go one better than Stephen Dedalus and awaken from the nightmare of history, rather as the subject of psychoanalysis can emancipate herself from the affliction of neurosis only by the painful process of working it through — which is to say, tackling the past in a way which makes it efficacious for the present. Indeed, neurosis is already a beginning to this process, as much therapeutic strategy as symptom. Freud admonished us that those who cannot remember the past are doomed to repeat it; and this, politically speaking, is the vacuous ideology of bourgeois Progress, which fails to recollect that the past has been for the most part a nightmare, and so rushes eagerly to commit the crime once more.

There are nations which are besieged by reminiscences, and there are those afflicted by amnesia. Ireland, some might claim, is currently in the process of moving from one condition to the other. Once a nation romantically in love with its own past, morbidly fixated on its ruinous history (or so a rather spurious argument runs), it has become since its recent affluence a briskly modernising society which wants nothing so much as to end up look-

ing exactly like Switzerland. Whereas once it could seem para-
lysed by its past, it is now in strident denial of it. Those who are
most precarious in their modernity are usually the ones who de-
nounce their own past most noisily.

Morbid nostalgia and brittle modernising are in a sense sides
of the same coin. A nation which cannot recollect its past without
hideous embarrassment, as at the moment at least some members
of the Irish nation appear unable to do, is just as much in thrall to
that past as one which can think of nothing else. It is when, as an
individual or as a nation, you can recollect your past in all its
glory and catastrophe, its hope and hurt, and do so with no danger of being accused of idealism, nostalgia or self-flagellation, that
you may be said to be genuinely free of it.

The point, then, is to be neither incarcerated by the past (afflicted with memories) nor to disavow it in a frenetic hunt for self-
invention, but to find a way of using it which will get you beyond
it. For the past is not of course a monolithic phenomenon, and
there are always those currents within it which, construed and
recollected in a certain way, may be induced to point to a desirable future. Any future which is desirable but not feasible simply
risks making us fall ill of longing. Any future which is simply a
repetition of the past is not a future at all. And any future which
depends on forgetting the past is not the future of *this* past. A
genuine future must be rooted in the present if it to be valid, the
subjunctive embedded within the indicative. We can discern the
shape of the future not in some effervescent dream of utopia, but
in the ways in which the present fails to be identical with itself, in
that which it has to discard as so much garbage, in the contradic-
tions at the core of its identity, in the gaps and silences with which
it is shot through from end to end. In the end, the only image of
the future is the failure of the present.

2

"Gloom and Grandeur" or the Threshing Floor: The Manufacture of Ecclesiastical Ruins in Nineteenth-Century Ireland

Máirín Ní Cheallaigh

In his book *In Ruins* Christopher Woodward asks us to imagine an abbey in the year 1540, when "the monks have been expelled, and wind and rain whistle through the gate, cloister and choir. The soaring stone vaults of the church are picked clean like the rib-cage of a whale" (Woodward, 2001: 110).[1] He continues with an evocation of the stripping of the physical carcass of the defunct abbey, and the sale and dispersal of its stonework and assets. Woodward's account not only describes the ruins of a "generic" abbey but also concentrates the mind on the moment of its dissolution or "death", the casting open of once enclosed spaces to the elements, and the dispersal of the physical fabric of the desecrated building into the profane worlds of domestic and agricultural activity. We might also see the death of the abbey as the

[1] The research upon which this paper is based was funded by the Irish Research Council for the Humanities and Social Sciences. The work was further assisted by the facilities made available to me in my capacity as Postgraduate Research Scholar at the Humanities Institute of Ireland, UCD. I also wish to acknowledge the kind permission of the Head of the UCD Department of Irish Folklore to cite material from the manuscript collection held in the department archives.

catalyst for changes in the settlement and political focus of its immediate neighbourhood. It might be seen as an opportunity for local people to perhaps inadvertently "reinforce" the void left by the ideological dismantling of the spaces of church and cloister by removing the walls that had once surrounded them.

Across Europe such ruins were almost obsessively presented and re-presented in numerous illustrated tomes and in plates and prints throughout the eighteenth and nineteenth centuries. They were also repeatedly visited, described and viewed by antiquarians, and as the nineteenth century progressed were favourite destinations of tourists and day-trippers, who often tethered their traps, carriages and charabancs alongside "famous" ruins, and consumed picnics while seated among headstones. Among such tourists and antiquarians were those enamoured of picturesque and romantic landscape settings, who sought in ecclesiastical ruins a measure of "gloom and grandeur" that was not to be found in the domestic spaces of everyday life (Bell, 1829: 56). In Ireland, however, despite the internationally recognised architectural excellence of such key buildings as St Canice's Cathedral in Kilkenny, St Cormac's Chapel, Cashel and the cathedrals of St Patrick's and Christchurch in Dublin, many of the smaller ecclesiastical sites did not "perform" well on the antiquarian stage as evidence of the past cultural sophistication of Irish ecclesiastics and society (Fallow, c.1894). Furthermore, the idea of the relative inferiority of many Irish ecclesiastical sites appears to have had some currency at the highest levels of the British establishment. In one of his speeches to Parliament during the debate over the Disestablishment of the Church of Ireland in 1869, William Gladstone remarked: "Unhappily in Ireland there are not copiously scattered, as in England, churches which are beautiful and wonderful specimens of art, and which form one of the richest portions of our national treasures", although he did allow that "here and there in Ireland there are churches of this class" (Gladstone, 1869: 29).

Although Gladstone may have in part been attempting to limit the number of churches which might have been proposed as legitimate recipients of maintenance funds, his observation can be seen to have been at odds with the cherished if often contested vision of Ireland as a land of saints and scholars. This national myth was frequently reinforced by reference to the number and importance of Irish church sites. Gladstone's remarks are also at odds with some of the assertions stemming from the processes of description, identification and representation of church sites undertaken by many nineteenth-century antiquarians, artists and clergymen, and which had already by the 1870s resulted in a large corpus of works on Irish ecclesiastical remains. Indeed, antiquarian and popular endeavours to collect evidence illustrating the value of Irish church sites may have been a competitive or defensive response to claims that they were "poor relations" of English examples (Bell, 1829: 20-22).

In creating this record of ecclesiastical sites in Ireland, antiquarians trawled through historical sources, ranging from more readily available popular texts to obscure unpublished manuscripts in Irish and Latin. They also spliced historical information onto descriptions of the dimensions, orientation and architectural features of the various structures found at ecclesiastical sites. Such efforts resulted not only in articles for publication in learned journals and notes written to accompany engravings in books of illustrated antiquities, but also in the construction of distinct forms of narratives. These facilitated the transformation of small, insignificant ruined structures into locations where saints and monks had founded schools and where "History" had occurred. They also facilitated the illusory reversal of the marks of time and decay, or — more prosaically — allowed walls, roofs and other spaces to be reconstructed in the mind's eye by projecting them upwards and outwards from barely visible remains. At Balgriffin in north County Dublin, for example, the Reverend William Reeves asserted that the outline of the medieval parish church was "still discernible on the sward at the left-hand side entering the avenue of Balgriffin Park", although not marked on the Ordnance Survey sheets of the 1830s. He continued that this church, and indeed the existence in this location of any form of ecclesiastical site, "might escape any eye but one accustomed to the shades of extinct churches" (Reeves, 1859: 5).

Lost ecclesiastical sites in the bloom and freshness of their past lives were not the only things conjured into imaginary existence in this fashion. Their churches and cloisters were peopled with imagined past inhabitants using techniques similar to that of the Reverend James Graves, whose mental ingenuity led him to "reconstruct from authentic data the dilapidated monastic pile, and call up before the mind's eye the manners and everyday occupations of its quondam inmates" (Graves, 1849-51: 41). As well as claiming the gift of seeing what was no longer physically present, some antiquarian and more popular accounts frequently detailed monuments which were understood as "mute witnesses" to historical episodes, or alternatively as "speaking" to those capable of hearing tales of past people and events. Those individuals with ears and eyes qualified to interpret the broken walls and fractured windows of church buildings could effectively create a narrative of the "original" use of such sites. While not actually restoring the monuments as "national treasures" in the sense delineated by Gladstone, such accounts created written records that gave sites printed genealogies. These in turn mimicked those created by the large collections of documents and manuscripts associated with the "premier" Irish churches such as St. Patrick's Cathedral. Irish church sites might thus be reconstituted and remade in represented form so that their former if not present glory could be set against the well-preserved "treasures" of other nations.

In Ireland as in Britain, however, the corporate claims to ownership of antiquities by the nation (however that nation was conceived) was somewhat complicated by the fact that the legal ownership of such sites more often than not rested in private hands (Cochrane, 1892; Chippindale, 1983). Since the sixteenth and seventeenth centuries, a significant proportion of surviving Irish medieval ecclesiastical sites had been used for the purposes of religious worship by Church of Ireland congregations. In practice, this meant that over the centuries repairs, extensions and rebuilding programmes had been carried out on the earlier medieval structures at these sites. The Church was particularly active in this regard in the later eighteenth and early nineteenth centuries and had in some instances totally demolished and replaced some of the older buildings in its possession. This was perfectly consistent with the relative absence of strongly formulated conservationist principles in the first half of the 1800s. It is likely, indeed, that the enthusiastic rebuilding programmes carried out by the Church of Ireland might not have taken the same form in the latter part of the century. By the 1830s modern churches had replaced earlier foundations at a large number of sites throughout the island, while at others, such as Rattoo in County Kerry, the walls of the old church were stated to have been "so modernized that it [was] impossible to recognise any part of the original work in them" (O'Flanagan, 1935: 9).

This remaking and rebuilding of medieval sites to accommodate contemporary congregations can be interpreted as a pragmatic response to the problems associated with ageing buildings. In the earlier part of the century, the renovation of medieval parish churches, rather than the construction of new structures adjacent to the old, may also have stemmed from confusion over whether such new buildings could be legally regarded as officially recognised parish churches.[2] With the building boom sparked by Catholic Emancipation in 1829, it is further possible that the remodelling of the fabric of medieval churches and sites by the Church of Ireland was in some sense a reaction to the proliferation of new Catholic churches — and indeed of Dissenting meeting-houses — which effectively created co-existing and occasionally competing "national" networks of recognised church sites.

The obliteration of medieval fabric that was frequently the result of nineteenth-century building programmes may have had the side-effect of rendering such sites less amenable to ideological or sectarian hijacking by opponents. For example, in the heated

---

[2] 'A Bill for explaining and clearing up certain Doubts respecting the Scites [sic] of Parish Churches within Ireland', *Parliamentary Papers* 1812-13 (157) I.639.

debates leading up to Disestablishment in 1869 pro-Catholic nationalists had highlighted the dilapidation and ruin of sites whose
medieval fabric had ostensibly been erected by the ancestors of
the Catholic rather than the Church of Ireland population. They
had also proposed that the decay of such sites formed a physical
analogue to what they ostensibly saw as the intellectual ruin and
enervation of the Church of Ireland itself (Gray, 1868: 30-50). Such
opponents, eschewing Romantic perceptions of the picturesque
nature of ruins, tended in a relentlessly pragmatic and functional-
ist way to view the dilapidation of sites as evidence that their contemporary guardians were incapable of maintaining the religious
purposes for which both churches and sites had originally been
constructed. Remaking or restoring ruined or decayed structures
could simultaneously contradict this assertion by facilitating their
use for contemporary religious purposes, while also in some sense
rearticulating and claiming the "original" impulses which had led
to the building's foundation. In 1900, for example, Sir Thomas
Drew effectively argued that the nineteenth-century restorers of St
Patrick's (of which he was one) had both literally and intellectu-
ally refounded the "original" church in the purity of its pristine
state (Drew, 1900: 125).

   Not only was this view somewhat controversial in contemporary architectural circles, but the physical removal of the surviving fabric and monuments on the sites was extremely problematic.
While tourists may have regarded the partial dismantling of ecclesiastical ruins with relative indifference (provided such actions
did not interfere with the picturesque nature or accessibility of
sites), for nationalists and learned antiquarian societies alike, the
destruction and alteration of monuments was something to be
roundly condemned. Such condemnation is unsurprising in an
international context where monuments were increasingly being
proposed as evidence of lengthy and coherent "national" pasts,
and where ruined or decayed structures were being re-used as the
building blocks from which the social history of Ireland was to be
constructed (Mease, 1849-51: 462; Smith, 1999). Attempts to create
such histories involved asserting the primacy of Newtonian linear

time, while threading a sometimes crooked and difficult path around obstacles formed by resistance within and outside the "nation" to the artificially homogeneous historical narratives proposed as "national" memory. The destruction of monuments in this context also destroyed the memories that were considered to reside in their fabric (Forty and Küchler, 2001: 2). Thomas Davis, for example, whose views reappeared in various guises, including Douglas Hyde's 1914 edited selection of his work, commented with some exasperation that money was being spent by Irish people on the study of Indian, Tuscan and Egyptian antiquities, while at home "pigs [were] housed in the piled friezes of a broken church, cows stabled in the palaces of the Desmonds, and corn threshed on the floor of abbeys" (Davis, 1914: 96).

We might, however, assume that many of the antiquarian and nationalist rhetoricians who were most active in seeking the preservation of ecclesiastical antiquities and sites were unlikely to have been representative of the entire spectrum of Irish rural society. Indeed its is likely that as antiquarians they were regarded with a somewhat sly amusement by many people who, in print at least, shared the popular view that antiquarians were more at home among the dusty, mouldering remnants of the past (*Dublin Penny Journal*, 1834-35; Chippindale, 1983: 13). In turn, individuals interested in the recording and preservation of ecclesiastical ruins were generally unsympathetic towards those who viewed semi-abandoned and almost forgotten churches as legitimate stone quarries or as structures suitable for use as cowsheds (O'Flanagan, 1927b: 26). Nor were antiquarians or those interested in a "national past" likely to have been sympathetic towards local assertions of moral, if not legal, ownership of the physical fabric of churches. Such assertions also encompassed the residual sacred power of carved stones, fonts and cross-shafts which rendered the re-use of elaborately carved fragments of ecclesiastical buildings as headstones a natural process.

Centralising historical narratives also had a tendency to negate or appropriate local narratives that might be interpreted as expressions of control over ecclesiastical sites. It is true that some sites had undoubtedly been forgotten by local communities, thus facilitating their incorporation into the newly-manufactured historical and linear narratives of antiquarians, churchmen and various other groups. Others, however, remained firmly integrated not only into the local agricultural economy but also into the dense networks of different sites in which, according to traditional understandings, the sacred was located (Ó Giolláin, 1991: 199). Stories that threatened supernatural vengeance against those who interfered with locally sacred church sites and burial grounds often circulated within different communities in various parts of the country throughout the nineteenth century, even as the names of other medieval parish saints and saints' days were forgotten (O'Hanlon, c.1875: 156; Kinahan, 1881: 105).[3]

Stories were collected by members of the Topographical Unit of the Ordnance Survey in the 1830s on the basis that they might, in the words of John O'Donovan, "throw the dimmest light upon Irish Topography" (O'Flanagan, 1927a: 67). Nevertheless, those engaged in the creation of national narratives, or in the pursuit of the "progress" beloved of nineteenth-century reformers, did not always mourn the passing of traditional stories associated with ecclesiastical sites. Some stories of vengeful saints were dismissed as superstition by those aspiring to modernity and upward mobility, while the active use of ecclesiastical sites as the focus of popular religious celebrations, such as patterns, were discouraged by clergy of all denominations. This was ostensibly to put an end to the periodic violence, drunkenness and other undesirable activities associated with them (Ó Giolláin, 1999: 214-17; Naughton, 2003: 26-28).

The replacement of "superstitious" religious pilgrims by "civilised" antiquarian or middle-class tourists in the aftermath of the decline of patterns meant that not only were the narratives surrounding Irish ecclesiastical sites remade or rephrased, but so also were the ways in which they were physically experienced. It is

---

[3] See also the Schools' Manuscript Collection, Department of Irish Folklore, UCD, Vol. 595, pp. 160-61, 164-65 and Vol. 505, pp. 14a-15a.

perhaps fanciful to liken the repeated circling of particular features and the traversing of ecclesiastical site boundaries to the definition of civic perimeters undertaken by town corporations during the early modern period (Kinahan, 1881: 119-21; Haddon, 1893: 360; Ó Giolláin, 1999: 205-06). It might, however, be less fanciful to regard the crossing of site boundaries and the definition of particular features through physical contact as a form of appropriation in which sites were (and are) made and remade according to specific understandings of their nature and significance. The suppression of such practices may have hastened the decline of local awareness of ecclesiastical sites, which simultaneously facilitated the remaking of these sites as part of historical or antiquarian narratives. In this context the replacing of medieval church buildings with modern Church of Ireland structures may have also facilitated the removal of these buildings from such popular cycles of remaking, as well as accommodating contemporary congregations more comfortably.

In conclusion, then, the antiquarian practices of measuring, sketching and describing ecclesiastical sites, while potentially very tiresome to perform and to read (as pointed out by John O'Donovan), resulted in both the creation of new historical "personae" for the sites and in the definition of new types of spaces (O'Flanagan, 1935: 2). That these spaces might be contested is unsurprising in a nineteenth-century Ireland where land and religion were conventionally considered to be the two great unsolved issues of the time. By locating ecclesiastical sites within new narratives of national glory, or within long-established aesthetic traditions of landscape appreciation, Irish ecclesiastical sites could, no matter how humble, be given an additional grandeur. They could also be ideologically removed from local agricultural and domestic economies, so that they might be made anew as part of the varied and contested historical and archaeological "heritage" of Ireland.

3

Late Nineteenth-Century Landscape Representation and the Development of Irish Fiction

Julie Anne Stevens

Pagan altars & pagan forts overlook monastic ruins & crosses carved with the Irish decoration of interwoven lines. In this confusion of survivals, the present loses weight, the Baal worshipper is revealed with the largeness of his time about him.[1]

The Irish land wars of the 1880s provoked the first novelistic treatments of the Irish peasantry by Emily Lawless (1845-1913) and Somerville and Ross, the joint pseudonym of Edith Somerville (1858-1949) and Martin Ross (1862-1915). Set in the Burren in Clare, *Hurrish* (1886) was Lawless's first Irish novel, her previous two having had English settings. *Naboth's Vineyard* (1891) saw Somerville and Ross move away from the ascendancy class, the focus of their first joint novelistic venture, *An Irish Cousin* (1889), to concentrate on a Catholic nationalist population

---

[1] Martin Ross, draft of "The Aras of the Sea", no. 3312-13, Manuscript Department, Trinity College Library, Dublin.

in west Cork. Both novels rely on journalistic reports to represent different kinds of agrarian outrage and incidents of land-grabbing amongst the peasantry, drawing on visual as well as textual material. Indeed, Somerville and Ross's satirical account of boycotting relies as much on theatrical representation as on factual reportage. The Caliban-like Mat O'Brady of *Hurrish* recalls simianized depictions of Land Leaguers in the English press, and *Naboth's Vineyard* echoes *Punch's* reviews of a farcical version of *The Tempest*, while also using newspaper accounts of the Parnell Commission of 1888-89. The violent Irish landscape is put to different uses in each novel, depending in part upon the tragic or burlesque elements of the authors' treatment. What unites these works, however, is their preoccupation with the ambiguity arising from the collision of different concepts of time stirred up by the "seething pot" of Irish politics and made manifest in place and space.

In dramatising the complex network of relations within rural agricultural communities, both *Hurrish* and *Naboth's Vineyard* highlight internecine peasant conflicts and divisions, thus undermining the notion of a unified Catholic underclass. Trouble is shown to originate from class divisions at ground level rather than from class oppression imposed from above by the Anglo-Irish elite. Lawless spells out the problem in *Hurrish*. Modern developments have distanced the younger generation of Irish peasants from their natural place in the world. Just as shop-bought clothing and whitewashed cottages look out of place in the Clare countryside, so too do new-fangled ideas disrupt the ingrained thought patterns of a predominantly agricultural community. In *Hurrish*, therefore, the natural world is shown to dominate as Lawless focuses upon an impoverished and embattled Irish landscape to investigate Darwinian notions of evolution, improvement and progress. Despite this emphasis upon place, however, the novel has traditionally been read within historical rather than environmental discourses, having first appeared alongside several other Irish texts concerned with late nineteenth-century agrarian outrages. Margaret Kelleher has described these novels as "factual fictions", texts which, by fictionalising specific acts of violence, offered themselves as vehicles for a better understanding of "the Irish question" (Kelleher, 1999). English readers were a particular target of such works; no less a figure than W.E. Gladstone was among those who expressed admiration for *Hurrish*, his imprimatur vindicating Lawless's intent to reinterpret the Irish situation for English readers (Brown, 1916).

Lawless's preoccupation with the Irish landscape as a site of "perfect mines and treasure-houses to the botanist" had been established early in her career with essays on Irish flora and fauna, including "An Upland Bog" (1881). Her study of bogland echoes earlier nineteenth-century commentary on the Irish landscape as a manifestation of Irish character (Croker, 1969: 13). The novelist also suggests that nature offers a larger commentary on progress in Ireland. For example, she speaks of passing a group of Scotch fir trees, "a sorry-looking company, undersized and ill-disciplined; anything, evidently, but secure in their position", and notes that these stunted firs are "much domineered over by the original possessors of the soil, in the shape of big thistles and long wiry grasses and briers, which have their own views on agrarian matters, and have no notion of surrendering possession to new-comers — especially Scotch ones!" (Lawless, 1881: 428). Lawless's representation of the landscape as a dramatic narrative echoing the struggles of Irish history follows Darwin's dictates, which she invokes when describing the flesh-eating flora of the bogland, including sundews, butterworts and bladderworts. She details the particular habits of such plants, which trap and devour insects in their broad viscous leaves as they enact the grisly process of adaptation and survival (Lawless, 1881: 423-24).

In the same way, *Hurrish* bears witness to a harsh, dynamic environment, using place as the central determining factor in narrative and character development, so that the protagonists seem more like insects than active, thinking human agents. Lawless's entomological and environmental determinism is especially evident in her treatment of the land wars and the conflicts they engendered. Like a thunderstorm or an avalanche, violence is shown to be part of a larger natural scheme that operates according to its own dictates rather than some progressive pattern. In a way, narrative serves nature; it appears to take its course from natural rather than artistic dictates. In *Hurrish* there is no further into the wilds that one can go than the Burren: "Wilder regions there are few to be found, even in the wildest west of Ireland" (Lawless, 1992: 3). Though the valley of Gortnacoppin dips within the desolate landscape, one has the impression of being on a height. "Standing in it," says the narrator, "you may fairly believe yourself in the heart of some alpine region, high above the haunts of men, where only the eagle or marmot make their homes." The valley has at its base a fertile oasis which results from the "mass of detritus, borne down from the hills". Sweet pockets of fertility arise out of the debris of the wasteland; opposites interact to create a landscape of complex parts. The artefacts of past traditions, moreover, have "melted into the surrounding stoniness" and the diverse forces of seemingly good and bad interact in a constantly fluctuating cycle (Lawless, 1992: 4).

The novel's protagonist, Hurrish O'Brien, demonstrates a textbook Celtic temperament: "poetic, excitable, emotionable [sic], unreasoning" (Lawless, 1992: 15). Half farmer and half fisherman, he comes from "that amphibious part of the island", and as a "contented giant" appears to be only half way up the evolutionary ladder, not far ahead developmentally of the resident "human orang-utang" Mat Brady, who manifests the traits of the worst type of Irish peasant as satirised by English cartoonists such as John Tenniel (Lawless, 1992: 9). Violent, red-headed and drunken, Brady is presented as the "most obnoxious of Calibans", who has replaced the pike for the gun: "Like every Irishman of his class — whether Coercion Acts are in force or whether they are not — he had an old gun hidden away in the thatch of his cabin"(Lawless, 1992: 63). He pursues Alley Sheehan whose mind, we are told, "was too simple, too inherently limited, to admit of any large or complicated variety of emotions" (Lawless, 1992: 27). Like Somerville and Ross's colleen in *Naboth's Vineyard*, Lawless's simple lass "was not given to introspection — that, happily, not being one of the vices of the class to which she belonged" (Lawless, 1992: 79).

Lawless's exaggeration of character, a perspective that enlarges the Irish world, relies upon familiar colonial stereotyping. The characters of *Hurrish* are carefully delineated as types. They demonstrate in their features and habits familiar categories of race and class, being sorted into groupings much as butterflies or beetles are arranged in glass cases in museums.[2] Yet Lawless's treatment of Irish character is determined as much by her naturalist bent as by her colonial eye. As types, her peasants possess both a scientific and a religious significance. On the one hand, they appear as specimens scrutinised by a distant narrator, as insects are under a microscope; on the other, they prefigure a larger Christian meaning. Alley Sheehan, for example, bears both a natural and Christian significance. Her type-casting issues from a mixture of colonial, scientific and religious discourses, in which setting is an all-important element:

> The little dells where the grass grew rich and thick; the wells full of offerings to their respective saints; the rifts into which she could plunge her hands, and bring them up filled with flowers; the isles of Aran opposite, where the saints used to live, and at which she looked in consequence with such reverence; the wild clearness of the sea, and great environing arch of sky. (Lawless, 1992: 79)

"Certain types repeat themselves eternally at all ages of the world," explains the narrator, "and hers was the type of all those gently ascetic natures which at every period and under all variations of circumstances have sprung up spontaneously" (Lawless, 1992: 78). Like the fertile oasis amidst the stony rocks of Gortnacoppin, Alley embodies qualities that temper the prevailing asperity. Moreover, she seems but an earthly cast for the larger kind

---

[2] Lawless's characterisation also borrows from Irish mythology, recalling stories of Fomorian giants waging war across the island, which she later incorporated into her novel *Maelcho* (1894). Thus, Mat Brady is not only a Caliban figure but also a "man-mountain" whose battle with the gargantuan Hurrish resembles a struggle between mythological figures who have more in common with the rocks and soil of the Burren than with present-day humans.

she worships, the Virgin Mother "who is the type of all mother-hood" (Lawless, 1992: 78).

In *Hurrish* a world of extreme contrasts is set within a larger dimension of sea and sky to become, at moments, spiritualised. The Western bluish light transforms place, character and action so that all appear to be enlarged, elevated to a different plane from that of ordinary reality. Throughout the narrative, knowledge re-sides in the landscape itself, as Lawless looks to nature to discover meaningful patterns of reality. The close scrutiny of the Burren demands an acknowledgement on the part of the reader of the pre-eminence of place as a source of understanding. Nature effec-tively tells the story, making the novel "place-centred" (Howarth, 1999: 511), not only in terms of natural phenomena and topog-raphical history but also in relation to its central argument which is based on land acquisition and social position. In other words, the driving force of the writer's analysis of Irish reality is place. Themes of land grabbing and social climbing shape the plot, while the landscape's history tells a larger story of conquest and coloni-sation. Thus, the subject matter of the novel, the struggle for land and social prestige, determines its treatment. Lawless's naturalist methods of character depiction, for instance, demonstrate the natural dictates of the landscape. The humans are part of nature, and her manner of individuating her peasants allows her to em-phasise the significance of the land in determining human behav-iour. The supposed closeness of the peasantry to the natural world gives Lawless the opportunity to exploit the land as a pri-mary source of meaning, so that her depiction of the peasantry as animal-like must be understood within the larger argument of the novel that makes place "function as a cultural and textual para-digm" (Howarth, 1999: 511).

When we turn to Somerville and Ross's satirical study of an equally contested terrain in west Cork, we recall that Edith Somerville, who had joined forces with Martin Ross only a few years previously, brought to their joint efforts her painting and illustration training in Düsseldorf and Paris (Bhreathnach-Lynch and Stevens, 2005). Ross accompanied Somerville on some of her art training stints and the pair shared a love of the grotesque and the comic. Indeed, Ross was directly connected to popular theatrical productions in Dublin and London. The writers' treatment of the Irish land wars, then, is influenced first by their European artistic training and second by their comic sensibilities. Furthermore, in writing *Naboth's Vineyard*, these two women writers were redressing a perceived imbalance in Lawless's work: while they admired her treatment of the Irish peasantry, they noted an absence of the humour they enjoyed in Maria Edgeworth's earlier representation of the Irish rural classes (Somerville and Ross, 1917: 139).

Nonetheless, Somerville and Ross's emphasis on place as a defining factor in human behaviour readily recalls Lawless's environmental determinism. Somerville's interest in landscape (she painted the west Cork countryside throughout her career) directs attention in the novel to the slowly evolving nature of the terrain and the jarring impact of sudden economic and political developments upon place and its human occupants. Significantly, she owned a copy of Darwin's *Expression of the Emotions in Man and Animals* (1872), and the emphasis on behaviour patterns in *Naboth's Vineyard*, on how people have evolved modes of behaviour that do not easily conform to sudden changes in position, reflects Darwin's argument that human or animal behaviour patterns evolve just as surely, and just as slowly, as do their shapes and forms (Darwin, 1965). At the same time, however, the depiction of characters such as the greedy shopkeeper couple, John and Harriet Donovan, the despised Caliban figure, Dan Hurley, who lusts after the poor widow's daughter, Ellen Leonard, and the rustic hero Rick O'Grady recall figures from popular theatre. Place in this novel also becomes a platform, a stage upon which the Irish peasant characters enact roles familiar from melodrama. The writers thus demonstrate a self-conscious redeployment of theatrical types in their depiction of agrarian agitation. In turn, their assessment of the conflict between progress and tradition which such agitation stirs up manifests itself in a grotesque realism that

shows the struggle between the "largeness of time" and the com-
pelling forces of a swiftly changing world.

Unlike their other fiction, Somerville and Ross's *Naboth's Vineyard* covers a short and specific time-frame — October to December 1883 — in which the focus is upon the daily measure of minutes. This period followed a particularly violent moment in Irish
politics, during which the country was convulsed by the Phoenix
Park murders of the new Chief Secretary, Lord Cavendish, and
his Under Secretary, T.H. Burke, in May 1882 and — much more
locally for Martin Ross — the massacre three months later of five
members of the Joyce family in Maamtrasna in Galway, close to
Ross House (Somerville and Ross, 1917: 38-39). If we look more
closely at one of the novelists' readily available sources, *Punch*
magazine, these dates may suggest a further significance which
gives ironic meaning to the emphasis on chronometric measure-
ment in west Cork. The writers' interest in pantomime and burlesque would have directed their attention to the *Punch* material
of October and December 1883, issues which also discussed the
plays of Ross's cousin, William G. Wills. On 20 October 1883
Punch hailed his play *Ariel* as a "triumphant Shakespearian bur-
lesque-fairy-drama". This, and the accompanying illustrations of
Ariel hovering above the waves and of Caliban and Miranda engaged in harmless dance, indicating the transformation of Shakespeare's play into light-hearted burlesque, may well have suggested similar manipulations to the two novelists — in effect, an
Irish version of *The Tempest*.

Two months later, on 22 December 1883, *Punch* printed Tenniel's notorious Irish caricature of O'Caliban — a brutal, degener-
ate ape-man representing the Irish Land Leaguers — and thereby
provided an entirely different version of the innocent, dancing
natives of the earlier review. In *Naboth's Vineyard* Somerville and
Ross may be said to have appropriated these *Punch* stereotypes
and restaged them on an Irish island — like Prospero's, one tem-
pest-tossed and subject to Donovan's patriarchal rule which both
a Miranda-like Ellen and a Calibanesque Hurley must endure.
With O'Caliban in mind, the writers conjure a Whiteboy lurking

in the background, while the novel's tempests become the boy-cotts and fires called up by Donovan and his superior wizard, the absent Parnell. In this way, the novelists rework a version of a timeless tale within a specific time and place, implying that how-ever new and revolutionary developments in Ireland may appear, they merely enact a much older pattern of human behaviour.

To conclude, then, it can be seen that *Naboth's Vineyard* reflects a series of images of Irishness rather than a particular Irish reality. It restages familiar burlesque material on a natural stage, the is-land of Ireland, while at the same time subverting picturesque versions of the Irish landscape. Its satirical treatment of Irish types — diminished rather than elevated, as in Lawless's work — counters idealised treatment. Most importantly, however, Somer-ville and Ross's early fiction, like Lawless's, maintains place as the central narrative force and ironically comments on a modern sense of time as progress. It is necessary to emphasise this point, since much recent commentary on these novels has noted the novelists' ambiguous treatment of Irish rural culture, often ascrib-ing it to colonial anxiety. However, while the three authors' in-volvement with British discourses about Ireland is clear, their dis-tanced perspectives and use of character types may indicate an environmental and aesthetic intent as much as a political one. Cer-tainly, different forces interact with the writers' cultural and po-litical awareness to create a landscape that is both distinctively Irish and reflective of broader late nineteenth-century European contexts. *Hurrish* and *Naboth's Vineyard* might therefore be fruit-fully analysed not only within Irish colonial discourse but also as part of a more general discussion of landscape as a transmitter of culture.

4

National Identity and Urban Topography in Joyce's and Kinsella's Dublin

Derval Tubridy

In her paper "Decoding Symbolic Spaces of Dublin" Yvonne Whelan describes the city of Dublin in terms of a "contested iconography" and argues for the "powerful role of landscape as a site of symbolic representation integral to the imaginative construction of national identity" (Whelan, 2003b: 48). This paper looks at the ways in which James Joyce (1882-1941) and Thomas Kinsella (b.1928) engage with the "contested iconography" of Dublin. It focuses in particular on the iconography of Sackville Street, that vibrant artery of the city which was renamed O'Connell Street in 1924 and which, as Whelan emphasises, "was to take on special significance as part of the nation-building agenda" of independent Ireland (Whelan, 2003b: 61).

In a letter written in 1905 James Joyce expressed surprise that his native city had never received the artistic representation that might have been expected on the basis of its antiquity, size and historical significance: "When you remember that Dublin has been a capital for thousands of years, that it is the 'second' city of the British Empire, that it is nearly three times as big as Venice it seems strange that no artist has given it to the world" (Joyce 1966: 122). This omission is more than adequately remedied by *Dub-*

liners (1914), *Ulysses* (1922) and *Finnegans Wake* (1939), works
which do not simply give Dublin to the world, but reinscribe the
city in terms of an emerging sense of identity instigated by Ireland's devolution from British control. In *The Irish Ulysses* Maria
Tymoczko argues that:

> Joyce retakes Dublin from the Irish Ascendancy, giving us a
> memorable Everyman's Dublin, an English-speaking
> Dublin upon which to build a free state. This attention to
> Dublin topography is an ironic expression of Joyce's
> nationalism, an expression not likely to be appreciated by
> the nativist nationalists who were interested in promoting
> and preserving a rural Irish Ireland. (Tymoczko, 1994: 159)

Here Tymoczko draws on a distinction, made by the historian
F.S.L. Lyons in his *Culture and Anarchy in Ireland 1890-1939*, between the cosmopolitan, urban nationalist on the one hand, and
the nativist, rural nationalist on the other hand (Lyons, 1982).
Emer Nolan eloquently criticises Lyons's characterisation of Joyce
as a cosmopolitan, "refusing equally the calls of 'Anglo-Ireland'
and 'Irish Ireland'", and argues instead for a more nuanced reading of the writer's relationship with both representative communities (Nolan, 1995: 48).

The interconnections between national identity and urban topography are evident also in the work of the contemporary Irish
poet Thomas Kinsella. Like Joyce, Kinsella was born and brought
up in Dublin and the city forms the focus of much of his poetry
throughout his long career. With an overlap of thirteen years between Kinsella's birth in 1928 and Joyce's death in 1941, the former can be seen as a writer who inherits what Len Platt describes
as Joyce's "very considerable investment in historical reconstruc-
tion, a motivation that was powerful, committed, even raw"
(Platt, 1998: 16). Kinsella's poetry exhibits a very strong commitment to the political and cultural development of the Republic of
Ireland, and his voice occupies a unique position within a generation who felt that it was truly in their hands to shape and form the
emerging nation. However, because of this commitment, Kinsella

has occasionally adopted the stance of a scathing social critic. For example, the 1968 poem "Nightwalker" characterises the politician Charles Haughey — who as taoiseach would have enormous influence on the development of the country throughout the 1980s but whose retirement would be stained by evidence of corruption — as:

> The Sonhusband
> Coming in his power, climbing the dark
> To his mansion in the sky, to take his place
> In the influential circle, mounting to glory
> On his big white harse! (Kinsella, 1996a: 80)

The unmistakable insult contained within the portmanteau word "harse" (formed from "horse" and "arse") takes issue with the implication of Haughey riding to hounds, his rise to power through marriage to a previous taoiseach's daughter, and his establishment of a large personal fortune through dubious means.

Kinsella's troubled nightwalker makes his way "toward the tower / Rising into the dark at the Forty Foot" and it is here that he invokes Joyce directly as both muse and mentor: "Watcher in the tower, / Be with me now. Turn your milky spectacles / On the sea, unblinking" (Kinsella, 1996a: 80). Joyce casts his unblinking gaze throughout Kinsella's work and is nowhere more evident than in the 1997 suite of poems, *The Pen Shop*. In these poems the poet-speaker journeys through the centre of Dublin, much like Leopold Bloom in *Ulysses*. Indeed, Kinsella explicitly references the "Hades" episode of that novel, as well as "Grace" from *Dubliners*. *The Pen Shop* uses the poet-speaker's peregrinations through a specifically delineated urban geography to explore the relationship between place and politics from the perspective of both the present and the past. And, as in *Ulysses*, the act of walking in a specific urban space allows for connections to be made between disparate times, enabling Kinsella to map Joyce's Dublin onto his own. With a reflexive movement of reiteration he folds the Dublin of the first decade of the twentieth century onto the Dublin of the last decade.

In *The Practice of Everyday Life* Michel de Certeau argues for an understanding of the city that focuses on the pedestrian, the very business of "walking in the city" (de Certeau, 1984). He wants to draw us away from a static, cartographic grasp of urban space — what he calls "an optical artifact" — towards an experience and comprehension of the city in terms of walking. By drawing this parallel between the acts of walking and speaking, de Certeau — in a move that is of particular relevance for our reading of literature — argues for an understanding of walking as "a space of enunciation" (de Certeau, 1984: 98). The pedestrians who populate the city describe a particular textuality, their bodies following "the thicks and thins of an urban 'text' they write without being able to read it" (de Certeau, 1984: 93). Through the act of walking both Joyce and Kinsella enunciate a similar textual geography of the city: the intersecting trajectories of Joyce's Bloom and Kinsella's speaker have, in effect, "a triple 'enunciative' function" (de Certeau, 1984: 97). They appropriate the topography of the city just as a speaker appropriates language; they enact the spatial dimensions of place just as a speaker acoustically enacts language; and they develop a system of gestural relations between differentiated positions just as a speaker develops a system of relations between interlocutors (de Certeau, 1984: 97-98).

I would like to suggest that *The Pen Shop* enunciates a topography of Dublin through which the poet draws together the strands of personal and public history into the nodal point of writing. Divided into two sections — "To the Coffee Shop" and "To the Pen Shop" — with a prefatory poem at the beginning of the pamphlet, *The Pen Shop* traces a journey from the General Post Office (GPO) on O'Connell Street, over the Liffey, into Westmoreland Street and on down to Nassau Street to the warm confines of a narrow establishment called the Pen Shop. This journey also traces a movement from the mythical history of Ireland which informed Kinsella's earlier volume *One* (1974), through a meditation on pre-independence history alluded to in sequences such as *The Messenger* (1978) and *St Catherine's Clock* (1987), to an assessment of the poet's family history and his own mortality. Ghosting Kinsella's speaker's journey down O'Connell Street is Bloom's own journey in the opposite direction. Kinsella's solitary speaker walks, while Joyce's protagonist rides in a carriage with his companions Martin Cunningham, Jack Power and Simon Dedalus up O'Connell Street towards Glasnevin Cemetery.

Kinsella's poem opens in the GPO as the speaker posts a letter to the muse-mother figure whose "fierce forecasts" provoke the response, "Rage, affliction and outcry!" (Kinsella, 1996b: 7). The GPO is a significant location in the history of modern Ireland in that it was the pre-eminent site of the 1916 Rising. The journey to the Pen Shop begins under its "cathedral ceiling" and the customers Kinsella's speaker sees there are envisaged as "souls" whose movements approximate Dantean circumambulation as they take their "places in line at the glass grills / or bowing at the shelves. / Following one another / out through the revolving doors" (Kinsella, 1996b: 7). These "souls" allude to the "silent shapes" glimpsed by Bloom as he passes the yard of "Thos. H Dennany, monumental builder and sculptor": "Crowded on the spit of land silent shapes appeared, white, sorrowful, holding out calm hands, knelt in grief, pointing. Fragments of shapes, hewn. In white silence: appealing" (Joyce, 1992b: 125). They also recall the shades of the dead who gathered around Odysseus in supplication when he arrives in Hades (Gifford, 1988: 115).

At the centre of the GPO stands a statue of Cúchulainn dedicated to all who died in the Easter Rising, which was unveiled on 21 April 1935 to commemorate the nineteenth anniversary of the event. The mythical figure of Cúchulainn is vaunted in the "Cyclops" episode of *Ulysses* and in Kinsella's "At the Western Ocean's Edge". He is familiar too from the poet's translation of the epic mythological cycle the *Táin Bó Cuailnge*:

> Around the bronze hero
> sagging half covered off his upright,
> looking down over one shoulder at his feet.
> The harpy perched on his neck. (Kinsella, 1996b: 7)

This bronze statue depicts a dead Cúchulainn who no longer turns his "struggle outward, against the sea" (Kinsella, 1996a: 302). Instead he is vanquished, though still upright in his dying moments, lashed to a stone pillar. It is only when the crow, symbol and manifestation of Morrígan, goddess of war, lands on his shoulder that his enemies know that he is dead. The crow, or "harpy" as Kinsella puts it, is also a version of the cailleach figure who can be read as Hecate or the Jungian Terrible Mother. By focusing on the representation of Cúchulainn depicted in the GPO, Kinsella situates an aspect of the Irish mythology which is fundamental to his poetry in a specifically political context. Through subject and situation he questions the use of mythology for political purposes, evoking the rhetoric of Pádraig Pearse, for whom Cúchulainn was "the great prototype of the Irish patriot-martyr" (Shaw, 1991: 593).

This rhetoric of blood-sacrifice embodied in the statue of the dead hero is subtly undercut in Kinsella's poem by the appearance of Joyce's pacifist "Mr Bloom". The introduction of Bloom adds a retrospective resonance to Kinsella's own, earlier description of himself in *The Messenger* as a "blackvelvet-eyed jew-child" who watches his father agitating against the fascist Blueshirts (Kinsella, 1996a: 222). On O'Connell Street Kinsella's speaker literally intersects with Bloom who travels northward to the Prospect Cemetery in Glasnevin. Kinsella writes:

> By Smith O'Brien. Dead thirty years, to the day,
> when Mr Bloom unclasped his hands in soft
> acknowledgement. And clasped them. About here.
> (Kinsella, 1996b: 8)

Drawing on the "Hades" episode of *Ulysses*, Kinsella joins the histories of mythological self-determination with those of a more recent political self-determination as he connects the statue of Cúchulainn with the statues of O'Connell Street, each of which commemorate a particular moment in Irish history. Here, Kinsella explicitly rewrites the following passage from Joyce:

> Mr Bloom unclasped his hands in a gesture of soft
> politeness and clasped them. Smith O'Brien. Someone has
> laid a bunch of flowers there. Woman. Must be his
> deathday. For many happy returns. The carriage wheeling
> by Farrell's statue united noiselessly their unresisting
> knees. (Joyce, 1992b: 116)

The statue Bloom notices as he passes is that of William Smith
O'Brien, Cambridge-educated MP for Limerick, who was involved in the insurrections of 1848 for which he was commemorated by a statue sculpted by Sir Thomas Farrell. On his way to
Glasnevin to attend Dignam's funeral Bloom passes another
statue by Farrell, that of Sir John Gray: "Mr Power, collapsing in
laughter, shaded his face from the window as the carriage passed
Gray's statue" (Joyce, 1992b: 117). Gray, of course, is the owner
and editor of the *Freeman's Journal*, a copy of which Bloom carries
in his pocket. Significantly for Kinsella's poem, it is in the offices
of the *Journal* that Stephen rejects the rhetoric of Irish nationalism.

Though Gray was commemorated for advocating land reform,
disestablishment of the Church of Ireland and free denomina-
tional education, he is now "unremembered on his pedestal" and
denigrated by the statement that "None of the Grays was any
good" (Kinsella, 1996b: 8). Here Kinsella quotes directly from
Joyce's short story "Grace", in which Mr Power — who in *Ulysses*
shares the carriage with Bloom as they travel to the cemetery —
pronounces that "None of the Grays was any good" (Joyce, 1992a:
170). In their book *John Stanislaus Joyce*, John Wyse Jackson and
Peter Costello note that this casual defamation is most probably
borrowed from Joyce's father who may have been "among the
party at the June [1879] unveiling of a statue of the late Sir John
Gray MP" (Wyse Jackson and Costello, 1997: 85). Terence Brown
reads the insult as an "especially ungracious remark", considering
the Gray family's "notable contributions to civic and national
life", but suggests that "Mr Power is probably recalling the fact
that in 1891 Edmund Gray's son deserted the Parnellite cause"
(Joyce, 1992a: 303-04).

The next statue encountered in *The Pen Shop* is that of the socialist activist James Larkin, who is described in redemptive
terms:

> Under Larkin with his iron arms on high,
> conducting everybody
> in all directions, up off our knees. (Kinsella, 1996: 8)

In *The Messenger* Kinsella remembers the role that Larkin played
in the development of his father's political consciousness: "He
reaches for a hammer, / his jaw jutting as best it can / with Marx,
Engels, Larkin" (Kinsella, 1996a: 226). Larkin's struggle against
capitalism rather than colonialism is seen, in these lines, to be in-
clusive and empowering. He stands outside the rhetoric of blood-
sacrifice promulgated by Pearse and provides a visual contrast,
"arms on high", with the "sagging" figure of the dead Cúchulainn. Kinsella's Joycean connection underlines a certain antipathy
to what Declan Kiberd, in his 1992 introduction to *Ulysses*, has
called "the Cúchulainn cult" which, he claims, was "objectionable
to Joyce because it helped to perpetuate the libel of the pugna-
cious Irish overseas, while gratifying the vanity of a minority of
self-heroicizing nationalists at home" (Joyce, 1992b: xii-xiii).

Just before crossing the River Liffey the speaker of *The Pen
Shop* encounters the statue of Daniel O'Connell aloft on his
twenty-eight foot pedestal. When the statue was unveiled in August 1882 the crowds that came out to cheer echoed the crowds of
O'Connell's own "monster meetings". On 9 August 1882 the
Freeman's Journal reported that a "mighty roar" went up "from ten
thousand throats when the veil fell at the Lord Mayor's signal"
(quoted in Whelan 2003b: 57). O'Connell is the "Hero as liberator"
of "At the Western Ocean's Edge" in the sequence *Personal Places*
(Kinsella, 1996a: 302) and also the "hugecloaked Liberator's form"
by which Bloom's carriage passes in "Hades" (Joyce, 1992b: 117).
O'Connell, member of parliament for County Clare and successful
agitator for Catholic Emancipation, stands "high in the salt wind"
that blows from the Liffey (Kinsella, 1996b: 8). The depth of his

commitment and his exceptional abilities as a politician are conveyed by his stance, "shirt thrown open and ready for nearly anything", and by his attitude, "with hand on heart and dealer's eye" (Kinsella, 1996b: 8). Below O'Connell's statue gather personifications of the warring forces and themes of his time: "Church and Education in debate / around the hem of his garment; Honest Toil at his heel" (Kinsella, 1996b: 8).

By ghosting *The Pen Shop* with "Hades" and "Grace", Kinsella strengthens his inquiry into the role of memory and the place of the hero in the formation of history. The shades which Odysseus meets in Hades become both the "souls" in the GPO and the statues that Joyce's and Kinsella's travellers pass as they move through the centre of Dublin. These statues, as Whelan explains, trace the movement from imperialism to nationalism within Irish history: "In the second half of the nineteenth century [Joyce's time], the 'supremacy in statuary' which imperial statues enjoyed was challenged both geographically and numerically by the unveiling of monuments dedicated to figures drawn from the contrary sphere of Irish culture, literature and nationalist politics" (Whelan, 2003b: 54). Yet by Kinsella's time, "monuments that had been erected with such choreographed ritual as symbols of a nationalist ideology would seem to have lost much of their symbolic potency" (Whelan, 2003b: 70). They are, as Kinsella himself puts it, "unremembered on their pedestals" (Kinsella, 1996b: 8).

To return, by way of conclusion, to de Certeau's parallel between urban typography and linguistic structures, we can see the intersection between the horizontal movement of Joyce's and Kinsella's protagonists on the one hand, and the vertical stasis of the statues and monuments encountered by them on the other in terms of synchronic and diachronic axes. De Certeau argues that the city as an architectural structure is irreducibly synchronic; like a proper name, "the city [...] provides a way of conceiving and constructing space on the basis of a finite number of stable, isolatable, and interconnected properties" (de Certeau, 1984: 94). If so, then the city of which Joyce and Kinsella write is not the static "optical artifact" that lends itself to a "panoptic administration" (de Certeau, 1984: 96). Created through an act of walking that is itself an enunciation, Joyce's and Kinsella's Dublin is a vibrantly diachronic textual space that interweaves the minor and the monumental, drawing together the threads of the private narrative and the public mythology to write a history of Ireland which can only be properly read from the perspective of the pedestrian.

5

"The Constant Reality Running through Our Lives": Commemorating Easter 1916

Róisín Higgins

The golden jubilee of the 1916 Easter Rising is now remembered as an orgy of unthinking nationalism and nostalgia. Writing on the occasion of the seventy-fifth anniversary of the Rising, Dermot Bolger opined: "For anyone who grew up in the 1960s, the Easter Rising meant 1966 and not 1916" (Bolger, 1991: 10). This a view endorsed by the poet Michael O'Loughlin, who was born in 1958:

> It is, I believe, almost impossible for any one of my generation to think about 1916 as an actual event in History, discrete and autonomous. The way in which 1916 had been presented to us was an important process in our understanding of the nature of our society, and of ourselves. For my generation, the events of Easter 1966 were crucial, so much so that I think it is almost possible to speak of a generation of '66. (Bolger, 1991: 227)

For O'Loughlin and other young people in 1966, the Rising was an abstract but defining event; for others, 1916 was part of living memory. In their 1965 proposal for a film to mark the event Gael-Linn suggested that "It is the constant reality of 1916 running through our lives that we wish to express".[1] The Irish-language film which resulted, *An Tine Bheo* (1966), begins with the recollections of five veterans of the rebellion:

> Veteran Voice 1: I remember Easter Week as vividly as if it happened last year.

> Voice 2: Oh, it's unforgettable — at times I think it's only a few months ago.

> Voice 3: I can visualise all the positions as if I was in them tonight.

> Voice 4: I feel it's part of my life, and a very lasting memory.

> Voice 5: It's indelibly impressed on my memory — every detail of it.[2]

The shifting mental time-frames of the speakers suggest a certain temporal confusion in remembering the Rising. Not only is the event itself both abstract and ever-present, the jubilee commemoration of it was situated at a significant juncture between past, present and future. At an official, political level, this temporal confluence allowed for an emphasis on pride in the past and confidence in the future, rather than a concentration on the difficulties of the present. In 1965 Taoiseach Sean Lemass told a Fianna Fáil gathering that for all those interested in the future of the country

> the celebration of the 50th anniversary of the 1916 Rising, while signifying primarily our understanding of its historical importance, will also be a time of national

---

[1] Taoiseach Papers, NAI, 97/6/157.

[2] Taoiseach Papers, NAI, 97/6/162.

stocktaking, and for trying to look ahead into the mists of
the future to see the right road leading to the high destiny
we desire for our nation.[3]

In his presidential address to the people of Ireland in Easter 1966,
President Eamon de Valera asserted: "We cannot adequately honour the men of 1916 if we do not work and strive to bring about
the Ireland of their desire."[4] The Rising was thus placed in a continuum of the struggle for Irish freedom which, de Valera reminded his listeners, was not political freedom alone but "an enabling condition for the gradual building up of a community".[5] The
jubilee year, therefore, offered an opportunity for the Irish population to use the example of the heroes of 1916 to recommit itself
to the ongoing project of Irish freedom. If the Rising was an attempt to invigorate Irish nationalism through extreme action, then
fifty years later it would be used to reinvigorate Irish patriotism
through extreme commemoration.

The government, however, was the target of criticism from
educationalists, artists, economic exiles, Irish-language groups
and, of course, those opposed to partition. Sinn Féin and the IRA
set up their own commemorative committee and held separate
events. Such was the anxiety in government circles that in the run
up to the jubilee Lemass wrote to the Minister for Posts and Tele-
graphs asking that the schedule for Radio Telefís Éireann be submitted soon "to ensure that these programmes will be suitable.
(This means in particular no O'Casey)".[6] The Abbey was also advised not to produce *The Plough and the Stars* during Easter week.[7]
The absolute conformity which Lemass urged did not materialise,
however, nor did the country at large abandon itself to the celebrations. In fact, articles critical of the prevailing condition of Ire-

---

[3] Taoiseach Papers, NAI, 97/6/159.

[4] Taoiseach Papers, NAI, 97/6/163.

[5] Taoiseach Papers, NAI, 97/6/163.

[6] Lemass to Joseph Brennan, Taoiseach Papers, NAI, 97/6/158.

[7] Report from the Commemoration Committee, Taoiseach Papers, NAI, 97/6/160.

land were carried in the *Irish Times, Dublin Magazine, Studies,* the *Irish Catholic, Campus* (the UCD student newspaper) and numerous provincial newspapers.

So, how was the Republic to mark the fiftieth anniversary of "a great and decisive event in Irish history", as Lemass described it at the launch of the programme of events? The official commemoration committee showed little originality in designing a schedule which included military parades, a pageant, religious services, essay and art competitions and the issuing of stamps and coins. In many ways the lexicon of republican remembrance was exhausted without being reinvented. Hunger strikes were held in Belfast and Dublin by Misneach, an Irish-language group protesting because they believed that the ideals of the 1916 generation had not been properly recognised. Nelson's Pillar was blown up by a republican splinter group and the Government secured an agreement with the national bus and rail company Coras Iompair Éireann (CIE) to remove "the Pillar" from their timetables and bus scrolls, replacing it instead with Árd Oifig an Phoist (General Post Office). CIE also agreed to rename principal railway termini after the executed leaders, and the newly built tower blocks of Ballymun in north Dublin were named in honour of the signatories of the 1916 Proclamation.

Luke Gibbons has suggested that in Joyce's depiction of the centenary of the 1798 Rebellion we can see a moment more akin to radicalism than romanticism, one that contained gestures towards other futures and alternative narratives of the nation (Gibbons, 2001). He contends that, rather than being fixed, these narratives could not even attain the condition of a monument, represented by that space in Stephen's Green "where Wolfe Tone's statue was not". There is the suggestion that colonised societies, in which the primary public voice is not that of "the nation", will find other ways to express their submerged identities within urban spaces. For Gibbons, the flâneur is clearly present in Joyce's Dublin, rejecting the prescriptions of official power, subverting imperial versions of history and place (Gibbons, 2001: 140-41). But what happens to the colony when it achieves statehood, when it takes control of those rigidly choreographed victory parades through the capital? While it can assert its own version of history through the renaming of streets and railway stations, does it simply replace the overarching imperial narrative with an equally linear version of the success of the newly constituted state, or does it provide space for those alternative narratives of the nation?

The Garden of Remembrance

The opening of the Garden of Remembrance was one of the central elements of the 1966 commemoration. It had been a long time in the making; the idea of creating a public park by the Rotunda hospital was first suggested in 1935 by the Dublin Brigade Council of the Old IRA, as it was on this site that the Irish Volunteers had been founded in 1913. In his speech at the opening of the Garden, de Valera also referred to its proximity to meeting places of the Gaelic League, the Irish Republican Brotherhood and to the Rotunda itself in which addresses had been given by members of the Irish Parliamentary Party, including Charles Stewart Parnell. On top of this series of references was placed layer upon layer of symbolism. The Garden is designed in the form of a cross, surrounded by a raised lawn. It is laid out as a basilica but with a western-facing apse within which an elevated platform accommodates the symbols of state rather than church. This raised area was designed to facilitate the Army Guard of Honour during ceremonies and is flanked by the national flag and those of the four provinces. The Garden's reflecting pool is also cruciform and contains a mosaic of six groups of weapons taken from Ireland's heroic age, which were broken to symbolise peace. The peace motif is further expressed in the railings that surround the pool. There, the Irish State Harp occupies the central panel, inset with an olive branch and a replica of the Ballinderry Sword pointing downwards. Further, at the eastern entrance to the Garden a limestone column is positioned, complete with a broken chain to symbolise release from bondage.[8] As such, the symbolism of the garden is clearly desig-

---

[8] Note from the architect Daithí Hanley, de Valera Papers, UCD, P150/3376.

nated; there is little scope in this space for the flâneur. Furthermore, movement within the Garden is channelled as if facilitating pilgrimage, the three aspects of which — tomb, basilica and Holy city — were all present in the 1966 commemoration.

The Garden of Remembrance can be seen as part of the reclamation of modern Dublin which bore the architecture, names and monuments of Empire. This included the overlaying of a different historical narrative on the Georgian and Victorian landscape and, with the Garden, the specific carving out of a space in the city which would reach back through time and into the future. The memorial is not appended onto the landscape in the form of a cenotaph or obelisk; rather, it has been sunk into the city, rooted in it (Whelan, 2003a: 177-85). At the official opening de Valera stated:

> the whole design of the Garden is symbolic. It represents faith, hope, peace, resurgence and is a challenge to all the generations that come, to make the Ireland of their day worthy of the Ireland of the past. All who enter here, or who pass this Garden by, will, I hope, as they murmur a prayer for the departed, pray also that God may preserve this old nation of ours, and have it always in his keeping.[9]

In its dedication — to all who gave their lives for Irish freedom — the Garden does not refer to a specific time-frame. Moreover, it extends the sense of anonymity beyond that of the "unknown soldier". The latter has been described as a specifically modern symbol, "saturated with ghostly national imaginings" (Anderson, 1983: 9) but it is nevertheless historically and gender specific. In fact, the sculptural centrepiece of the Garden of Remembrance has no military resonances. It is a representation of the mythical story of the children of Lir. The artist Oisín Kelly was influenced by the poetry of Yeats and the idea that men at certain moments of history are "transformed utterly".[10]

---

[9] De Valera Papers, UCD, P150/3376.

[10] Included in a statement from the Government Information Service, Taoiseach Papers, NAI, 96/6/193.

Kelly's design was finally sanctioned by the Government in 1965. He had won an open competition to undertake the sculpture in 1950 but work had been delayed due to the reservations of politicians that the theme was based on a pagan legend and had no apparent relevance to the purpose of the memorial. It was accepted by the Lemass administration, however, on the strong recommendation of the Arts Council which argued:

> With sureness of vision Oisín Kelly has realized that the longest series of sacrifices that have gone into the making of a free Ireland could only have been adequately expressed sculpturally through some great 'myth'. History cannot be carved; the thousands of mouldering long-forgotten historical statues in every land give sad proof of this fact.[11]

Kelly himself was drawn to the subtle ambiguity of the subject. He explained to the Office of Public Works: "I should like a memorial which does not attempt to bully my countrymen into having splendid thoughts and noble feelings, but rather one whose message is implicit, a hint rather than a shout" (Hill, 1998: 158). The choice of the children of Lir was indeed ambiguous. A note to the taoiseach on possible inscriptions for the sculpture includes a reminder that one connected to the children would be problematic, as Kelly depicts the swans streaking upwards into triumph, though in the myth the transformation of the children into swans was a cruel act of jealousy striking them down to disaster.[12]

It is in this ambiguous space that the Garden might be said to depart from prescriptive nationalist symbolism, in so far as the sculpture is open to individual interpretation. It uses an old Irish legend from Ulster which is conveyed through contemporary design. The figures are transfixed as well as transformed, the tension of the piece representing a revolution suspended, incomplete.

---

[11] Recommendation from the Arts to the Office of Public Works, Taoiseach Papers, NAI, 96/6/193.

[12] Taoiseach Papers, NAI, 96/6/193.

And although it implicitly references Irish independence and the heroism of 1916, the symbolism, in reaching back to the children of Lir, evades nationalist chronology while also underlining that ancient nation to which de Valera referred in his opening address (Bhreathnach-Lynch, 1999).

The statue itself was not unveiled until July 1971, on the fiftieth anniversary of the Anglo-Irish truce, against the background of burgeoning conflict in the North. The theme of Irish freedom as an ongoing project became, therefore, more explicitly a statement about partition. At the unveiling Taoiseach Jack Lynch made a call to the British Government to declare their interest in the unity of Ireland, returning to this theme three years later when in opposition. In a Dáil debate he had tabled on events in Northern Ireland following the breakdown of the Sunningdale Executive in 1974, Lynch accused the taoiseach, Liam Cosgrave, of having lost focus on Irish unity and concluded with lines from John Hewitt's "An Irishman in Coventry":

> This is our fate: eight hundred years' disaster,
> crazily tangled as the Book of Kells;
> the dream's distortion and the land's division,
> the midnight raiders and the prison cells.
> Yet like Lir's children banished to the waters
> our hearts still listen for the landward bells.
>
> (Hewitt, 1991: 98)[13]

Through the political context of its unveiling, the statue of the children of Lir thus shifted in meaning. The Troubles transferred fresh ambiguity to the surrounding Garden, with its symbolism of bonds severed and violence ended.

Kilmainham Jail

The Garden of Remembrance was just one of a whole range of symbolically significant sites to come to prominence during the

---

13 Dáil Debates, Vol. 273, 26 June 1974.

golden jubilee in 1966. I would like to turn now to another iconic site, one that is situated within quite a different time-frame, Kilmainham Jail in Dublin's western outskirts. The jail itself was built in 1796 as an extension to the existing jail on the gallows hill. The opening of the new jail at this time coincided with the emergence of the United Irishmen and was dubbed the "Irish Bastille" by Charles Teeling. Indeed, almost from its beginning Kilmainham was depicted as a site of both oppression and liberty. The Ireland in which it was built was not simply a colony but a nation speaking a language of European republicanism. Unlike the Garden of Remembrance, therefore, Kilmainham offers itself as a monument to modern concepts of nationhood: that which was articulated, not through symbol, but through word and gesture by the United Irishmen, and instituted by proclamation at the General Post Office over a hundred years later.

The jail was finally closed to inmates in 1924 and fell into disuse until the engineer Lorcan Leonard suggested in the late 1950s that it should be restored and converted into a museum. He wrote to Sean Dowling, chairman of the Association of the Old IRA, of his desire to "elevate that weed-grown, debris strewn yard [...] to the most holy spot in Ireland. [...] What was once a monument to heroic endeavour is now the silent mocking cavern to the indifference of our age."[14] Yet Kilmainham stood for more than the sum of its parts. That it vividly represented imperial power was most efficiently symbolised in the East Wing, built in 1861. Although an imperfect panopticon, it was designed in the spirit of that disciplinary gaze. The booklet issued during the restoration stated:

> Over the gate of Kilmainham Jail there is a device in bronze representing the demons of crime restrained by the chains of Law and Justice. [...] It may afford the visitor some ironic amusement to wonder whether they who commissioned the design had any special crimes in mind and whether they included patriotism (Kilmainham Jail Restoration Society, 1961).

[14] Leonard to Dowling, 9 June 1958, Kilmainham Jail Archive.

But Kilmainham Jail was not simply restored; it was reconstituted. The building itself was imbued with new meaning. The chains of British Law and Justice, divested of power, were now given an ironic twist. The imperial project literally lay in ruins and was to be rebuilt in a not-so-silent mocking of a different age.

At meetings to discuss the organisation of a voluntary effort to restore the jail, it was agreed that in order to preserve unity of purpose, nothing relating to events after 1921 would be introduced into any activity or publicity in connection with Kilmainham.[15] In jettisoning the period of the Civil War, the jail would become a much less contested site within Irish politics, while at the same time underlining its place of importance in the struggle against British rule. So the panoptican, a system which attempted to catalogue and process prisoners in a bid to control not only their bodies but their minds, became a very different space. The institution became a vessel, not of conformity, but one within which individual stories echoed. In a place which might have been dehumanising, it was the humanity of the inmates that was pressed on the memory: Joseph Mary Plunkett, writing a proposal of marriage on the back of his will, or the mathematical equation which de Valera wrote on his cell wall, presumed by the authorities to be a republican hieroglyphic. Within the museum exhibits, the prisoners are seen to conform, not to any penal system, but rather to the expectations of Irish nationalists. It would be several decades before the stories of non-political prisoners would be included in the history of the prison.

Throughout its history Kilmainham was "home" to a host of Irish nationalist leaders, with the notable exceptions of Daniel O'Connell and Michael Collins. The jail, therefore, lent itself to a linear depiction of Irish history, in which each act commemorated that which had gone before. The building also invited the collapsing of temporal and ideological divisions in the modern struggle for Irish freedom, effectively becoming a single site where they

---

[15] L.C.G. Leonard, *The Kilmainham Project as I Dreamt it and Lived it*, [no date], Kilmainham Jail Archive.

could be depicted seamlessly. Furthermore, the narrative arch incorporated in Kilmainham appeared to reach its end at the opening of the museum by Eamon de Valera, the former prisoner now returning as President of Ireland. According to an *Irish Press* report of the event, he told those assembled: "I am not strange to this place. I have been here before, but it was not as bright then as it is now". But history it is not quite so simple. De Valera had indeed been there before, the last time in 1924, when he was imprisoned by his former comrades. So Kilmainham was the backdrop not only to the battle for authority between the British and Irish, but also to power struggles between the Irish themselves. Thus, the ideological differences between Irish nationalists were ignored rather than resolved.

It is precisely this lack of resolution which is so central to the way in which the jubilee commemorations functioned. Despite attempts to provide an overarching narrative of the march of the nation, cracks appeared, largely because the meanings attached to the Rising, like those attached to the two sites discussed above, are not fixed but change through time. In commemorating the Rising, the lines between the details and the meaning of that specific event, and a more general memory of the quest for Irish freedom, were blurred. Thus, the 1966 pageant at Croke Park opened with scenes of the United Irishmen; the official commemorative programme included the unveiling of statues in Dublin to Robert Emmet and Thomas Davis; memorials were built throughout Ireland to a variety of republicans with little or no link to the Rising; and the commemorative supplement of the *Irish Independent* carried a full-page photograph of the late John F. Kennedy at Arbour Hill. In short, the meaning of the Rising was porous. As a political event it could be used as a standard by which to judge subsequent Irish history or it could act as a floating symbol of the much more elusive idea of Irish freedom. Viewed in such symbolic terms, its commemoration could provide an opportunity to celebrate loosely defined moments of Irish heroism and martyrdom stretching from the children of Lir and to the presidency of JFK.

Towards the end of 1965, as the restoration of the jail was in progress, Leonard again wrote to Dowling, saying: "As far as the 1916 Jubilee is concerned, I do not wish to be brought into it; at the best, it can only be a melancholy remembrance, as we, right and wrong sections, have fallen so far short of the minimum."[16] Here lies the paradox of 1966. Involvement in the commemoration of the Easter Rising did not necessarily mean an endorsement of the Ireland of the present (which is not to say it never did). Rather, the jubilee could represent a moment of longing for the ideals of the past and moment of hope in a dream of the future.

---

[16] Leonard to Dowling, 12 November 1965, Kilmainham Jail Archive.

6

"The Glorious Dead"?: Commemorating the Security Forces in Northern Ireland

Catherine Switzer

On 23 September 2003 the first major public memorial commemorating members of the security forces who died during the Northern Ireland Troubles was dedicated at the National Memorial Arboretum in Staffordshire, England. The Ulster Ash Grove consists of a central stone hewn from Mourne granite, surrounded by six boulders, one from each county of Northern Ireland. Spreading from this centre is an area planted with a total of 846 ash trees. 808 of these represent the serving and retired members of the armed forces killed during the conflict, and each of them bears a tag with an individual's details. A further 29 trees were planted by the Northern Ireland Prison Service, one for each prison officer killed, while the 38 trees planted by the Police Service of Northern Ireland (PSNI) represents the former subdivisions of the Royal Ulster Constabulary (RUC). These trees, chosen from species native to Ireland, are intended to "represent lives lost between 1969-2001 and form an ever-changing backdrop to the stone circle and granite plinth".[1]

---

[1] Northern Ireland Office Press Release, dated 23 September 2003. http://www.nio.gov.uk/press/030923b.htm.

The past decade has seen the creation of a relatively large number of memorials honouring victims of the Troubles. One component of this complex but fragmented memorial landscape comprises monuments dedicated to the locally-recruited security forces. This landscape of security force commemoration has not been created in isolation. On the contrary, Loughlin contends that over the course of the Troubles, unionists have drawn on their perception of two World Wars "to provide a mode of understanding — and added legitimisation — for their struggle with militant republicanism, with the scope of the remembrance ritual itself being extended to include security force personnel and civilians killed by republican paramilitaries" (Loughlin, 2002: 147-48). But it would be wrong to assume that security force commemoration draws uncritically on the pre-existing commemorative tradition. The security forces have indeed been woven into the fabric of public commemoration, but while some threads have been picked up, others have been dropped. These interconnections and fractures provide the focus for this paper. I begin by examining the discourses surrounding security force commemoration and the inscriptions employed on security force memorials in public places. I then address the ways in which these commemorative practices both draw on and depart from the already established tradition of public conflict commemoration, before moving to a more detailed consideration of the implications of security force commemoration.

Setting Troubles Commemoration in Context

Troubles commemoration today takes place in a political context which has seen levels of violence in Northern Ireland decrease as the region moves towards a "normal" society. The peace process has had of necessity to deal with questions relating to how the conflict and its victims will be remembered. In 1998 Sir Kenneth Bloomfield, in his role as Northern Ireland Victims' Commissioner, published a number of such recommendations. The Bloomfield Report recommended that the best form of physical memorial would be a "beautiful and useful building within a peaceful and harmonious garden" (Bloomfield, 1998: 51). This idea was innovative in that until very recently there have been few large-scale efforts to commemorate the Troubles in a comprehensive manner. This is due in large measure to the highly contentious political context whereby victim and perpetrator are commemorated in the same landscape and where the definition of each may be dependent on one's political viewpoint. Consequently, a great deal of Troubles commemoration has been very piecemeal, with responsibility for memorials being taken on by particular groups which are often quite selective in who they choose to commemorate.

The commemoration of the security forces represents one important component of the commemorative landscape. Although in general usage the term "security forces" is ill-defined, it refers here to members of the Ulster Defence Regiment (UDR) and its successor the Royal Irish Regiment (RIR), along with the RUC. The UDR was an infantry regiment of the British Army which recruited and operated solely within Northern Ireland (Ryder, 1992; Potter, 2001). The RUC was the police force of Northern Ireland, controversially rebadged and renamed in 2000 as the Police Service of Northern Ireland (Ryder, 2000). The overwhelming majority of members of both the UDR and the RUC were Protestant, despite efforts on the part of both organisations to recruit Catholics. The landmark publication *Lost Lives* finds that of a total of 3,636 deaths up to the summer of 1999, 1,012 were members of the security forces (McKittrick *et al.*, 1999). Of these, 206 belonged to the UDR or its successor the RIR, and 303 were members of the RUC or its reserve forces. Within Northern Ireland a number of different groups are active in commemorating these deaths. These include local government bodies, the Royal British Legion, loyalist organisations and the families of the dead, alongside the various branches of the security forces themselves. The activities of these groups have resulted in complex patterns of memorialisation, much of it quite low-key given that many of the memorials are located inside security force premises (Leonard, 1997). In fact, the contentious political context often makes it impossible to commemorate the security forces in public space. As a result, in many towns commemoration is invisible to the general public.

Like many other territories with a British imperial past, Northern Ireland has adopted a number of conventions for publicly commemorating deaths in warfare. The memorials erected during the 1920s provided a focus for what has been termed "the sorrow and the pride" (Maclean and Phillips, 1990). They were a place "where people could mourn. And be seen to mourn", providing "first and foremost a framework for and legitimation of individual and family grief" (Winter, 1995: 93). Yet these memorials were also political symbols tied up with the workings of British nationalism. The memory of the war was reconstructed into "a myth which would draw the sting from death in war and emphasise the meaningfulness of the fighting and sacrifice", just as the experience of the war was made "acceptable, important [...] above all for the justification of the nation in whose name the war had been fought" (Mosse, 1990: 6-7). Ultimately, however, war memorials embody a whole range of meanings about power, social status and ideology. They are composite sites of which the commemorative element is only one of many possible readings. In Northern Ireland these war memorials and commemorative ceremonies constitute a tradition which has been and continues to be seen largely as the preserve of the Protestant community. In the words of Keith Jeffery, commemorating the First World War provided "an opportunity to confirm loyalty to the British link and affirm Ulster's *Protestant* heritage" (Jeffery, 2000: 131, original emphasis). It is this tradition which in turn provides a framework and backdrop for much security force commemoration.

Memorial Inscriptions

Memorials to members of the security forces in public spaces can be divided into five principal categories: "stand alone" memorials commemorating only the security forces; security force-specific memorials placed beside existing war memorials; names of security forces added to the list of names on existing war memorials; security forces commemorated obliquely on new war memorials; and security forces commemorated as an integral part of new war memorials. The location of security force memorials alongside existing war memorials provides one obvious link between the two conflicts, as does the common use of poppies as a symbol of remembrance, but my focus here is on the inscriptions employed on security force memorials. These can provide a productive area for study since they indicate the intended meanings of the memorial. The tradition of public commemoration as it developed in the aftermath of the First World War is reliant on what Fussell has called "high diction" which gave meaning to the war and instruction to the public on how to understand it (Fussell, 1975: 21). Memorials might exhort "Glory to the dead" or be dedicated to the "Memory of our fallen heroes".[2] However, the poet Michael Longley has written that this language of "high diction" actually contributes to a process of forgetting; it "encourages us *not* to remember how shrapnel and bullets flay and shatter human flesh and bones" (Longley, 1997: 122, original emphasis). In this view, the brutal and bloody truth of death in warfare is effectively hidden from view.

Although a number of inscriptions make use of sentiments borrowed from existing war memorials, such as "Lest we forget" and "We will remember them", security force memorials tend to be devoid of high diction. Individuals are not usually construed as having died for any of the ideals commonly invoked on existing war memorials, such as "freedom", "honour" or "glory". Instead, less elevated language is usually employed. Some invite the viewer to dwell on the manner of death of those being commemorated. One common inscription, which also appears on security force gravestones, is "Murdered in the execution of their duty", a phrase with many potential meanings which hinge on the different ways in which execution can be carried out. Police officers and

---

[2] Inscriptions taken from First World War memorials in Armagh and Gilford respectively.

soldiers, it is implied, execute their duty, while terrorists, although not explicitly identified, execute human beings. Several
memorials use the word "killed" as an alternative to "murdered",
but this does not bring them much closer to high diction. A stone
at the base of the memorial clock tower in Rathfriland, County
Down, commemorates those who "made the supreme sacrifice",
but it appears to be the only public memorial to the security forces
bearing this more traditional inscription. There seems to be a re-
luctance to use the word "fallen", commonly employed on First
World War memorials, perhaps because its use would imply a
level of dignity at odds with the construction of these deaths as
cold-blooded murder. Assertions that those commemorated
"gave" their lives are relatively rare, again conveying the impression that these people had their lives violently taken from them.

These inscriptions represent deceased members of security
forces not so much as the "glorious dead" as the "dutiful, murdered dead". This may be partially explained by unionist attitudes to the status of the Troubles. The conflict may be conceived
of as a war by Irish republicans directed against the British state.
Members of the security forces are regarded as part of the state
apparatus, the British presence in Ireland, and therefore as legitimate targets. For unionists, however, as one RUC widow put it,
"We keep being told by the Shinners [Sinn Féin] that this is a war
[...] [but] I don't see this as a war. I see this as a terrorist campaign."[3] From this perspective, the security forces are concerned
with the maintenance of law and order, and individuals within
those organisations "weren't involved in conflict, they were simply doing a day's work".[4] The vast majority of these individuals
were Protestant, and for unionists, violence directed by militant
republicans against the security forces is therefore sectarian (Fay
et al., 1998: 16). This perception is particularly relevant in the ap-

---

[3] Iona Meyer, RUC Widow's Association.
http://archives.tcm.ie/irishexaminer/1999/09/20/ihead_300.htm

[4] Iona Meyer, RUC Widow's Association.
htttp://archives.tcm.ie/irishexaminer/1999/09/20/ihead_300.htm

parent targeting of UDR soldiers by the IRA in Border areas, a process seen by many unionists there as tantamount to ethnic cleansing. Memorials commemorate the dead, but in another sense they commemorate the violent acts of terrorists, since implicit in the list of names is a record of violent acts. Commemorating the "murdered" dead as such serves to commemorate violence against the Protestant or unionist community.

Implications of Linking the Memory of Different Conflicts

The Bloomfield Report noted that "in our society commemoration itself can too easily take on a confrontational quality" (Bloomfield, 1998: 11). Many aspects of Troubles' commemoration are indeed controversial, and security force commemoration is not immune to this. One of the most obvious points is that the linking of the predominantly Protestant security forces with the war dead through commemoration could be seen as "claiming" it for the Protestant or unionist community. As Edna Longley has observed, commemoration "honours *our* dead, not your dead" (Longley, 1991: 29, original emphasis). But amongst the people I interviewed, all of whom described themselves as unionists, the linking of security force commemoration with that of the war dead was not particularly controversial. It did not constitute a political statement; the existing memorials and rituals were simply the accepted means of public commemoration. War commemoration in Northern Ireland has been seen traditionally as predominantly the preserve of unionists, so even if security force memorials do serve to claim it more unequivocally, would it matter?

One of the most important implications relates to the ways in which the common Irish experience of the First World War has, in recent years, become a much-vaunted symbol for reconciliation in Ireland. Since the dedication of the Island of Ireland Peace Tower in Belgium in 1998, there has been some evidence that remembrance ceremonies in Northern Ireland are assuming a more overtly cross-community character than might previously have been the case. Although the First World War could act potentially as a symbol of reconciliation, the integration of the security forces into commemoration has the potential to disrupt whatever fragile possibilities exist. Nationalists might be able to recognise and accept the service of Irishmen in the First World War, but they are less likely to publicly acknowledge this through participating in commemoration at sites where the security forces are also honoured. Unionists, on the other hand, might come to see beyond the heroes of the Somme and recognise the participation of Irishmen with other political aspirations, but for them commemoration is developing in a different direction. First World War commemoration is being reshaped, but not in a unified or unproblematic way.

It is clear that the commemorative landscape currently being shaped by unionists is informed by the belief that "their" Troubles victims, of which the security forces would be seen as a major group, are being forgotten *on purpose*. This belief has been further strengthened by a number of enquiries into particular killings. For some unionists, such enquiries are perceived to be rather one-sided, and to encourage the remembrance only of those seen as belonging to the nationalist tradition. One interviewee commented:

> Whilst unionists and their victims are told to forget and forgive and move on, nationalists on a daily basis lobby and campaign for enquiries into Bloody Sunday, Pat Finucane, Rosemary Nelson, the guy [Robert] Hamill in Portadown — the list is endless. So on the one hand we're told to put the past behind, and yet there are millions of pounds being spent on Bloody Sunday.[5]

At the heart of this viewpoint is a belief that unionist victims are being purposely sidelined, while those who murdered them are set free from prison. Moreover, it suggests that nationalist victims are being kept in the public eye through government-funded en-

---

[5] Personal communication with anonymous interviewee, September 2000.

quiries, while at the same time unionist commemorative endeavours are not subject to the media gaze.

Conclusion

Troubles commemoration is inevitably controversial. While its divided and piecemeal nature does not totally preclude the possibility of Bloomfield's commemorative building in honour of all Troubles' victims, it certainly complicates the matter, and points to the difficulty of reconciling individuals, communities and their pasts. However, the meanings of the memorials and the rituals which take place around them are not set in stone; instead they are fluid, conditioned and influenced by numerous factors. Commemoration is after all, as Roy Foster has noted, "always present-minded" (Foster, 2001b: 68). But these changing meanings do not make these memorials meaningless; they are fought over and contested both internally and externally for a variety of reasons. Memorials to members of the security forces, like the existing war memorials, are sites at which the purely commemorative is only one of a number of possible readings — which takes us back to the Ulster Ash Grove in Staffordshire.

All of the planning for the memorial and the careful stage-management of its dedication could not prevent criticism from a number of sources. Prison Service widows resented the lack of acknowledgement of the service by name on the central memorial stone, getting no official invitation or financial assistance for the trip to England, and having to bring their own chairs to the dedication ceremony. Police widows and mothers were angered at the RUC being represented only through a tree for each sub-division, rather than one for each police officer killed. Politicians pronounced that the memorial was "tainted with half-heartedness and would be viewed by many as just another attempt to airbrush from history the memory of the sacrifice of the police, Army and Prison Service" (*Belfast Newsletter*, 2003). On the other hand, much of the official talk surrounding the dedication focused on the positive legacy of the security force dead. "Without their dedication, bravery and commitment," said Secretary of State Paul Murphy, "we would not be where we are today on the road to lasting peace and stability."[6] This sentiment was reflected in the emphasis placed on the living nature of the memorial. Yet while trees have often been incorporated into memorials because of their association with regeneration and continuing life, the satirical *Portadown News*, in its edition of 30 September 2003, saw them as particularly appropriate in this case for another reason: "Trees are the perfect memorial to the security forces. [...] They have bark but no bite, many special branches and end up being treated like planks." Like any memorial, this one was open to multiple readings.

---

[6] Northern Ireland Office Press Release, dated 23 September 2003. http://www.nio.gov.uk/press/030923b.htm

7

Origin and Oblivion: Representations of Death in the Poetry of Medbh McGuckian and Eiléan Ní Chuilleanáin

Borbála Faragó

The central objective of this paper is to investigate the poetic methodology of exploring death as the origin of work, life and identity formation in selected poems by Medbh McGuckian (b.1950) and Eiléan Ní Chuilleanáin (b.1942). Representing death as a formative idiom poses several challenges to a reader. Death can never surpass its symbolic significance as the ultimate collapse of meaning: there can be life after death and before death, but the moment of death, as a black hole, carries with it a finite negation of existence. To overcome this negative economy, death is often represented as a threshold of meaning, a transitory phase between different modes of existence. The classical story of Orpheus, which has had a major influence on the shaping of elegiac poetry, offers a suitable allegorical representation of this point (Zeiger, 1997: 2). When Orpheus's wife Eurydice dies from snakebite, he mourns her and in his grief descends into the Underworld. There, with his speech and sweet music he persuades Hades to release her from the dead. Hades agrees on one condition: Orpheus must not look back at her before they reach their own house. Orpheus fails, and with his backward glance casts Eurydice back to the black hole of the Underworld. Eurydice thus dies twice and Orpheus mourns twice. The acts of dying and mourning are duplicated, creating a heightened sense of everlasting grief, failure and absence. Orpheus's eventual death symbolises his entrapment in disjointed sentiment: he is torn apart limb by limb by a group of females known as the Maenads, and has his head thrown into the sea; eventually it is washed up at the island of Lesbos, where it continues to sing until the Lesbians bury it.[1] Death, both for Orpheus and his wife, is thus represented as the threshold that connects the anxiety of life to the grief and mourning of after-death-life.

The central question of the story, however, is why Orpheus turns to look at Eurydice. Such weakness seems out of character for a powerful and successful poet (Zeiger, 1997: 12). Simon Critchley, following Blanchot, interprets this as the crucial moment of identity formation:

> the paradox of Orpheus' situation is that if he did not turn his gaze on Eurydice he would be betraying his desire and thus would cease to be an artist. Thus, the desire which destroys his art is also its source. (Critchley, 1997: 42)

The close association between death and desire, lack and fulfilment characterises that crucial moment of identity formation, when one becomes fascinated by the vanishing face of Eurydice, caught in the double bind of origin and oblivion.

In the context of contemporary Irish poetry, death is often represented as a reservoir of identity formation, as in Seamus Heaney's bog sequences, and also as an ultimate collapse of meaning, as in some of Ciaran Carson's Belfast poems. Medbh McGuckian, in her poem "Forcing Music to Speak", revisits the death of Robert Emmet and the story of Orpheus (or rather, his severed head) to muse upon identity. Although the title could be interpreted as a reference to Orpheus' speech to Hades in the Un-

---

[1] The gender implications of the myth are not lost on McGuckian, though for reasons of space they are not considered here.

derworld, the poem opens with a quotation from the Bible, depicting Christ's funeral gear: "And the napkin, which was about his head, not lying with the linen cloths, but rolled up in a place by itself" (McGuckian, 2003: 102). The imagery of absence, lack, negation and displacement set the tone for the poem. Jesus has left, and the napkin is without its "content" and context, not with the other clothes but all by itself. As a fragmented signifier, its purpose is to highlight the absence of Christ. At this crucial moment, the disciples only know that Christ is gone; "as yet they knew not the scripture, that he must rise again from the dead". As such, the napkin induces grief in Mary and joyous belief in one of the disciples.

The poem opens on this precarious threshold between death and life, grief and belief. The first three stanzas describe a church as "the shell of the bride of Christ", emphasising again the discrepancy created between the signifier and that which it is supposed to signify.[2] Like the head napkin of Christ, the empty church is deprived of its meaning; the void this creates evokes "illness spirits", voices of the Underworld. At this point life and meaning prevail, though the narrative "I" has "no ear for their whispering" and is unaffected by their proximity. Stanzas seven to nine see the appearance of a "young man" who turns out to be Venantius Fortunatus, the sixth-century poet who recorded and celebrated the life of St Radegund and her spiritually adopted daughter Agnes. Throughout his poetry, he rejoices in life's little pleasures, and the chestnut and butter he receives from the two women symbolise the contrasting existences inside and outside the convent (the food having been sent from within, where it cannot be enjoyed, to be consumed outside). The print of Agnes's finger in the butter reinforces the discrepancy which exists between actual and signified presence.

Up to this point the poem is structured around ambiguities: Christ, the church and Fortunatus's poetry represent ambivalence

---

[2] This church is St Catherine's on Dublin's Thomas Street, in front of which Emmet's execution took place in September 1803.

spaces between life and death. As an embodiment of this hesitancy, stanza 11 describes the indistinct face of a man: "We cannot see his eyes, and can discern / only a hint of his mouth." The "harp" in stanza 13 suggests that he is Orpheus, "delivering his body, his whirling, / musical body, musical glove, to the music / he knew in the sky". In the Underworld, pleading for his wife, he invokes his music, which "answers to every touch". Stanza 15, however, explicitly evokes the figure of Emmet, to whom the volume *Had I A Thousand Lives* (2003) is dedicated. Emmet, like Orpheus, creates his identity in and through death. His famous proclamation, "when my country takes her place among the nations of the earth, then, and not till then, let my epitaph be written", contextualises his significance in terms of the politics of death. In following his dream and desire, he has taken the first steps towards his destruction ("his head / is cast in shadow and his lower body melts") and subsequently becomes "post-human", "without a body, / broken in two by his fall" (a reference to his hanging and subsequent beheading). Significantly, however, the black hole of death is circumnavigated. Orpheus (who represents Emmet) emerges from the Underworld, and even after being pulled apart is "free of all body, his breath / giving out before his song" (McGuckian, 2003: 103-04).

The encounter with the abyss of annihilation creates an identity for Emmet as a national "saint". This identity is no longer congruent or harmonious, however. Anxiety, loss and mourning are inseparable parts of it, and the dead hero's voice, "with something dark and thirsty about it, [...] states this lack clearly". The ambivalence of the first part of the poem is taken a step further here. Not only are life and death divided, but their essential interpretation also founders. Death, as a giver of meaning and identity, ceases to fulfil its singularly destructive function, and life, because it is filled with the grief of encountering death, is no longer the blissful harmony represented by chestnuts and butter. Orpheus comes to life as an artist in this harrowing ambivalence, though his human body is torn apart: "His severed head continues to sing

/ as it floats down the Heber / and is immersed in stagnant winter water" (McGuckian, 2003: 104).

In a political context, Emmet's Irish identity and significance are created by his refusal to accept life or death in singular terms. The only epitaph that duly captures his significance is this poem of ambiguities, which successfully depicts the universal impenetrability of the concept of identity. The identity of the poet Orpheus/Emmet is precariously balanced between origin and oblivion and its true realisation does not come about until he is no more (or less) than a floating head landing on the island of Lesbos. Here he is "winnowed and purged and stellified – / true forge embroidered in gold and writing". The last two stanzas situate the speaker back at the moment of initiation in the Underworld, where, glancing at death, the poet says to Orpheus what Orpheus says to Eurydice:

> I don't want,
> I don't want you
> to rest in the leisure times of the cosmos:
>
> for we do not sing 'Requiem'
> for such a soul,
> but the 'Gaudeamus' Mass. (McGuckian, 2003: 105)

Eurydice, the face of death, the ultimate threshold between origin and oblivion, gives meaning to the concept of identity, which can only be seen, claimed and articulated at that vulnerable moment when her face is still visible though swallowed by darkness. In this poem, standing on the docks, awaiting his death, Robert Emmet writes his own epitaph.

The "Deadest Deaths are the Best" has a somewhat more direct approach to mortality. The title is a quotation from Montaigne's 1575 essay "That To Study Philosophy is to Learn to Die", the central thesis of which is that facing death takes away its greatest power over humans: fear. Montaigne argues that incorporating the thought of death into his life allows him to use his time wisely and without fear. Thus, encountering death is the fulfilment of life. The deadest deaths are the best, because they portray mortality as total and immediate oblivion, and with that gesture liberate the mind. McGuckian opens her poem with the image of a corpse: "You lay, quiet, / herded into a ring / by the exploded tree" (McGuckian, 2003: 47). The dead body, perhaps that of Judas, is described as being "comely as a church". "But it was I who was / nailed there firmly", says a Jesus-like voice, and this saviour/betrayer juxtaposition sets the tone of the poem. As in "Forcing Music to Speak", therefore, duality shapes the conceptualisation of identity from the outset.

The next stanza introduces Narcissus, or, more precisely, his reflection:

> His arms mark
> the beginning of an embrace,
> the embrace that is
> only a splash. (McGuckian, 2003: 47)

The goddess Nemesis cursed Narcissus to fall in love with his own reflection, because he had ignored all the girls and nymphs who loved him. He subsequently glimpsed himself in a spring and died of longing. Again, death happens through a fatal glance. Orpheus looks back to Eurydice and Narcissus looks at himself. Both men see death at "the beginning of an embrace", and both men's identity is formed by that encounter. "Deadest Deaths are the Best" reads like a love poem to Robert Emmet, whose epitaph informs the crux of this volume. Created at the instant of departure, Emmet epitomises and frames the Christian and classical references McGuckian lists in these two poems. He is created when he is destroyed, his art and memory coming to life with his demolition. "Image and spectre [...] / snake within each other", so that Emmet's undoing becomes the foundation for a national narrative. His name is saved from Lethe, the ancient river of forgetting, where the shades of the dead have to drink to forget about their past lives on earth. Emmet is thus rescued from oblivion and is portrayed as "the aisleless horizon" of remembering. Achieving his goal in an unwritten epitaph, he symbolises the diverse pressures on claiming a singular identity. In other words, stating the lack clearly is sometimes all it takes to be heard.

Eiléan Ní Chuilleanáin introduces the theme of death as a site of identity formation through the concept of gender politics in her poem "Translation", which was written "for the reburial of the Magdalenes", the used and abused mothers of "illegitimate" babies who died in the now infamous laundry houses. This reburial becomes the act of translation from forgotten to remembered, from silenced to heard. The poem opens with the imagery of the graves:

> The soil frayed and sifted evens the score –
> There are women here from every county,
> Just as there were in the laundry.
>
> (Ní Chuilleanáin, 2001: 25)

The underground corpses and the women of the laundry are intricately fused in this imagery. As spectre, one haunts the other, the corpses foretelling both the future and the past of the living women (Butler, 1993: xi). "There *are* women here", dead and/or alive, depending on the reader's perspective. The soil, so often clichéd as the womb or grave of humanity, assumes both roles simultaneously; sifting "evens the score", becoming the ultimate female materiality of expression. The second stanza gently shifts the focus to the laundry, where the identities of the women are "bleached out" and disappear like fragile spirits in the steam:

> White light blinded and bleached out
> The high relief of a glance, where steam danced
> Around stone drains and giggled and slipped across water.

The bodies of the women are immaterialised in the eerie surroundings of the wet laundry-room. Their existence in this stanza is purely textual, their identities slipping away from definition. The third stanza attempts to reconstruct the struggle of the women for self-expression. As they search "for their parents, their names, / The edges of words grinding against nature", they remain unheard and unidentified. The female body, which gives

identity through birth, is here robbed of it. However, it is the silence of the unheard which eventually gives way to a single voice:

> As if, when water sank between the rotten teeth
> Of soap, and every grasp seemed melted, one voice
> Had begun, rising above the shuffle and hum
>
> Until every pocket in her skull blared with the note.
>   (Ní Chuilleanáin, 2001: 25)

The rising of the "one voice" is reminiscent of Lazarus's return
from the dead, carrying with him the decay of the grave.[3] The
soap and water subvert their function of keeping the living clean
to assisting in the decomposition of defined identity. The physi-
cality of the bodies seems "melted" in the scum of the laundry.
The voice, which is heard above the "shuffle and hum", speaks
through the "rotten teeth" and "skull" of the dead-living women.[4]
However, what we hear is "sharp as an infant's cry". It is the birth
of an identity, not the death of it. The function of the female body
is yet again paradoxically subverted: the living women give birth
to their identities in and through their death. The ultimate act of
translation in the poem is deciphering the voice of the dead for
the living. This happens in the synchronised processes of birth
and death, "While the grass takes root, while the steam rises".
This instant is reminiscent of the Lacanian recognition of subjectivity of a child in the mirror. As Jane Gallop argues: "This moment is the source not only for what follows but also for what
precedes. It produces the future through anticipation and the past
through retroaction. And yet it is itself a moment of self-delusion,
of captivation by an illusory image" (quoted in Landry and Mac-
Lean, 1993: 159).The identity formed in this poem thus remains

---

[3] Ní Chuilleanáin's poem "Autumn" revisits the site of Lazarus's burial place,
refocusing the attention from his rising to his ultimate death.

[4] Toril Moi, paraphrasing Hélène Cixous, claims that "the voice in each woman
[...] is not only her own, but springs from the deepest layers of her psyche: her
own speech becomes the *echo* of the primeval song she once heard" (Moi, 1985:
114, emphasis added).

illusory and fragmentary, a simultaneous loss and gain. The para-
phernalia of the laundry (soap, water, steam) symbolises the collective loss of identity and also its emerging articulation.

The last section of the poem, with its staccato lines, follows the
processes of death, life and death again, recalling the development of identity formation. From death ("clean of idiom")
emerges an identity ("temporary name") which comes to life
("parasite that grew in me") and turns back into death again ("I
lie in earth sifted to dust"). The next line, quickening the tempo,
encompasses images of birth burdened with death — "Let the
bunched keys *I bore* slacken and *fall*" (emphasis added) — before
the ultimate collapse of meaning in the last line of the poem: "I
rise and forget • a cloud over my time." Yet, this language still
resides in the realm of the dead. As Julia Kristeva argues: "the
work of death as such, at the zero degree of psychicism, can be
spotted precisely in the *dissociation of form* itself, when form is dis-
torted, abstracted, disfigured, hollowed out: ultimate thresholds
of inscribable dislocation and jouissance" (Kristeva, 1989: 27,
original emphasis). Thus, the act of forgetting becomes synony-
mous with remembering, just like the physical reburial of the
Magdalenes is "dissociated" in the final image of the cloud.

"Translation" captures the absurdity of transmitting meaning
in/to death. Associating the act of translation with the act of reburial ensures that the significant language of the silenced women
remain in the realm of the dead. However, the "message" is not
entirely negative. The invocation of the reader to "assist" the
women in finding their voices and subsequently "hear it" indicates the existence of another sphere of communication. This is
located in the distinct moment of translation, at the threshold of
language, which is situated between sender and receiver, signifier
and signified. The collective identity of the women emerges from
and simultaneously embodies this threshold of language. This
formulates an ethics of constructing a self which is unstable but
recognisable, political yet fundamentally poetic.

The imagery of death in Medbh McGuckian's and Eiléan Ní
Chuilleanáin's poems characterises the dynamics of identity for-

mation. Identity, interpreted here as a construct of continual change and development, incorporates its own undoing. The political pressures of identity formation evoke a poetic reshuffling of conventional metaphors of self. Death, in this context, is no longer interpreted only as the ultimate obliteration of life. Seen as a threshold, "washed clean of idiom", death occupies centre stage as the ultimate conjunction of space and time which defines human and poetic expression.

Part 2

GEOGRAPHIES OF BELONGING

8

Teaching Irish Spaces in Different Times and Places: Reflections of a Peripatetic Irish Historian

Elizabeth Malcolm

One of the stated aims of the conference held at the University of Ulster's Academy for Irish Cultural Heritages in Derry in March 2004 was to examine the relationship between concepts of space and time and issues of place and identity in Ireland and among the Irish abroad. This aim set me pondering differences in how Ireland, the Irish and Irish Studies have been perceived in Ireland itself and elsewhere, and how these perceptions have changed over recent decades. Do perceptions vary substantially according to place? Are there different Irelands and different types of Irish Studies depending upon where an individual is located: whether, say, in Dublin or Belfast, in Liverpool, in Sydney or Melbourne, or, even, in Trondheim or Tromso? I list these cities because they are all places in which I have lived and worked for significant periods of time over the last 30 years. And how does time affect perceptions? The Ireland of the 1970s was definitely a very different place from the Ireland of the 2000s. But, equally, the perceivers of the 2000s are different from those of the 1970s, being either now an aging baby-boomer generation or a new, younger generation, some actually born during the 1970s.

In this paper I want to challenge the notion that there is one accepted Irish space and an agreed canon of Irish Studies,[1] and I want to do so by using my own pedagogical life as text and discussing the different student constituencies I have taught and their varying responses to Ireland and Irish Studies over the period of a generation. A brief autobiographical sketch at the outset might be helpful to the reader in situating me in terms of place and time. I come from an Irish family in Australia. My father was born and grew up in the north of Ireland and my mother was the descendant of several generations of southern Irish immigrants to Australia, going back to the Great Famine of the 1840s. I first studied Irish history in Sydney at the University of New South Wales. I then spent nearly 15 years researching and teaching in Ireland: first at Trinity College in Dublin and then at Queen's University in Belfast, with a couple of years in between working at universities in Norway. After that I worked for ten years in the Institute of Irish Studies at the University of Liverpool, before returning to Australia in 2000 to take up a new chair of Irish Studies at the University of Melbourne. So, personally, I have had substantial experience of teaching Irish history in Ireland itself, in England and northern Europe, and also in Australia.

---

[1] Of course the term "Irish Studies" was not widely used when I first began teaching Irish history in the 1970s, although at that time I did join the American Committee (later Conference) for Irish Studies, which had been established during the 1960s. I also worked in the Institute of Irish Studies at Queen's University, Belfast in the 1980s, which was another product of the 1960s. The first published guide to Irish Studies I can remember appeared in 1988. With a collection of chapters offering introductions to Irish history and literature, it seemed to me to be particularly geared to American students, who had been exposed to the concept of Irish Studies at universities in Boston, New York and Washington and who were increasingly attending Irish summer schools during the 1970s and 1980s. I would like to thank Dr Christina Hunt Mahony of the Catholic University, Washington DC, for information on the development of Irish Studies in the USA. See also Bartlett *et al.* (1988) and Harte and Whelan (2006).

Norway in the Late 1970s

The first time I ran my own courses on modern Irish history, rather than teaching on courses designed by others, was in Norway during the late 1970s. This was the only time I taught large numbers of students who were not predominantly of Irish birth or descent. I recollect that Norwegians found Irish history difficult to comprehend, especially the Troubles in Northern Ireland, which by then had been dominating the news from Ireland for nearly ten years. Many students took my Irish courses specifically because they wanted a better understanding of the Troubles than was being offered in the media.[2] They regarded the twentieth-century history of Northern Ireland as far more interesting than the history of the Republic. Like a lot of students I've encountered, the Norwegians tended to see the Troubles as either a religious conflict or as an anti-colonial one. Yet they had problems with both approaches. Norway is an overwhelmingly Protestant country and I found that students knew little about Catholicism and what they did know was decidedly unflattering. They struggled to comprehend the importance of religion in the formation of Irish identities and viewed the powerful influence of the Catholic Church in the south with suspicion.

They found it somewhat easier to understand the Troubles as an anti-colonial struggle. But, at that time, only a little over 30 years after the end of the Second World War, most students had parents and grandparents who had lived through the German occupation of Norway. They regarded the English as liberators. My students were English-speaking; they were majoring in English

---

[2] Given the lack of scholarly study of Northern Ireland at that time, I found myself relying heavily on newspaper articles I had collected from the Irish and English press and on books by journalists in order to teach the Troubles. The articles of Mary Holland in *The Observer* were especially helpful, as were works by Coogan (1971), the *Sunday Times* Insight Team (1972) and Dillon and Lehane (1973). Additional historical context was provided by Stewart (1967), de Paor (1970), O'Brien (1972) and Bell (1972). Vivid personal accounts of the outbreak of the Troubles from a nationalist perspective were offered by Devlin (1969) and McCann (1974).

language and literature and most had been to England. I don't remember any having been to Northern Ireland, for, while media reporting had not succeeded in explaining the Troubles, it had certainly succeeded in scaring off tourists. Those who had been to the south were usually shocked by the poverty of the country and especially the sight of beggars in the streets, which were then un- heard of in Norway. Catholic Ireland seemed a very foreign coun- try to them, whereas Protestant England was much more familiar. This generally pro-English sentiment meant there was a reluc- tance to be too critical of British governments in terms of Anglo- Irish relations — in other words, the students demonstrated an unwillingness to believe the worst about the English. They cer- tainly had some sympathy with Irish nationalism, but at the same time they were very ready to accept stereotypes of the Irish as poverty-stricken, priest-ridden, drunken, ignorant and excessively belligerent. They recognised that there had been discrimination against Catholics under Stormont, but they regarded the IRA's violent methods as totally unjustified.[3]

This first experience of teaching Ireland abroad made me con- scious that perceptions of the country were very much influenced by students' backgrounds and the values of the society from which they came. Norway was in the 1970s a prosperous, largely non-Catholic country with an anglophile culture and a deep commitment to the peaceful resolution of political conflict. Thus, Ireland's long and often bloody relationship with England posed serious problems for Norwegian students, in terms of both com- prehension and interpretation. And these problems were espe- cially acute given that the 1970s had witnessed hundreds of vio- lent deaths in Northern Ireland. Studying a polarised political situation inevitably invites the observer to take sides. I felt that

---

[3] I would stress that these are recollections of experiences nearly 30 years ago and I suspect that my remarks would no longer be accurate as regards Norwe- gian students. Irish Studies have developed very considerably in the Scandina- vian countries in recent years. There is now a Nordic Irish Studies Network and centres for Irish Studies at the universities of Aarhus in Denmark and Dalarna in Sweden, while a journal, *Nordic Irish Studies*, began publication in 2002.

my Norwegian students wanted to side with the Irish as the underdogs in an anti-colonial struggle, but their cultural anglophilia and pacifism kept getting in the way. Thus, as many of them told me, Irish history was "hard".

Belfast in the 1980s

During the 1980s I lived and worked in Belfast and mixed with students a good deal. I remember a pervasive sense of hopelessness, produced of course primarily by the Troubles, which seemed to go on endlessly with no prospect of resolution. Many students were keen to finish their degrees as soon as possible so that they could leave Northern Ireland.[4] Many took summer jobs in England, Europe or the USA and relished the freer and more optimistic atmosphere that they found abroad. I encountered many students who expressed a disinterest in, if not an actual hostility towards, Irish history. On more than one occasion I was asked why I didn't teach Australian history as that was seen as far more interesting. Australian history was a success story; Irish history, in the context of 1980s Belfast, clearly was not. I could certainly well understand that students who were living with the Troubles on a day-to-day basis — many of whose families had suffered — did not want to sit in a classroom hearing more about Ireland's violent history. Some of course did. I worked in the History Department and the Institute of Irish Studies at Queen's University and both had many students studying Ireland throughout the Troubles. But I definitely encountered a significant number of history students with the attitude: *I'm interested in any history but Irish history.*

Identity was also very polarised among students in Belfast, as among the rest of northern society. Given the highly segregated

---

[4] Even in 2001 the Census of Northern Ireland showed a sharp dip in the population aged in their twenties, which presumably indicates that the flight of the young from the province has continued. In the Republic, on the other hand, according to the 2002 Census, the population's age profile reached a peak in the late teens and early twenties, reflecting the fact that around 40 per cent of the south's population is under 25 years of age. See Central Statistics Office (2003), p. xxiv.

nature of schools and housing in Northern Ireland, university was
for many students the first time they found themselves working
and even living in close proximity to members of the other community. This new experience often generated tension, especially
after upsurges in violence. I was warden of a student hall of residence for two years and on their application forms for accommodation students were asked to specify their nationality — not their
religion. Overwhelmingly they opted for British or Irish. There
were a few who said Northern Irish or Ulster, but British or Irish
were far and away the principal categories. It seemed then that
there could be no accommodation between the two; I don't recollect any hyphenated identities.

An obvious question to ask was whether students identifying
as Irish were more inclined to study Irish history or other aspects
of Irish Studies than students identifying as British. Did political
and cultural divisions dictate academic preferences? One would
presume so, but unfortunately I was not in a position to investigate this important issue. Unlike all other places in which I have
worked, I did not question students in Belfast during the Troubles
about their identities or their reasons for taking particular courses.
There were many questions it was not wise to ask people in Belfast at that time.

Liverpool in the 1990s

Perceptions of Ireland changed quite markedly during the 1990s. I
was in Liverpool then and found there a far greater interest in and
enthusiasm about Ireland than I'd experienced in Belfast. Partly
I'm sure that this reflected greater optimism about the future of
Northern Ireland fostered by the peace process. The rise of the so-
called "Celtic Tiger" economy in the south and the growing popu-
larity of Irish culture among the young were also important developments. But I think the difference was not just a matter of
changing times; for me it was also a matter of a different place
which gave rise to very different attitudes towards Ireland. Most
of the students I taught in Liverpool fell into three categories, in

terms of their backgrounds. The largest group were the children and grandchildren of Irish immigrants to England; the second largest were English-born students without Irish ancestry; and then there was a smaller group who had been born and had largely grown up in Ireland. Some of the latter were from the north and preferred tertiary education in England to Northern Ireland or the Republic.

The second group of English-born and English-descended students seemed to me to be largely motivated by curiosity, tinged with guilt. Like the students I'd taught in Norway years earlier, they had grown up with reports of the Troubles dominating the media, but the media did not provide answers to such fundamental questions as why the Troubles had occurred and why they had lasted for so long. Some of my English students had spent holidays in Ireland, especially in Dublin, and had had a wonderful time there. During the 1990s Dublin gained a reputation among the young as a great city for parties. Budget airlines like Ryanair offered cheap, direct flights from Liverpool, a mere 35 minutes away. Weekends in Dublin for birthday or stag parties, mainly held in the many pubs, clubs and restaurants of the Temple Bar area, became extremely popular among the youth of England. My English students were certainly keen to understand the Troubles, but, unlike the Norwegians, they had a very positive view of the south. To them the south, which usually meant Dublin, was a young, modern, vibrant place, not at all the run-down, impoverished and conservative city experienced by many of my Norwegian students during the 1970s.

I did encounter some anti-Irish feeling in Liverpool during the 1990s but not a great deal; certainly not on a par with the hostility towards the Irish evident in other English cities during the 1970s and 1980s. Being Irish in large parts of England at that time, especially if you had a Northern Irish accent, could be a very unpleasant experience indeed (Hickman and Walter, 1997: 116-28). There was no hostility among the students I taught; on the contrary, if anything they tended to be very uncritical of Ireland. I remember, when teaching the Famine to students of English background, that they would sometimes express anger, guilt and deep regret for what "England had done to Ireland". Despite the new "revisionist" history of the Famine, they were inclined to favour John Mitchel's interpretation that "the English created the Famine" (Donnelly, 2001: 11-40). So if they indulged in stereotyping of the Irish, it was of a decidedly positive kind.[5]

Generally, Liverpool took pride in its Irish heritage. The decline of sectarianism in the city after the 1950s and the close working relationship between the Catholic and Anglican archbishops during the 1980s and 1990s were held up as models that Northern Ireland could learn from. When the Famine was commemorated in the late 1990s, Liverpool stressed how it had taken in and looked after huge numbers of Irish famine refugees (Malcolm, 2001: 11). I also suspect the fact that Liverpool was never subjected to major bombing during the Troubles may well have played a role in the more benign attitude towards Ireland that existed there.

The largest group of students I taught in Liverpool were of Irish ancestry — some came from Liverpool, but by no means all. In many ways this group was the most interesting. I used to ask them why they were doing courses in Irish Studies and whether they regarded themselves as Irish or English (Mulligan, 2004).[6] Many opted for a compound identity: English but Irish; Irish but English — some a combination of the two. Yet there is no hyphenated identity, Irish-English or Irish-British, in the way that there is a widely-recognised hyphenated identity of Irish-American. A few students opted to describe themselves as Liverpudlian, but the majority, it appeared, wanted somehow to be both English and Irish, while being very aware that the two did

---

[5] For a useful warning against the dangers of "positive stereotyping" and "defensive positioning" in terms of teaching Irish Studies in Britain, see Sharkey (1997).

[6] Mulligan warns teachers against asking students why they are undertaking a particular course, yet at the same time he has some intriguing comments on the reactions of his Kentucky students to Irish Studies. I would like to thank Professor Mulligan for sending me a copy of his paper.

not sit at all comfortably together.[7] Obviously the fact that they had chosen to take university courses on Irish Studies demonstrated a continuing identification with Ireland; and I presume that the courses in turn reinforced that identification. I was struck that many knew Ireland well and said that their families holidayed there regularly. Their parents were often members of that generation of Irish who had immigrated to England in large numbers during the late 1940s and 1950s in search of work (Delaney, 2000: 160-225). So the personal links these second-generation Irish students had with Ireland were often very close indeed. The proximity of Liverpool to Dublin and the advent of cheap flights allowed the students to visit Ireland at least once a year, if not more often.

The way in which my two main groups of students experienced Ireland appeared rather different to me. To the English students, Dublin was essentially a package-holiday destination that offered them "fun", while to those of Irish-descent, who normally ventured beyond Dublin, Ireland represented "roots", family and, in a certain sense, home. And yet the package-holiday experience had played a role in inspiring many of these English students to decide to take up Irish Studies, so it probably should not be dismissed as simply a deplorable manifestation of the "commodification" of Irish culture. (It might be worth investigating if Spanish package holidays, which were even more popular among the young during the 1990s, helped boost Spanish Studies in Britain.)

In terms of courses, I found the students of Irish descent very interested in Irish history, but less interested in the history of the Irish abroad. Courses taught by my colleagues on the Troubles, Anglo-Irish literature, Irish film, Irish archaeology and on the Irish language were also very popular. I wondered if the students' interest in Ireland itself, rather than in the diaspora, was a reflection of the strength of their identification with Ireland and their problematic identification with England. The various commemo-

---

[7] For an important study of identities among English-born students of Irish descent in London and Liverpool, see Hickman (1999).

rations of the 1990s, especially those of the Famine and the 1798 Rebellion, plus the publicity given to the peace process in Northern Ireland, certainly focused attention squarely on Ireland rather than on the Irish abroad. Important developments in women's history, in historiography and in cultural studies also extended and enriched the Irish Studies curriculum very considerably during the 1990s.

There were certainly major advances in Irish Diaspora Studies during this decade as well (O'Sullivan, 2003), but in terms of England, much of this new work painted a very bleak picture of the Irish community in both the nineteenth and twentieth centuries.[8] In what was something of a reversal of my experiences during the 1970s and 1980s, I suspected that students preferred to look at Ireland itself, which to them offered an optimistic picture, rather than to address the hardship, deprivation and ill health which were so characteristic of the story of the Irish in England. When I did teach the Irish abroad, I noticed that many students opted to write essays about the Irish in America or in Australia, rather than in Britain. Admittedly, students also complained that they found my comparative course on Irish migration to Britain, the USA and Australia difficult. One American academic teaching the diaspora has recently argued that students find the topic challenging because it lacks an overarching narrative (Mulligan, 2004). I think there is a lot of truth in this observation. The experience of the Irish in different countries did vary considerably and it is not easy to create a coherent overview without resorting to theory, which students often have trouble grasping.

---

[8] I could cite various authors to illustrate this point, but the work of David Fitzpatrick comes especially to mind. Fitzpatrick has argued that the Irish in England were in a sense "failed" immigrants from the outset, as most would have preferred to have gone elsewhere, but were simply too poor to do so. Note his use of the words "curious" and "peculiar" in the titles of his two major 1989 essays (Fitzpatrick, 1989a, 1989b).

Melbourne in the Early 2000s

Going to Melbourne in 2000, not having lived in Australia for over 20 years and never having lived in Melbourne, I was conscious that I would be facing a new student audience — most born after I had left the country — and was interested in what their perceptions and reactions would be. The majority of the students I've taught over the last five years have been of Irish descent, although I've certainly had some students of Italian, Greek and Chinese origin as well.[9] I do get a number of American exchange students, but most of them are also of Irish descent. It troubles me at times that Irish Studies in Australia does not appear to have yet escaped the diasporic community to appeal to a broader non-Irish audience, the way it has in some other places. Australian students are different from English students in important respects. They are more likely to be of Irish descent, yet when I ask their nationality, they are in no doubt that they are Australian — certainly not Irish or even Irish-Australian, just Australian. Time and place have, I am sure, played an important role in the construction of their identity. Their links to Ireland are not as strong or close as those of my Liverpool students. Their ancestors mostly came to Australia in the late nineteenth or early twentieth centuries and so they look back to Irish grandparents, or more often to great or great-great grandparents. Most never knew their Irish immigrant ancestors personally. In Liverpool, on the other hand, many students were the children or at most grandchildren of Irish immigrants. These students knew their Irish forebears and often retained close links to family still in Ireland. To my Melbourne students their Irish ancestry is generally an historical artefact, not a matter of lived, personal experience. Thus they identify unequivocally as Australian.

Yet, while my Melbourne students are more distanced from Ireland in various ways, I have been surprised at how many of

[9] When writing a history of Ireland specifically for Australians in the mid-1990s, the late Oliver MacDonagh estimated that about 20 per cent of the population had some Irish ancestry. See MacDonagh (1996), p. xi.

them have been to Ireland. International travel by Australian students has increased substantially since I was an undergraduate there during the 1960s. Even so, given the great distance involved, their trips are fewer and not as regular as those of my Liverpool students. Australian students' experience of Ireland is usually that of a young backpacker, spending a week or two in Dublin and parts of the south-west, while in the process of coming from or going to Britain, Europe or the USA. Thus, despite their Irish ancestry, Ireland is essentially a package-holiday or tourist destination for them.

Like the English, they are interested in the Troubles, which they too have grown up with and have difficulty comprehending. But my impression is that they are more interested in migration and the diaspora than were many of my Liverpool students. This may have something to do with the fact that they see themselves as Australian, and thus as part of an immigrant culture, and not as Irish. All non-indigenous Australians are of course comparatively recent immigrants or the descendants of such immigrants.[10] Perhaps it is because of this strong identification as Australian that my Melbourne students have generally demonstrated far less interest in learning the Irish language than did my Liverpool students.

In Melbourne, more than in Liverpool, I have developed contacts outside the university with various Irish community organisations and groups. This has made me acutely aware that even in the same place and at the same time, perceptions of Ireland among the descendants of immigrants can be very different indeed. Different generations see things differently. Irish commu-

---

[10] Currently some 25 per cent of the Australian population of 20 million have been born overseas. Terms like Italian-Australian, Lebanese-Australian and Vietnamese-Australian are often used to describe post-1945 immigrants and their descendants. Academics have recently invented the term "Anglo-Celt" in an attempt to describe Australians of British and Irish descent, whose ancestors arrived before 1945 and usually before 1900, but so far it has not caught on. For studies of the various immigrant communities that form the non-indigenous Australian population, see Jupp (2001).

nity groups tend to be dominated by older, often quite elderly, people. Some are immigrants, others the children of immigrants, but many seem to me to live in a time warp. Theirs is an Ireland of the past, of their childhoods in the 1930s or 1940s or even of their parents' youth in early twentieth-century Ireland. As such, they are very different from my students, who are certainly interested in Irish history, but are also very aware of and excited by the Ireland of today. This older diasporic generation is also more Catholic and more republican than my students, and its cultural tastes more traditional and conservative. It prefers sentimental ballads to current Irish rock or folk music: Tom Moore rather than U2, Sinéad O'Connor or the Corrs. Older Irish-Australians concede that *Riverdance* popularised Irish dancing but worry that it also compromised standards. To them Northern Ireland is occupied territory and a united Ireland is both essential and inevitable. They are very anti-unionist and anti-English, which most of my students are not.

If the different diasporic generations have different readings of Ireland, they also have different readings of the history of Irish Australia. One of the great heroes of the older generation is Archbishop Daniel Mannix, a fervent nationalist and former president of Maynooth College, who was appointed archbishop of Melbourne in 1913, a post he filled for 50 years. The older generation relishes Mannix's Irish nationalism: how he dramatically defied the British both in Ireland and in Australia. The younger generation — if they know anything about him at all — views him much more critically, no doubt because he was deeply conservative on social and political issues. His anti-communism during the 1940s and 1950s helped to split the Australian Labor Party and keep a conservative government continuously in power in Australia for more than 20 years.

To conclude, then, I would say that my own personal experience of looking at Ireland from different perspectives — from different places and times and through the eyes of different groups and generations — has made me very suspicious of attempts to construct agreed definitions of Ireland, the Irish or of Irish Studies. To me such definitions can only be temporary constructions, flimsy shelters for the peripatetic scholar, not solid, permanent habitations. Ireland is an unstable entity and *what* it is depends very much on *who* you are, *where* you are and *when* you are.

9

"A Dialogue in Hibernian Stile": Controlling Language and Constructing History in Early Eighteenth-Century Ireland

James Ward

A story told about a member of the Irish Parliament offers a fitting image for an historical moment.[1] Cornelius O'Callaghan, MP for Fethard, was a convert from Catholicism who, through his "assimilation to the dominant Protestant order [...] personified the trend which reformers wished to intensify and accelerate" in eighteenth-century Ireland (Barnard, 2001: 198). While he was attempting to secure a wife for himself, O'Callaghan was asked where his estates lay. In reply he "was alleged to have stuck out his tongue and pointed to it" (Johnston-Liik, 2002: 377). This gesture could be taken to refer to what O'Callaghan had left behind as well as what he stood to gain. Its significance for the present discussion lies in its identification of language as an estate, since the metaphor of estate-management is an apt one for the duties assumed by the dominant order in the decades after the Williamite settlement. In the time of a "new co-

---

[1] Research for this paper was assisted by a postgraduate bursary from the British Association for Irish Studies. I am grateful to Professor David Fairer of the University of Leeds for his comments.

lonial settlement dedicated to the 'improvement' of confiscated territories", landowners were prevailed upon to improve their estates by fencing, planting and draining. Language also became a terrain that must be rigorously altered in response to the question of "how and under what conditions, land politics and religion could be 'improved', administered or parcelled out" (McMinn, 1998: 129).

Perhaps the most famous schemes of language "improvement" in the early eighteenth century are found in the third part of Swift's *Gulliver's Travels* (1726). Projects underway in the Academy of Lagado include a machine for writing books, a plan "to shorten Discourse by cutting Polysyllables into one" and "a Scheme for entirely abolishing all Words whatsoever" (Swift, 1965: 185). This aspect of Swift's satire is routinely linked with the English Royal Society but some of the work in progress in the Academy recalls projects then being mooted as means to alter the linguistic contour of Ireland. Swift made several contributions to the debate on this subject, one of his most famous pronouncements being also an overt statement of Ireland's deleterious influence on the linguistic competence of his junior colleagues in the Anglican clergy.

In "A Letter to a Young Gentleman, lately enter'd into Holy Orders" (1720) Swift complains that the "Stile" of his recipient and many others like him has been corrupted by the "barbarous Terms and Expressions" of the locality:

> I could [...] have been glad, if you had applied your self a little more to the Study of the *English* Language, than I fear you have done; the Neglect whereof is one of the most general Defects among the Scholars of this Kingdom, who seem to have not the least Conception of Stile, but run on in a flat Kind of Phraseology often mingled with barbarous Terms and Expressions peculiar to the Nation. (Swift, 1968: 65)

To correct such defects of "Phraseology" Swift asserts that "Proper Words in proper Places, makes the true Definition of a

Stile". This formulation may have become almost proverbial but its Irish context is often overlooked. In one of the first London printings of this letter, a note on the title page states that "the following Treatise was writ in Ireland by the Reverend Dr Swift". To identify the nation in question as Ireland clarifies both Swift's remark about "defects among the Scholars of this Kingdom" and his observation that their language is "often mingled with barbarous Terms and Expressions peculiar to the Nation".

Sometime in the 1730s Swift began work on a piece that exemplifies the "mingled" discourse he complains of in the letter of 1720. A truncated Irish counterpart to Swift's *Polite Conversation* (1738), entitled "A Dialogue in Hibernian Stile", the precise date of which is unknown, is a brief manuscript fragment containing an exchange between two members of the English-speaking landowning class. Even such a limited sample reveals their "Hibernian" style of speech to be a hybrid discourse. It includes words taken directly from Irish such as "Frawhawns" (bilberries), as well as others like "Sowins" (flummery), which may be either from Irish or Scottish Gaelic, while others still, such as "Bear" (to mean barley) are dialect forms from the north of England or Scotland (Swift, 1973: 277-78). This combination of different codes reflects both the speakers' origins in Britain and their present situation in a time when, to quote another of Swift's works, "many gentlemen among us, talk much of the great convenience to those who live in the country, that they should speak Irish" (Swift, 1973: 281). The mixture of Irish, English and Scottish terms, non-standard usages and archaisms in "A Dialogue" offers an instance of style that disrupts the epigrammatic concision of "Proper Words in proper Places", showing how that definition hinges on the notion of propriety — a term that comprises not only the idea of correctness but of belonging. "Proper" words can either be correct ones or words unique to an individual, a time, a place or a community. "Hibernian Stile" brings these two denotations into conflict. Out of the dialogue comes a dialectic, a clash that Swift's "true Definition of a Stile" cannot successfully resolve.

These conflicting versions of style call to mind an intriguing, if glancing, use of the term by Edward Said, whose close engagement with Swift's notion of style is often overlooked. In *Orientalism* (1978) Said initially defines his titular concept as "a *style* of thought based upon an ontological and epistemological distinction made between 'the Orient' and [...] 'the Occident'"; it is, he continues, "a Western *style* for dominating, restructuring, and having authority over the Orient" (Said, 1991: 2-3, emphasis added). Swift's notion of Hibernian style is rooted in an analogous distinction between English and Irish modes of speech and thought, which is itself grounded in a comparison with Roman theories of colonisation. Even though Hibernian style is properly seen as a mixture of Irish, English and Scottish elements, Swift identifies the Irish language as the sole contaminant of an otherwise "pure" English, a deviant style that militates against the adoption of properly civilised styles of life and speech. The most efficient means of dominating, restructuring and having authority over these wayward styles was therefore to abolish Irish. Swift endorsed this policy in a piece called "On Barbarous Denominations in Ireland":

> The Legislature may think what they please, and that they are above copying the Romans in all their conquests of barbarous nations; but I am deceived, if any thing hath more contributed to prevent the Irish from being tamed, than [the] encouragement of their language, which might easily be abolished, and become a dead one in half an age, with little expence, and less trouble. (Swift, 1973: 280)

Thanks to the legislature's failure to adhere to the Roman model, the work of conquest has been left unfinished. As a result, the persistent influence of Irish has begun to blur what Seamus Deane calls the divide "between barbarians and civilians", as even clergymen begin to adopt a discourse laden with "barbarous" terms (Deane, 1985: 42). The *OED* reminds us that the Greek word *barbaros* "had probably a primary reference to speech, and is compared with Latin *balbus*", meaning stammering. A barbarian is thus someone who does not speak correctly; a practitioner of an unacceptable style. Swift was not the only churchman to fear that the distinction between the "Romans" and "barbarians" of post-Williamite Ireland had begun to dissolve. In *The Querist* (1735-37) Bishop Berkeley asked "[w]hether the upper part of this [Irish] people are not truly English, by blood, language, religion, manners, inclination, and interest [...]; Whether we are not as much Englishmen as the children of old Romans, born in Britain, were still Romans?" (Berkeley, 1901: 430). When it came to language, the question could no longer be answered confidently in the affirmative. Swift's response to this contingency was to extinguish the source of the "barbarous" terms he abhorred.

His claim that the legislature must make a more concerted effort to eliminate Irish is often seen as an ironic exaggeration in the mould of *A Modest Proposal* (1729), and as a result it is seldom taken seriously (Fabricant, 1986: 245; Harrison, 1999: 153). However, Swift's view that Irish could and should be "abolished" was not unusual for a member of the Anglican Church at this time. The use of Irish as an evangelical tool had been enshrined within the canons of the Church of Ireland since the seventeenth century, but by the 1720s this policy was falling from favour. In its place came a policy of promoting English through charity schools (Connolly, 1992: 294-307; Barnard, 1993: 260). As early as 1711, the Dublin House of Commons had cited this method as one whereby "the Irish Language may be utterly abolished" (Richardson, 1712: 60). An adherent of this method wrote in 1717 that "all the young Irish can understand and speak English [...] And 'tis in Schooling such Irish Children the whole Hopes of Converting the Irish People must lie" (Anonymous, 1717). By 1734, the charitable initiative had received government sanction when the Incorporated Society in Dublin for Promoting English Protestant Schools in Ireland received its royal charter (Connolly, 1992: 304; Milne, 1997). Although little was actually said about the suppression of Irish, it seems nonetheless to have been an "implicit policy" of the charter schools (Milne, 1997: 133). One of its keenest champions was

Henry Maule, Bishop of Dromore. Shortly before the Society was formally constituted, he announced in a sermon that:

> The poorer sort of Irish most cheerfully send their children
> to the English Protestant Schools, provided they are taught
> gratis: the Irish language, as to the reading of it, is now in a
> manner become a dead letter to the natives, and the
> characters of it as little understood [as] the Danish or Runic.
> It is now not read, or made use of by the Irish themselves,
> who are all desirous to read, write and to speak the English
> tongue. (quoted in Milne, 1997: 131)

Maule's claims may be a little exaggerated but the perception that Irish was becoming "a dead letter" to the natives was not confined to those who were hostile towards it. In his *The Elements of the Irish Language* (1728) the soldier, poet and lexicographer Aodh Buí Mac Cruitín explains that the ensuing text is designed to rescue his native language from oblivion and preserve it for posterity: "[I] am hereby moved to use al [*sic*] my Endeavours and Industry, to publish a more full and correct Grammar of the said Language, now in its decay, and almost in Darkness, even to the Natives themselves" (MacCurtin, 1728: vi). Mac Cruitín, who published this and other English-language texts under the anglicised name Hugh MacCurtin, was embarking on a project motivated by an emotional sense of loss, one that he has been "moved" to undertake because his own is falling into "decay" and becoming unintelligible even to the "Natives". This use of the word "native" verges on metonymy, gesturing towards the term "barbarian" in the sense of one who lies outside the pale of linguistic respectability. The underlying distinction between the civilized and the barbarous was not entirely alien to Gaelic culture. As Sean Connolly notes, the "Gaelic literati" were an intellectual elite whose manuscript-based culture was wholly separate from "the despised oral tradition of the lower classes" — or, as Mac Cruitín calls them, "the Natives" (Connolly, 1998: 6).

Mac Cruitín's fears about the decay of Irish provide a link with Swift's most famous work on language, *A Proposal for Correcting,*

Improving and Ascertaining the English Tongue (1712). This *Proposal* asserts that the "Roman Language arrived at a great Perfection before it began to decay". English, however, is at a different stage on this trajectory:

> But the English tongue is not arrived to such a Degree of Perfection, as [...] to make us apprehend any Thoughts of its Decay: And if it were once refined to a certain Standard, perhaps there might be Ways to fix it for ever, or at least until we are invaded and made a Conquest by some other State: And even then, our best Writings might probably be preserved with Care, and grow into Esteem, and the Authors have a chance of Immortality. (Swift, 1973: 8-9)

It is interesting to find that Swift not only proposed the abolition of Irish but looked with equanimity on the possibility that English might become a dead language preserved only in writing; that he saw this as the corollary of being "invaded and made a Conquest by some other State". Mac Cruitín's preface finds Irish undergoing a version of this fate. Having reached a state of perfection, it has entered its decay and is threatened by encroaching darkness: "most of our Nobility have abandoned [Irish], and disdain'd to learn it this 200 years past". Against such indifference he announces his aim to be the "promotion of our language and the preservation of our Ancient Monuments" (MacCurtin, 1728: ix, xi). But for whose benefit were such works of promotion and preservation to be undertaken?

Mac Cruitín's grammar was published at Louvain, possibly under the auspices of St Anthony's Franciscan College, and was dedicated to John James Devenish, a major-general in the service of Louis XV. The nobility he refers to is therefore the exiled Catholic aristocracy, but his work may also have had a wider appeal. In his preface he states that his work is aimed at "the studious and other ingenious Gentlemen, lovers of Antiquity", adding that he craved "the favour and acceptance of the curious seekers of Antiquity and of all generous learned students, to whom these my Endeavours may prove in any way serviceable" (MacCurtin, 1728:

xi). Increasingly such "curious seekers of antiquity" could be found among the Protestant elite in Ireland as much as among the old order in Europe. Cornelius O'Callaghan, mentioned at the start of this paper as the man whose estates lay in his tongue, had in his library a copy of Mac Cruitín's *Brief Discourse in Vindication of the Antiquity of Ireland* (1717) as well as Dermot O'Connor's recent English translation of Geoffrey Keating's *Foras Feasa ar Éirinn*. O'Callaghan also had eight volumes of the *Spectator* — a combination that might indicate that Irish culture before the Norman invasion was becoming an acceptable subject of polite interest (Barnard, 2001: 198).

In this context it may be significant that O'Connor published his translation of Keating under the title *A General History of Ireland*, placing it within a historiographic genre that, alongside natural and ecclesiastical history, would have been a recognised category to Anglophone readers and publishers. Karen O'Brien notes an increasing demand in England "for works of polite literature" and especially "a steady growth in the readership for demanding lengthy histories", often "in expensive multi-volume folio formats" such as James Tyrell's *General History of England* (1696-1704) (O'Brien, 2001: 105-06). The need for an Irish equivalent was widely felt. "[A]s to the History of Ireland I am very sensible there is one wanting", Archbishop King of Dublin wrote to Henry Maule, the champion of the charity schools whose comments on this subject were quoted earlier. Maule seems to have been keen to undertake the project of compiling a history, although he was warned by King that it would be a "more Difficult work than you imagine". King's comments on the subject further imply that the writing of Ireland's history was a task that fell naturally to the Protestant clergy and gentry. As if to confirm them in this role, it was to the clergy and gentlemen of Derry that King left his library in his will.[2]

---

[2] W. King to H. Maule, 8 May 1722, 26 May 1722, TCD MS 750/7, pp. 104, 117. King's own interest lay mainly in natural history, a discipline that combined elements of geology, geography, quantity surveying and civil engineering. He envisioned a county-by-county survey of Ireland's natural resources and investi-

Others did take cognisance of the native scholars' efforts. William Nicolson, one of King's successors in the see of Derry, commented favourably on O'Connor and Mac Cruitín's books in his *Irish Historical Library*, a survey of materials that, to quote his title, "may be serviceable to the Compilers of a General History of Ireland" (Nicolson, 1724). As this further suggests, however, Nicolson did not cast either of the two in the role of such "Compilers". Their works may have been useful preliminaries, but the compilation of an authoritative historical account was a project that awaited completion. O'Connor and Mac Cruitín's attempts to promote the monuments of their culture also met with open antagonism. Mac Cruitín found a rival historian in Sir Richard Cox, author of the stridently xenophobic *Hibernia Anglicana* (1689-90). It may have been for his criticism of the latter work, and its attempt to "prove the *Irish* Language to be a Mixture of other Languages" (MacCurtin, 1717: xiii), that Mac Cruitín was denigrated by Cox. O'Connor's book, meanwhile, was denounced in print by his patron, the Anglican cleric Anthony Raymond, as "a spurious Edition of Doctor Keating's General History of Ireland [...] printed after a vile and incorrect manner" (Harrison, 1999: 117). Such tensions show that the correlation between the Hibernian and the stylish should not be over-emphasised. Antiquarian enquiry may have gained a certain polite status by presenting Gaelic culture as a museum piece, but the living version could still meet with suspicion and incomprehension. The taint of barbarism lingered and there was concern that the project of instilling civility could easily falter.

Just before he wrote to Henry Maule to advise him on his projected history of Ireland, Archbishop King warned another acquaintance that "it is much observed that your family is altogether Papists, and that you live as much after the old Irish manner, as

---

gations into the feasibility of public works such as improving Dublin's harbour and making the Liffey navigable by barge. King's own paper on loughs and bogs, written for the Dublin Philosophical Society, was published as part of *A Natural History of Ireland* [...] *by Several Hands* in 1726.

the merest Irish man in the Kingdom".[3] Ironic confirmation that lifestyles had not been brought to the required level of civilised respectability came inevitably from the pen of Swift, who in 1730 wrote "The Answer to the Craftsman" — a kind of follow up to *A Modest Proposal* — which, following William Petty, argued that Ireland should be evacuated and transformed into a giant cattle ranch. The scheme would be supervised by "our inhabitants the graziers" who, Swift's proposer argues, will be well suited to their employment by their diet of "Bonnyclabber, mingled with the Blood of Horses", which was until recently the staple food of the Irish: "until about the Beginning of the last Century Luxury, under the Form of Politeness, began to creep in, they changed the Blood of Horses for that of their black Cattle; and, by Consequence, became less warlike than their Ancestors" (Swift, 1971: 178). In Swift's version of the Irish historical narrative, politeness makes a minimal intervention as the native Irish become marginally less barbarous through an expedient that literalises the idea of "fresh blood". For Swift, as for many of his Anglican contemporaries, Hibernian style was a discourse that had yet to undergo extensive — not to say drastic — revisions.

---

[3] King to Lord Kingston, 9 January 1722, TCD MS 750/7, p. 128.

10

Moving Titles of a Young Ireland Text: Davis, Duffy, McGee and the Origins of *Tiocfaidh Ár Lá*

Brian Lambkin

The Young Ireland text to which my title alludes, "The Irish Chiefs", is a ballad poem that used to be well-known by nationalists throughout Ireland and its diaspora. It was written by the Young Ireland leader Charles Gavan Duffy (1816-1903), who first published it in 1846 under the curiously suggestive title "Time was, and is, and is to be". This paper investigates this change of title and also considers the relationship between "Time was, and is, and is to be" and the now well-known republican slogan "Tiocfaidh ár lá" ("Our day will come", a phrase which was "used originally as a kind of slogan by supporters of Sinn Féin and of the PIRA, but is probably now used more widely by nationalists, if sometimes a little ironically" (Dunn and Dawson, 2000: 269).

Duffy wrote this ballad poem of six ten-line verses in response to the sudden death of Thomas Davis (1814-45) on 15 September 1845. He published it five months later on 28 February 1846 in *The Nation* newspaper, which he edited, above one of his pseudonyms "The O'Donnell", under the title "Time was, and is, and is to be". Later that same year the poem was republished, with some slight textual alterations, in the *Book of Irish Ballads*, edited by Denis Florence MacCarthy (MacCarthy, 1874: 215-17). Under Mac-Carthy's editorship it was given the title by which it has been known subsequently, "The Irish Chiefs". MacCarthy's book, which included four other poems by Duffy, was intended as a se-quel to Duffy's own *Ballad Poetry of Ireland* (1845) in which the au-thor had included none of his own poems. By this time Duffy was well known both as editor of *The Nation*, which he had founded jointly with Davis and John Blake Dillon, and as one of the new group of Young Ireland *Nation* poets. Indeed, his "Faugh-a-Ballagh" or "Fag A' Bealach" ("Clear the Way") had inspired Davis to write one of his most famous poems, "Lament for the Death of Owen Roe O'Neill", which Duffy first published in *The Nation* in November 1842 (Duffy, 1968a: 64).

Whether it was Duffy, the author, or MacCarthy, the book edi-tor, who was mainly responsible for the move of title from "Time was, and is, and is to be" to "The Irish Chiefs" is not clear. How-ever, it seems likely that Duffy was content with the move and that it was probably made because the longer title was considered too clumsy — not immediately memorable — or too obscure. By contrast, "The Irish Chiefs" was both simple, being taken from the first line ("Oh! to have lived like an Irish Chief..."), and direct, referring to the four named chiefs in the poem: Brian Boru, Owen Roe O'Neill, Henry Grattan and Davis. Relatively few readers could have been expected to recognise that "Time was, and is, and is to be" alludes to the Three Fates or *Moirai* of Greek mythology, who "as they spin, they sing, with the Sirens, the music of the spheres; Lachesis the past, Clotho the present, Atropos the future" (Greene, 1944: 315-16). Fewer still might have been expected to discern an allusion to the Three Norns of Norse mythology, maid-ens who dwelt by the well of Fate tending the destinies of men and whose names were Urd (Past), Verdandi (Present) and Skuld (Future) (Ellis Davidson, 1964).

What is clear is that Duffy fully intended his original title to al-lude to the ancient tripartite personification of time, especially as depicted in Norse mythology. In this he was expressing the profound influence on his own thought of Thomas Carlyle, which was particularly acute at the time he wrote the poem. In the early 1840s Duffy read Carlyle's *Miscellanies* and in 1845 published John Mitchel's review of Carlyle's *Life of Cromwell* in *The Nation* (Pearl, 1979: 10, 43). As well as this, Duffy and two Young Ireland colleagues, John O'Hagan and John Pigot, met Carlyle at his home in Chelsea in April 1845, describing themselves as his "sworn disciples" and explaining that their purpose was to make him their advocate "before England and the world" (Kaplan, 1984: 336; Wilson, 1925: 283). In September 1845, just before Davis' death, Duffy went on an excursion to Ulster with O'Hagan, Mitchel and John Martin, during which they usually finished the day with what Duffy described as "tea and Thomas", meaning that while they sipped their tea, one of them would read aloud from Carlyle's *Sartor Resartus* (1834) (Pearl, 1979: 50). In October Carlyle sent Duffy a copy of his book *Past and Present* (1843) and early in 1846, when his poem was first published, he helped Carlyle with *Cromwell* — extraordinarily for a nationalist considering Cromwell's reputation in Ireland — by correcting the Irish names for the second edition (Pearl, 1979: 45; Wilson, 1925: 314). It was in the works of Carlyle, therefore, particularly in his developing ideas on the nature of time, that Duffy found the inspiration for his original title, "Time was, time is and is to be".[1]

In *Sartor Resartus* Carlyle introduced his concept of time with that same distinctive tripartite formula, and with words that might be especially comforting for those coming to terms with death, as Duffy was in late 1845:

> The curtains of Yesterday drop down, the curtains of tomorrow roll up; but Yesterday and Tomorrow both *are*. Pierce through the Time-element, glance into the Eternal. Believe what thou findest written in the sanctuaries of Man's Soul, even as all Thinkers, in all ages, have devoutly

---

[1] Another title that may have been influenced by Carlyle was an essay by the Young Irelander Michael Barry, "Ireland As She Was, As She Is, and As She Shall Be", published in 1845.

read it there: that Time and Space are not God, but creations of God; that with God as it is a universal Here, so is it an everlasting Now. [...] Know of a truth that only the Time-shadows have perished, or are perishable; that the real Being of whatever was, and whatever is, and whatever will be, *is* even now and forever. (Carlyle, 1863a: 160, original emphasis)

In *The French Revolution* (1837) he tried a variation on this formula, replacing "is" with the more active "do" ("All that has been done, All that is doing, All that will be done [...]: the All of Things is an infinite conjugation of the verb *To do*") and connecting it with weaving and a movement towards doomsday: "how we stand enveloped, deep-sunk, in that Mystery of Time; and are sons of Time; fashioned and woven out of Time; and on us, and on all that we have, or see, or do, is written: Rest not, Continue not, Forward to thy doom!" (Carlyle, 1842: 429-30). Three years later, in his lecture "The Hero as Divinity", quoting this same "active" variant of the tripartite formulation, Carlyle went on to develop his famous image of time as a great tree, which he derived from Norse mythology:

I like, too, that representation they [the Norsemen] have of the Tree Igdrasil. All Life is figured by them as a Tree. Igdrasil, the Ash-tree of Existence, has its roots deep-down in the kingdoms of Hela or Death; its trunk reaches up heaven-high, spreads its boughs over the whole Universe: it is the Tree of Existence. At the foot of it, in the Death-kingdom, sit Three Nornas, Fates — the Past, Present, Future; watering its roots from the Sacred Well. [...] It is Igdrasil, the Tree of Existence. It is the past, the present, and the future; what was done, what is doing, what will be done; 'the infinite conjugation of the verb *To do*.' (Carlyle, 1863b: 199-200)

And in *Past and Present* Carlyle again returned to this theme: "Time was, Time is [...]; and withal Time will be. There are three

Tenses, *Tempora*, or Times; and there is one Eternity" (Carlyle, 1893: 55).

From this we can clearly see the Carlylean influence on Duffy's original choice of poem title. Surprisingly, perhaps, it appears that Carlyle's tripartite formulation ("whatever was, and whatever is, and whatever will be") was unprecedented. Although the Fates and Norns are represented as singing in Classical and Norse literature, there is no instance of them making such an oracular utterance about time.[2] So although Duffy's original title would have resonated strongly with devotees of Carlyle, those who were not may well have found it obscure. But what probably clinched the case for replacing the original title with the relatively simple "The Irish Chiefs" was the allusion of the latter to something much less obscure: *The Scottish Chiefs* (1810) by Jane Porter, which Duffy's mother read to him as a boy and which is credited with being one of the first true historical novels and the inspiration for Sir Walter Scott's Waverley series (Dennis, 1997: 9).

Even if given the chance, however, Duffy's original title was not likely to have stuck in the popular mind in the way that Davis's "A Nation Once Again" did. Nevertheless, "Time was, and is, and is to be" and the poetic ideas it encapsulated continued to be influential. In later life Duffy returned to its formula in reflecting on the achievement of starting *The Nation* when "new and engrossing hopes [were] created which have not ceased, and which shall not cease" (Duffy, 1968a: 79). In similar vein he reminded his Young Ireland colleague Thomas D'Arcy McGee (1825-68) of "the pleasant summer rambles we have enjoyed together, speculating on the dead past and unborn future" (Duffy, 1968b: 24).[3] In this they, and Davis, were no doubt strongly influenced by Carlyle's reading of Norse mythology. One of Davis's

---

[2] Remarkably, the American poet James Russell Lowell has the following in "The Washers of the Shroud": "I looking then, beheld the ancient Three / Known to the Greek's and to the Northman's creed, / That sit in shadow of the mystic Tree, / Still crooning, as they weave their endless brede, / One song: 'Time was, Time is, and Time shall be'".

[3] Their first ramble occurred shortly after they first met in the summer of 1845.

essays, edited and published immediately after his death by Duffy in 1846, was called "The Sea Kings", based on Samuel Laing's three-volume translation of Snorro Sturleson's *Heimskringla or Chronicles of the Kings of Norway* (1844).

Davis, Duffy and McGee were probably also familiar with an important source of Carlyle's interest in the Three Norns, "Gray's fragments of Norse Lore" (Carlyle, 1863b: 31). The Three Norns were also the subject of Gray's "The Fatal Sisters". Published in 1768, it was the first English language version of the medieval *Darradarljód*, a "lay" inserted in the late thirteenth-century *Njal's Saga*. In it, a man called Darradar has an awful vision in Caithness of women weaving on a loom where "men's heads were used in place of weights, and men's intestines for the weft and warp; a sword served as the beater, and the shuttle was an arrow" (Magnusson and Pálsson, 1960: 349-51). Duffy, Davis and McGee had a particular interest in this poem because of its relevance to Brian Boru, the first named chief in Duffy's poem, and the Battle of Clontarf: Darradar had his vision on the morning of the battle, Good Friday 1014, and the women he saw were Norns or Valkyries determining the fate of those in the battle.

This vision of "The Fatal Sisters" became widely known, first through the work of McGee, who reported it in some detail in his two-volume *Popular History of Ireland* (1862), along with a verdict on the importance of Boru as an "Irish Chief" in terms that invoke Carlyle's concept of time, which is in the gift of "Fate": "Not from the Anglo-Norman invasion, but from the day of Clontarf may we date the ruin of the old electoral monarchy. The spell of ancient authority was effectually broken and a new one was established. Time, which was indispensable, was not given" (McGee, 1869: 102-03). McGee's Carlylean view of time and fate, which he adopted from Duffy, proved more widely influential, largely as a result of it being amplified in the work of A. M. Sullivan, who relied on McGee's *Popular History* as one of his two principal sources for his bestselling *Story of Ireland* (1867) (Foster, 2001a: 1-22). Sullivan's book opens with his hope that his young fellow-countrymen at home and abroad "will not fail to read aright the lesson which is taught by *The Story of Ireland*" (Sullivan, 1898: 5-6). In case this lesson is lost, he ends by explaining that it is about the "doings" of "Time", "Providence" and "Destiny" personified:

> Time as it rolls onward will always be adding to its chapters. Let us hope it may be adding to its glories. The lesson which the "Story of Ireland" teaches is, Hope, Faith, Confidence in God. Tracing the struggles of the Irish people, one finds himself overpowered by the conviction that an all-wise Providence has sustained and preserved them as a nation for a great purpose, for a glorious destiny. (Sullivan, 1898: 7)

Sullivan's view that time is an agent capable of determining Ireland's destiny, and that lessons about the nation's destiny can be learned from its past, is an outworking of Carlyle's overall project, which was "from the Past, in a circuitous way, [to] illustrate the Present and the Future" and so, by engaging in the proper study of History, "to predict the Future, to manage the Present" (Carlyle, 1893: 33). This was the project taken up so enthusiastically by Davis, Duffy, McGee and the other Young Irelanders who contributed to the "Library of Ireland" and the "Ballad History of Ireland" in order to popularise that history. At the heart of that project was a distinctive, quasi-religious view of time and Ireland's "fate" or "destiny". Sullivan summed it up in the title of his final chapter: "The Unfinished Chapter Of Eighteen Hundred and Sixty-Seven. How Ireland 'Oft Doomed to Death' Has Shown That She Is 'Fated Not To Die'." The endpoint of this "unfinished chapter", Sullivan explained, is the coming of a particular day when, in the words of Davis, "Orange and Green shall carry the day", "we'll have our own again" and "be a Nation once again". This is the same day to which Duffy refers in the final lines of "The Irish Chiefs": "Let a king arise / And a holier day is come."

This optimistic view of the future contrasts with the un-Carlylean despair of "Dirge and Prophecy", quoted by Sullivan, which was written on the night the Act of Union was passed in 1800:

> There are marks in the fate of each clime —
> There are turns in the fortunes of men;
> But the changes of realms, and the chances of time,
> Can never restore thee again.[4]

Space does not permit discussion of the antecedents of this optimistic idea of a coming day, or a detailed tracing of its descent in nationalist literature (especially through Pearse). Perhaps the most powerful encapsulation of it emerged in the 1970s with the coinage in Irish of the slogan "Tiocfaidh ár lá", attributed to Bobby Sands.[5] In giving a graphic account of its use in Long Kesh during the Blanket protest, Sands illustrates its connection with Davis and the Young Irelanders:

> 'Tiocfaidh ár lá' bounced and rebounded in frightening echoes off the walls [...] 'Our day will come!' That's what it meant and our day would come, I told myself. [...] 'Tiocfaidh ár lá!' I screamed out the door. One of the boys down the wing began to sing. *A Nation Once Again* resounded and echoed from behind every door. (Sands, 1983: 59-60)

Whether Sands read Davis, Duffy and McGee directly, or indirectly through Sullivan or his many imitators, his poem "The Rhythms of Time" returns us to the Young Irelanders and their Carlylean sense of time and fate:

> There's an inner thing in every man,
> Do you know this thing my friend?
> It has withstood the blows of a million years,
> And will do so to the end. (Sands, 1998: 177-79)

---

[4] Sullivan (1898: 533) explains that this verse is "by some attributed to the pen of Moore, by others to that of Furlong".

[5] For illustrations of its use, and that of the variant "Béidh Ár Lá Linn", on wall murals, see Rolston (1991). Note also that "Our Day Will Come" was a hit for Ruby and the Romantics in 1963.

Sands then lists a sequence of historical exemplars of this "inner thing" which takes in the exile of the Jews in Babylon, the Crucifixion of Jesus, Wat Tyler's Peasant Revolt and the French Revolution. Like Duffy's roll-call of Irish chiefs — Boru, O'Neill, Grattan, Davis — who belonged to times "when hearts were fresh and true", Sands' sequence illustrates the working of the eternal "spirit" that "lies in the hearts of heroes dead".

Evidently, the Young Irelanders' tripartite formula (heroic past, present suffering, future reward) continued to move nationalists, not least through the writings of Sullivan and Sands. Sullivan's source, as Foster correctly notes, was the "early-nineteenth-century treasurehouse of Irish Romanticism: Tom Moore's historical ballads, Samuel Ferguson's bardic fantasies and the writings of John Mitchel" (Foster, 2001a: 8). But for his core view of Ireland's "sacred destiny" Sullivan owed more to Davis, Duffy and McGee. To the protagonists of later Troubles, in the 1970s especially, the Young Ireland language of time, fate and destiny came to sound a little old-fashioned. Something simple and direct, like "The Irish Chiefs", but more suited to the less spiritual, "sound-bite" culture of the late twentieth century was needed; and so a snappier slogan, encapsulating all that Duffy had summed up in his abandoned "Time was, and is, and will be", was found in "Tiocfaidh ár lá".[6]

---

[6] It is unlikely that Duffy ever considered translating "Time was, and is, and is to be" into Irish. Even though his mother knew Irish and as a boy he plagued her to tell him stories such as those of the Irish chiefs, he never learned it from her. As an adult, notwithstanding his "Fag A' Bealach", he "behaved as if Irish did not exist", according to León Ó Broin (1967: 147, 153).

11

"His Lights Are Not Ours": W.B. Yeats and the Wartime Poems of Louis MacNeice

Richard Danson Brown

My title comes from the penultimate paragraph of Louis MacNeice's (1907-63) *The Poetry of W.B. Yeats* (1941): "The spiritual lesson that my generation (a generation with a vastly different outlook) can learn from Yeats is to write according to our lights. His lights are not ours" (MacNeice, 1967: 197). This approach — a form of generational criticism which locates the older man as a powerful but dangerous figure — is anticipated by *The Oxford Book of Modern Verse*, where Yeats reads MacNeice generationally: "Ten years after the war certain poets combined the modern vocabulary [...] with the sense of suffering of the war poets. [...] Day Lewis, Madge, MacNeice, are modern through the character of their intellectual passion" (Yeats, 1936: xxxv-xxxvi). Despite his suspicion of most forms of "intellectual passion", Yeats reacted favourably to MacNeice, praising him as an apocalyptic "anti-communist" and including a more generous selection of his work than he did of either Auden or Spender, whom he excludes from his generational summary (Yeats, 1936: 419-33). A sense of being part of opposed literary generations was common to both poets.

Ireland and Irishness underpin these transactions. In recent years, MacNeice's affiliations have been re-evaluated by critics reacting against the complementary over-simplifications that either he was not sufficiently Irish (because of his English education and residence) or that, in Samuel Hynes's formulation, he was a "professional lachrymose Irishman" (Hynes, 1992: 332). MacNeice's reading of Yeats has figured prominently in revisionist accounts. Edna Longley argues that despite their differences of background and allegiance, "MacNeice is the major Irish poet after Yeats who follows him in broad cultural orientation" (Longley, 1996: 28). The differences between Yeats and MacNeice — one an ascendancy nationalist, the other the Ulster-born son of southern Protestants — are, in this reckoning, ultimately subsumed by similarities of "cultural orientation". Peter McDonald suggests that MacNeice operates almost as an inverse of Yeats: as "Yeats used Ireland to construct a dominant myth of the self, MacNeice undermined the self to complicate and qualify the myth of 'Ireland'" (McDonald, 1991: 227-28).

Both Longley and McDonald tend to privilege MacNeice over Auden and Spender: Longley has written wittily of her dream that there should be books called *The MacNeice Generation* and *MacNeice and After* (Longley, 1988: 6), while McDonald problematises the conventional hierarchy which defines Auden as "major" and MacNeice as "minor" (McDonald, 1991: 2-4). Yet MacNeice's conclusion indicates that his sense of belonging to a generation was more than just a rhetorical convenience, or inconvenience. As in *Modern Poetry* (1938), "my generation" meant chiefly Auden and Spender. "His lights are not ours" is suggestive of an ongoing generational friction and of MacNeice's primary allegiance to values he shared with his English contemporaries. Writing to in 1964, Auden admitted that Yeats "has become for me a symbol of my own devil of unauthenticity, of everything which I must try to eliminate from my own poetry" (quoted in Smith, 1994: 155). MacNeice never felt this paranoiac sense of the culpability of Yeats's poetry, yet the relationship between the two remains vexed and provocative in terms of what it implies about literary generations and national affiliations. This paper explores MacNeice's response to Yeats during the war years, when the question of allegiance was at the forefront of his mind and when he tried to write a non-combatant's war poetry which seeks to capture some of the charge of Yeats's work. This is not simply a question of poetic influence, but rather of the critical and creative dialogue which MacNeice conducts with Yeats.

Portents of War

MacNeice's struggle to assimilate Yeats's influence was arduous and had ramifications for the whole of his poetic project. Long before *The Poetry of W.B. Yeats* he was a significant presence in MacNeice's thinking. In 1935 he warned would-be imitators of the plays that Yeats "is a very single-minded or whole-minded artist. Take hints if you like but for God's sake don't imitate him. You would have to be him first, which you're not" (MacNeice, 1935: 8). John Engle has suggested that there was little connection between Yeats's poetry and MacNeice's, observing that *Autumn Journal* (1939) shows "no trace" of Yeats's influence (Engle, 1993: 73). Yet this assertion is complicated by the literary contexts of the poem. Deriving from his collaboration with Auden on *Letters from Iceland* (1937), *Autumn Journal* forms part of MacNeice's project to write what *Modern Poetry* calls a long poem of "serious criticism in the lighter manner" (MacNeice, 1938: 188). As *The Poetry of W.B. Yeats* indicates, MacNeice's central interest was in Yeats's shorter poems (MacNeice, 1967: 17). The wartime volumes, *Plant and Phantom* (1941) and *Springboard* (1944), include shorter poems which recall Yeats's manner; *The Last Ditch*, which gave a dry run to several poems collected in *Plant and Phantom*, was published in 1940 by Yeats's sisters at the Cuala Press (Stallworthy, 1995: 277-78).

MacNeice became more conscious of Yeats as a positive influence as he moved away from *Autumn Journal*; indeed, Stallworthy suggests that Yeats's death liberated MacNeice from the fear of being adversely influenced (Stallworthy, 1995: 253). *The Poetry of W.B. Yeats* admits that *Modern Poetry* had "over-stressed the half-truth that poetry is *about* something" (MacNeice, 1938: 15, original emphasis). The ambition realised in *Autumn Journal* and theorised

in *Modern Poetry* was for an *"impure"* poetry embroiled in the everyday (MacNeice, 1938: v, original emphasis). As MacNeice acknowledged, "Yeats all his life was a professed enemy of facts,
and that made my generation suspicious of him" (MacNeice, 1967:
18). While he never abandoned the notion that "Everydayness is
good" (MacNeice, 1979: 353), the events of 1939 were a significant
challenge to such assumptions: "I had only written a little of this
book when Germany invaded Poland. On that day I was in Galway. As soon as I heard on the wireless of the outbreak of war,
Galway became unreal. And Yeats and his poetry became unreal
also" (MacNeice, 1967: 17).

   This sense of estrangement leads to the realisation that the fate
of Yeats's poetry is that of all poetry, including that of MacNeice's
generation:

> war spares neither the poetry of Xanadu nor the poetry of
> pylons. I gradually inferred, as I recovered from the shock of
> war, that both these kinds of poetry stand or fall together.
> War does not prove that one is better or worse than the
> other; it attempts to disprove both. (MacNeice, 1967: 18)

Though McDonald suggests that he distances himself from the
"Auden generation" through *The Poetry of W.B. Yeats* (McDonald,
1991: 99), MacNeice maintains his earlier proposition that the poet
is closer to the ordinary man than the mystic, while seeking to
qualify *Modern Poetry*'s poetics of communication through the
study of a poet who is resistant to that model (MacNeice, 1967:
24). Yet MacNeice's Yeats remains congruent with *Modern Poetry*'s
sense that poets need to write from an intellectual perspective. A
key passage rebukes escapist accounts of Yeats:

> He was neither so simple-minded nor so esoteric nor so
> dilettante a poet as he is often represented. I have met
> people whose attitude is: 'Yeats was a silly old thing but he
> was a *poet*.' This is a foolish attitude. No silly old thing can
> write fine poetry. A poet cannot live by style alone; nor
> even by intuitions alone. Yeats, contrary to some people's

opinion, had a mind. (MacNeice, 1967: 31, original emphasis)

Auden's "In Memory of W. B. Yeats" lurks below the surface: "You were silly like us: your gift survived it all" (Auden, 1977: 242). Where for Auden, Yeats's silliness establishes his kinship with the rest of humanity, MacNeice brings out the condescension implicit in the term. The drift of his study is precisely that Yeats was neither "silly" nor "like us" yet remains a significant poet whose work demands more generous theoretical support than *Modern Poetry* provided. As the opening paragraphs demonstrate, *The Poetry of W.B. Yeats* recognised, in a way the brasher *Modern Poetry* had not, that "both these kinds of poetry stand or fall together". War threatened poetry *tout court*: MacNeice's theory had to encompass Yeats's "extraordinary force of personality" — crucially, not his silliness — on something like Yeats's own terms (MacNeice, 1967: 31).

These concerns underlie "The Coming of War", a sectional poem which recalls "Meditations in Time of Civil War".[1] "Dublin" in particular has been seen as a key text in MacNeice's dialogue with Yeats. As McDonald observes, "Dublin" recalls the rhythms and stanzaic form of "Easter 1916": it revisits the locus and invokes the pitch of Yeats's poem (McDonald, 1991: 100-01). That process of revisiting encompasses Yeats's reconnection with militant Irish republicanism in the aftermath of the Easter Rising and MacNeice's very different position in the late summer of 1939. "Dublin" can be read as a response to "Easter 1916", which dramatises MacNeice's distance from Yeats's politics. Where "Easter 1916" constructs a martyrological lament for "MacDonagh and MacBride / And Connolly and Pearse", "Dublin" petrifies the heroes of the past, be they Irish patriots or English admirals, as "Declamatory bronze[s]":

---

[1] Since the sequence was substantially revised through publication, I quote from the fullest version in *The Last Ditch* (1940) where it runs to ten poems.

Grey brick upon grey brick,
Declamatory bronze
On sombre pedestals —
O'Connell, Grattan, Moore —
[....]
And Nelson on his pillar
Watching his world collapse.

This was never my town,
I was not born nor bred
Nor schooled here and she will not
Have me alive or dead. (MacNeice, 1940: 2-5)

For McDonald, MacNeice's speaker is an inveterate outsider: "'Dublin' has no room for any 'terrible beauty'; it leaves the poetic voice separated from its subject" (McDonald, 1991: 100-01). Yet since the poem's form and subject invoke "Easter 1916", it must also be read in terms of the time lapse between 1916 and 1939. In this context Yeats's revolutionary contemporaries are "ghosts" as historical as "O'Connell, Grattan, Moore" on their "sombre pedestals". The differences between the poems are connected with their different brands of historicism. Where Yeats provides a heroic litany for the rebels against the backdrop of Georgian Dublin, for MacNeice the city incarnates his conflicted allegiances and is itself a hybrid construction. The third stanza emphasises the overlapping liaisons between apparently opposed camps:

And the mist on the Wicklow hills
Is close, as close
As the peasantry were to the landlord,
As the Irish to the Anglo-Irish,
As the killer is close one moment
To the man he kills,
Or as the moment itself
Is close to the next moment.

Such formulations resist classic nationalist binaries and emphasise Dublin's cultural hybridity. The city embodies conflated histories, identities and allegiances: "Fort of the Dane / Garrison of the Saxon, / Augustan capital / Of a Gaelic nation." For MacNeice, the conflicts of "Easter 1916" are over, while the present "toppling hour" claims, yet fails to elicit, a more committed response. The comic juxtaposition of the statues of Irish patriots with Nelson's recognises that none of them is adequate to the moment at hand. Nelson is "Watching *his* world collapse", but "Dublin" insinuates that, in the broader terms of the Cuala volume, his is not the only paradigm which is currently "Bundled up in the last ditch" (MacNeice, 1940: v).

Casualties of War

In contrast to the ambiguities of "The Coming of War", *Springboard* conveys the hardening of MacNeice's attitudes to Irish politics. During 1940 he considered emigrating to America. *The Strings are False* (1965) articulates his dilemma: "In Ireland most people said to me 'What is it to you?' while many of my friends in England took the line that it was just power politics" (MacNeice, 1965: 21). MacNeice's subsequent commitment to the Allied cause entailed choosing between Ireland and England, or between the foreign policies of Churchill's government and de Valera's. MacNeice's work at the BBC initially involved propaganda. "Neutrality" demonstrates that he had developed a clear sense of ethical priority. Ireland's neutrality affronted his increasingly dualistic interpretation of the war. While the third stanza includes a line which mimics Yeats's idiom ("Intricacies of gloom and glint"), the force of the poem lies in its subjection of the conventions of Yeatsian pastoral to sardonic treatment. That "the neutral island" finds in its heart "a County Sligo" or "ducats of dream and great doubloons of ceremony" does not obviate the perfidy of non-alignment. The final stanza juxtaposes the "archetypal sin" of Nazi-dominated Europe with the image of Atlantic mackerel "fat — on the flesh of your kin" (MacNeice, 1979: 202-03). This unequivocally answers the question posed by MacNeice's Irish friends. War means the slaughter of "your kin"; Ireland's foreign policy refuses to recognise the claims of kinship and proximity between Ireland and Britain.

MacNeice's dialogue with Yeats is most striking in "The Casualty". As has often been observed, this poem works in the same tradition as "In Memory of Major Robert Gregory". It commemorates one of the victims of the Atlantic war, MacNeice's friend, Graham Shepard, whose corvette was torpedoed in 1943. Jon Stallworthy's account of the poem as a failed pastoral elegy exemplifies the critical consensus about the relationship between the two poems: "MacNeice knew and liked Shepard better [...] than Yeats knew and liked Robert Gregory but, ironically, it is his honesty — and his respect for Shepard's honesty — that undermine his poem and prevent it from taking its place with [...] Yeats's masterpiece of rhetorical inflation" (Stallworthy, 1995: 322). MacNeice's unimpressed reading of Yeats's elegy complicates such criticisms:

> Yeats [...] treated [...] Gregory in the same way that Shakespeare treated his tragic heroes and heroines; the hero is conceded full individuality; his Marxist conditioning is ignored. This means simplification, means [...] the elimination from the tragic figure of all psychology except some simple trends, it means the explanation of a man not by his daily life but by one or two great moments. (MacNeice, 1967: 110)

For MacNeice, Yeats's concession of "full individuality" to his protagonists misrepresents them. "The Casualty" shoulders the burden not only of trying to elegise a close friend, but of correcting Yeatsian simplification. In its sequence of "snapshots" MacNeice constructs a patchwork of images which attempt to recapture aspects of Shepard's life and to distinguish his act of poetic commemoration from Yeats's:

> Look at these snapshots; here you see yourself
> Spilling a paint-pot on a virgin wall

Or boisterous in a sailing-boat or bubbling
At a Punch-and-Judy show or a music-hall
Or lugging Clausewitz from a public shelf
To make your private notes, thumbing and doubling

His corseted pages back. Yes, here and here
You see yourself spilling across the border
Of nice convention, here at a students' dance
Pinching a girl's behind — to reappear
A small boy twined in bracken and aprance
Like any goatfoot faun to propagate disorder.

(MacNeice, 1979: 246-47)

In place of Yeats's elaborate eight-line stanzas with their mesh of couplets and interlaced rhymes, "The Casualty" is cast in six-line stanzas in which the rhyme scheme shifts restlessly and the syntax is frequently at odds with line length and metrical order. It is not only Shepard who "spill[s] across the border/ Of nice convention": the text overflows conventional boundaries in imitation both of Shepard and "the mid-Atlantic swell" which killed him. And in place of Yeats's abstract assertion of Gregory's scholarly and military prowess — "Soldier, scholar, sportsman, he" (Yeats, 1997: 63) — MacNeice particularises. Shepard's reading of Clausewitz is metaphorically enriched by his delight in "silken legs", as the physical form of the military treatise is treated as though it were a woman to be coaxed out of her corsets. Shepard fails to approximate to Yeats's hyperbole, yet this is precisely MacNeice's point. Rather than "Our Sidney and our perfect man", Graham Shepard comes through as a genial anarchist, happy "to propagate disorder".

Such a reading problematises the idea that "The Casualty" unsuccessfully replicates "the method of Yeats's poem" (McDonald, 1991: 126). Further, though the poem does not read Shepard's death ideologically, the wartime context infiltrates the text in ways in which the First World War does not impinge on "In Memory of Major Robert Gregory". Yeats presents Gregory's death as a terrible surprise — "a thought / Of that late death took all my heart for speech" (Yeats, 1997: 63) — but avoids explicit contextualisation. In contrast, MacNeice's title connects the poem with others in *Springboard* such as "The Conscript" and "The Mixer", which locate their protagonists as participants in "'this second war'" (MacNeice, 1944: 7). "The Casualty" mirrors these texts with the difference that where they present imagined characters against the background of the early 1940s, this poem elegises a real individual who symbolises the war's many casualties.[2]

The structure of *Springboard* is also pertinent. *Collected Poems* (1966), edited by E. R. Dodds after MacNeice's death, follows *Collected Poems 1925-1948* (1949), which dismantled the ordering of *Springboard*. "The Casualty" is the first poem in the second section of the original volume; it faces "The Springboard", a parable which imagines a diver poised "High above London" (MacNeice, 1944: 40-41; Brown, 2002). So the physical form of *Springboard* establishes a connection between the existential predicament of the diver and Shepard's death. The diver is caught between his sense that the "circumstances called for sacrifice" and his own scepticism, having long ceased to believe "In any Utopia or in Peace-upon-Earth; / His friends would find in his death neither ransom nor reprieve / But only a grain of faith — for what it was worth (MacNeice, 1979: 213). Similarly, Shepard's death is subservient "to circumstance" (MacNeice, 1967: 109): the war against Nazi Germany places him in the "mid-Atlantic" just as surely as it perches the hero of "The Springboard" "There above London where the gargoyles grin". "The Casualty" may not be a thorough Marxist rebuke of "In Memory of Major Robert Gregory", yet it is a poem which demands to be read and appreciated contextually — through the circumstances of its production and the circumstances to which it responds.

---

[2] See for example "The Mixer" ("in this second war which is fearful too, / He cannot away with silence") and "Bottleneck" ("When I saw him last [...] he was standing / Watching the troopship leave").

Conclusion

In September 1948 Yeats was reinterred in Sligo's Drumcliff churchyard. His body was exhumed during the war by local authorities in Roquebrune "without anyone informing the family" (Foster, 2003: 656). Rumours persisted that the remains which eventually made their way to Drumcliff were not in fact Yeats's. MacNeice was prominent among those who believed that the authorities had got the wrong man: "They had dug up the body of a Frenchman with a club foot [...]. What do you think should be done? we asked. Can't do anything now, [MacNeice] said" (Collis, 1970: 85). In this paper I have shown that MacNeice's response to Yeats was serious about the value of his poetry yet critical of his values. This dialogue informs the poetry MacNeice wrote during the war, in which his commitment to the Allied cause is at odds with Yeatsian nationalism. MacNeice's refusal to collude with the events of September 1948 is a characteristic coda to their relationship. Yeats's reburial aspired to make life mirror art: in Roy Foster's words, it "announced that WBY's reputation belonged neither to government nor family, but to the country whose consciousness he had done so much to shape" (Foster, 2003: 657). In Maurice Collis's account, MacNeice appears as a mischievous party-pooper, hungover and dishevelled, failing to behave as befitted "the most able poet present" (Collis, 1970: 84). MacNeice's relationship with Yeats is a narrative punctuated by such moments of resistance. Yet this is not simply a case of poor funereal etiquette. MacNeice's allegiances, both to his own literary generation and to the struggle against fascism, make his lights as prominent in their exchange as Yeats's own.

12

Beyond the Cartesian Imagination: Placing Beckett

Charles Travis

Samuel Beckett's (1906-89) first novel *Murphy* (1938) provides an idiosyncratic examination of the human mind and its perception of the experience of social alienation inhabiting the architecture of Cartesian space. The novel also provides a map with which to plot the intersection between geography and the psychoanalytical development of the early Beckett style. Influenced by the literary explorations of Beckett's contemporary James Joyce, *Murphy* charts the peripatetic mental wanderings of an Irish emigrant living in London. Despite his love for a prostitute named Celia, the protagonist longs for the detachment suggested by postmodern theorists Deleuze and Guattari who, in their critique of the Cartesian framing of space, enigmatically claim that "the schizophrenic voyage is the only kind there is" (Deleuze and Guattari, 1983: 223). However, Murphy discovers through his work as a medical orderly in a lunatic asylum the ultimate spuriousness of Deleuze and Guattari's claim. Accordingly, it can be said that Beckett wrote from a nebulous space located beyond the debate between Enlightenment discourses of rationality and the postmodernist response.

Murphy was written in the early 1930s at a time when Beckett was undergoing psychoanalysis in London, a treatment which was then illegal in the strongly Catholic milieu of the Irish Free State. The publication of the novel illustrated that he was actively engaged in the trope of his own devising and would endeavour from then on to "write as an inmate in the asylum of the *solus ipse*, rather than as an Irishman in his native tradition" (Kearney, 1988: 59). This native tradition comprised the Irish Literary Revival, which contributed to the gestation of an independent Irish state during Beckett's formative years. He was raised as an upper-class Dublin Protestant who boarded in private schools before reading modern languages at Trinity College Dublin. Estranged from the ethos of the Free State as a result, he was acerbically critical of its polity. He regarded nationalistic tropes as "faeces", wryly noting in his later fiction that "wherever nauseated time has dropped a nice fat turd you will find our patriots, sniffing it up, on all fours, their faces on fire" (Beckett, 1974: 30-31). He was particularly scathing of the 1929 Censorship Act, accusing the government of promoting "sterilisation of the mind" (Beckett, 1983: 87). However, in rejecting the mythologies of Irish cultural nationalism, which subordinated the individual to the collective ideological tropes of an idealised heritage, Beckett was not repudiating Irishness *per se*, as most of the characters in his oeuvre have names and personalities which are idiosyncratically Irish. Further, by setting *Murphy* in London with a cast of Irish emigrants he not only undermines the nationalist construction of Irish identity in cultural *bas-relief*, but also questions the very premises underlying the perception and representation of experience and space as they have emerged in Platonic and Cartesian perspectives.

The Mind, the Street and the Asylum

In his early work *Proust* (1931) Beckett considered the perception and representation of experience drawn from the faculties of memory and habit, derived from the perspective of the Cartesian narrator. He observed that voluntary memory "is of no value as

an instrument of evocation, and provides an image as far removed from the real as the myth of our imagination or the caricature furnished by direct perception", adding that "Habit is a com-
promise effected between the individual and his environment"
(Beckett, 1965: 14, 18). He also contended that there are individuals who seek a demythologised experience of life and, as one critic
has it, "are willing to undergo the agony of insecurity for perceptions of things as they are and an experience of time as it is, un-
manacled from Memory and Habit" (Abbott, 1973: 3). Thus, what
is experienced will resist rational examination, having more to do
with what Proust termed "the imposition of our own familiar soul
on the terrifying soul of our surroundings" (Beckett, 1965: 40-41).
Both Beckett's experience of psychoanalysis and his writing of
Murphy echo this observation of Proust in a number of significant
ways which I propose to examine in this paper.

Beckett sought psychoanalysis after the death of his father in
1933 and presented his analyst W.R. Bion with symptoms that included "a bursting, apparently arrhythmic heart, night sweats,
shudders, panic, breathlessness and, at its most severe, total pa-
ralysis" (Knowlson, 1996: 176). Bion's treatment, named "reduc-
tive analysis", had an immediate impact. Beckett noted:

> I certainly came up with some extraordinary memories of
> being in the womb. Intrauterine memories. I remember
> feeling trapped, of being imprisoned and unable to escape,
> of crying to be let out but no one could hear, no one was
> listening. I remember being in pain but being unable to do
> anything about it. (quoted in Knowlson, 1996: 177)

Reliving his intrauterine memories, the writer intuited a caesura
in the Cartesian logic of dualism with its "suggestion that reason-
ing, and moral judgement, and the suffering that comes from
physical pain or emotional upheaval might exist separately from
the body" (Damasio, 1994: 249-50). During the course of his psychoanalysis he attended one of a series of lectures given by C. G.
Jung, in which Jung commented that "you can read a writer's
mind when you study the characters he creates" (Wakeling, 1984:

8). Through the character of Murphy, we are allowed a gaze into the *solus ipse* of Beckett's mind and it can be seen that Bion's therapeutic course "probably helped Beckett to see how his solipsistic attitudes could be mined fruitfully in his writing" (Knowlson, 1996: 181).

In *Murphy* Beckett is preoccupied with questioning the rational Cartesian framing of space and experience, along with its construction of identity as "a self-contained thinking subject (or *Cogito*)" which posits a mind-body split (Kearney, 1988: 66). Accordingly, there is a distinct contrast between the geographical settings of the novel, which are firmly situated in Cartesian space, and Beckett's representation of Murphy's perceptions as he moves through the sphere of his mind, the streets of London and the wards of a lunatic asylum. This contrast is underscored by an exchange at the outset of the novel: "'Murphy, all life is figure and ground.' 'But a wandering to find home,' said Murphy" (Beckett, 1993: 6). As an aspiring *Cogito*, Murphy's mind "pictured itself as a large hollow sphere, hermetically closed to the universe without", so that he "felt himself split in two, a body and a mind" (Beckett, 1993: 63-64). To aid his quest for self-sustained detachment, he would often tie himself to a rocking chair and "as he lapsed in body he felt himself coming alive in mind, set free to move among its treasures" (Beckett, 1993: 65). In such a state he would picture his mind as a place comprised of "three zones, light, half light, dark, each with its speciality" (Beckett, 1993: 65). Moving into the dark zone Murphy can intimate the "tumult of non-Newtonian motion" and the solipsistic experience of "willlessness, a mote in its absolute freedom" (Beckett, 1993: 66).

Accordingly, Murphy's wanderings occur not only within his mind, but across a geography of London that is plotted with a cartographer's precision. During the course of his therapy Beckett himself took long and frequent walks in the city. His biographer James Knowlson tells us that he "got to know the area down by the Embankment in West Brompton and Chelsea where he lived particularly well and used to cross the Thames by Battersea Bridge or the Albert Bridge to circle nearby Battersea Park [...]. But he could cover as much as twenty miles in a day and knew the more distant Hyde Park and Kensington Gardens like the back of his hand" (Knowlson, 1996: 204).[1] This familiarity with place finds its way into the construction of the novel, as characters traverse a highly particularised landscape:

> She [Celia] walked to a point about halfway between the Battersea and Albert Bridges and sat down in a bench between a Chelsea pensioner and an Eldorado holey-pokey man, who had dismounted from his cruel machine and was enjoying a short interlude in paradise. Artists of every kind, writers, underwriters, devils, ghosts, columnists, musicians, lyricists, organists, painters and decorators, sculptors and statuaries, critics and reviewers, major and minor, drunk and sober, laughing and crying, in schools and singly, passed up and down. (Beckett, 1993: 12-13)

Mikhail Bakhtin's concept of the chronotope, a spatial/temporal motif expressed artistically in literature, can plot the confluence of Beckett's interests as they echo through the non-linear narrative of the novel, which is constructed in flashbacks and jump-cuts, to reflect the peripatetic nature of Murphy's mind. Within the chronotope "time as it were, thickens, takes on flesh, becomes artistically visible; [and] likewise, space becomes charged and responsive to the movements of time, plot and history" (Bakhtin, 1984: 84). Accordingly, dates and places, often aligned with the signs of the zodiac, anchor the idiosyncratic narrative of *Murphy*. For example, within the chronotope of the road, in which "people who are normally kept separate by social and spatial difference can accidentally meet [and] the most varied fates may collide and interweave with one another" (Bakhtin, 1984: 244), Beckett creates a space where Celia first spies Murphy under the star sign of Cancer: "It was on the street, the previous

---

[1] It should also be noted that Beckett's knowledge of his surroundings and its demographics coincided with his interest in astrology, which peaked when he discovered that Jung advised his patients to have their horoscopes cast as part of their therapy.

midsummer's night, the sun being in the Crab, that she met Murphy" (Beckett, 1993: 11).

As a result of the physical relationship which develops between them, Murphy's sense of identity, "split in body and mind", comes into conflict with itself. When Celia threatens to return to street-walking unless he finds gainful employment, Murphy leaves her to take a job in a lunatic asylum, a place that anchors Beckett's interrogation of the Cartesian perception of space.[2] His use of a lunatic asylum as a setting to evoke social alienation, as well as provide a critique of the positivist medical approach to mental illness, anticipates Michel Foucault's *The Birth of the Clinic* (1963), in which the term "institutional spatialisation" was coined to depict the construction of places in which a medical gaze maintained a "continuous supervision of social space" (Philo, 2000: 16). Murphy's impression of the asylum as a church — "the layout of the wards was that of the nave and transepts" (Beckett, 1993: 95-96) — is echoed in Foucault's observation that "the asylum is a religious domain without religion" (Foucault, 1991: 148). Within its wards individual patients display a variety of symptoms which are "hierachised into families, genera and species" (Philo, 2000: 12). Like Dante's Virgil in *The Inferno*, the novel lists the ailments and behaviours of the socially damned whom Murphy encounters in the wards:

> Melancholics, motionless and brooding, holding their heads or bellies according to type. Paranoids, feverishly covering sheets of paper with complaints against their treatment or verbatim reports of their inner voices. A hebephrenic playing the piano intently. A hypomaniac teaching slosh to a Korsakow's syndrome. An emaciated schizoid, petrified in toppling attitude as though condemned to an eternal *tableau vivant*, his left hand

---

[2] In 1935 Beckett's friend Geoffrey Thompson became house physician at the Bethlem Royal Hospital in Beckenham. Beckett paid several social calls to him and on a few occasions was given access to the wards, where he observed institutionalised patients. The Magdalen Mental Mercyseat, which "lay a little out of town, ideally situated in its own grounds on the boundary of two counties" (*Murphy*, p. 90), was based on his impression of the clinic.

rhetorically extended holding a cigarette half smoked and out, his right, quivering and rigid, pointing upward. (Beckett, 1993: 96)

Just as Foucault was critical of medical models in which "patients were seemingly looked upon more as objectified sources of data than as unwell individuals" (Philo, 2000: 17), Murphy resents the medical establishment's "textbook attitude towards them, the complacent scientific conceptualism that made contact with outer reality the index of well being" (Beckett, 1993: 101). Congruent with Foucault's underlying assertion that medieval religious pieties had been replaced by enlightenment rationalist practices, Beckett (perhaps anticipating the postmodernist perspective) observes through the eyes of Murphy: "The men, women and children of science would seem to have as many ways of kneeling to their facts as any other body of illuminati. The definition of outer reality, or of reality short and simple, varied according to the sensibility of the definer" (Beckett, 1993: 101).

Thus, Murphy compares his aspiration to dissociate his mind from his body to the detached mental state of the patients. Consequently, his "experience as a physical and rational being obliged him to call sanctuary what the psychiatrists called exile and to think of the patients not as banished from a system of benefits, but as escaped from a colossal fiasco" (Beckett, 1993: 101). Beckett later noted that his construction of the novel was reflected in the formulations of the philosopher Arnold Geulincx and the writer Andre Malraux:

> I shall have to go to into TCD after Geulincx, as he does not exist in National Library. I suddenly see that *Murphy* is [a] break down between his *Ubi nihil vales* [,] *ibi* [*etiam*] *nihil veils* (position) [where you are worth nothing, you will wish for nothing] and Malraux's *Il est dificile a celui qui vit hors du monde de na pas rechercher les siens* (negation). [It is hard for someone who lives outside society not to seek out his own]. (quoted in Knowlson, 1996: 219)

Murphy's denouement as an aspiring *Cogito* comes about as a result of a chess match he plays with Mr Endon, a "schizophrenic of the most amiable variety" who possessed a "psychosis so limpid and imperturbable that Murphy felt drawn to it as Narcissus to his fountain" (Beckett, 1993: 105). The match takes place during Murphy's night shift, in which his duties require of him to complete a round of the patients' cells, take a "panoptic" gaze through the Judas hole in the door, and press a light switch that electronically registers the visit in the head nurse's chamber, leaving a record of the rounds. Upon each visit to Endon's cell, he moves his chess pieces in response to the schizophrenic's, thinking that in some way he is communicating with an individual whom he believes has achieved the ultimate state of solipsism. However, "the sad truth was, that while Mr Endon for Murphy was no less than bliss, Murphy for Mr Endon was no more than chess" (Beckett, 1993: 135). Conceding the match, Murphy swoons. Endon leaves the cell and catatonically completes Murphy's rounds, pressing the light switches at the door of each cell "determined by a mental pattern as precise as any of those that governed his chess" (Beckett, 1993: 138). The impression gathered by the head nurse in his chamber the next day is that Murphy "went mad with his colours nailed to the mast" (Beckett, 1993: 139).

This conclusion, drawn from the empirical data recorded by the panoptical system in the lunatic asylum, is belied by Murphy's recognition of the viability his own sanity, after realising that Endon's schizophrenia provides him with "immunity from seeing anything but himself" (Beckett, 1993: 140). In contrast, Murphy "is aware of the exigencies of the body and of the social world, while professing to hate them both" (Keatinge, 2004). During one of his visits to the Bethlem Royal Hospital, Beckett encountered a patient diagnosed with schizophrenia whom he compared to "'a hunk of meat. There was no one there. He was absent'" (quoted in Knowlson, 1996: 209). Murphy, after peering into Endon's eye and seeing his own reflection, registers a similar impression of the solipsistic dilemma:

'the last at last seen of him
Himself unseen by him
And of himself'. (Beckett, 1993: 140)

Murphy's last alienated words in the novel before he is killed in a gas explosion in his garret are: "Mr Murphy is a speck in Mr Endon's unseen" (Beckett, 1993: 140).

Conclusion

Murphy typifies the Beckettian hero in which "tramps, clowns, alcoholics, failures and misfits are, singularly and collectively, the tormented often demented Samuel Beckett" (Junker, 1995: 16). In this, his first novel, Beckett projects his own *solus ipse* onto the space of a lunatic asylum to provide a critique of the Enlightenment discourse of rationality, which is one foundation for the Cartesian framing of space that allots separate places for the social misfits who do not adhere to its premise. Instead of critiquing this discourse from a postmodernist notion of solipsistic relativity, however, Beckett draws on his experience of psychoanalysis and migration,[3] grounding his critique within the contingencies of time and place. Consequently, he writes from the perspective of the alienated existentialist, tearing down the walls and opening the cages of the mental prisons devised by the self and society, in order to catch a glimpse of the quixotic "first landscape of freedom" (Beckett, 1993: 48). This Beckettian style places the idiosyncratic personality above the heritage of traditions enshrined in the "rational" performances of memory and habit. It is a notion that opts for an interrogation of the subject and the object, whether "current, historical, mythical or spook" (Beckett, 1983: 70), and relegates these fictive constructions of experience to the voluntary falsifications of the Cartesian imagination.

---

[3] Knowlson tells us that Beckett "hated London and was infuriated by the patronising English habit of addressing him in the pubs and shops as 'Pat' or 'Paddy'" (*Damned to Fame*, p. 186).

13

"The Beckett Country" Revisited: Beckett, Belonging and Longing

Seán Kennedy

In 1986, with the publication of Eoin O'Brien's *The Beckett Country*, Beckett scholars admitted to being surprised by the extent to which the playwright's texts were rooted in the specific area of Dublin in which he was born. *The Beckett Country* was a coffee-table book that rooted out the numerous references to places and people in Beckett's oeuvre and placed them beside photographs of those people and places in order to re-assert "place", and, more importantly, Irish places, as a significant feature of the writer's work. James Knowlson admitted in his foreword to being "startled" by the extent to which the texts were immersed in this area, "even Beckett's mature, more abstracted landscapes" (O'Brien, 1986: xvi). Knowlson's "even" here indicates the broad-based assumption that as Beckett's texts grew more radical and universal in scope, they became correspondingly less Irish in setting, an assumption that underpinned almost all critical work up until the 1980s. Ruby Cohn suggested that Beckett's setting was "vaguely" Ireland (Cohn, 1973: 63), while John Fletcher contended that the "stories take place in no definite country, but if it is anywhere, the setting is Ireland" (Fletcher, 1964: 103). The preferred setting was "everywhere and nowhere", implying that Beckett was gradually liberating himself from his Irish cultural predicament and facing broader issues of identity and epistemology.

O'Brien's book startled proponents of this view, though it has proved enduring. Since 1986 it has proved impossible to ignore Ireland's presence in Beckett's writing, yet it has been equally difficult to assess its significance. Ireland tends to be both there and not there in Beckett scholarship, so that Culik can refer to Beckett's "residual Irish landscape" while also maintaining that the novels are "carefully arranged" so as not to disclose their settings (Culik, 1982: 95). Others argue that his Irish settings are utterly transformed, "turned into landscapes of writing with no other existence than their precarious uncertainty as figments of alien words" (Hill, 1990: 39). This last contention indicates a common view of landscape in Beckett, which becomes dissolved, like almost everything else, in the "unalterable whey of words" (Beckett, 1999: 30). However, all this really says is that Ireland in Beckett is being re-presented: the same assertion that Magritte made with his painting of a pipe that proclaimed "This is not a pipe", the point being, of course, that it is a representation of a pipe. Yet the painting still relies on a referent, a real, for its effect. Similarly, I cannot think that Ireland is merely dissolved in Beckett's work into a figment of alien words: to privilege problems of language it is not necessary to depreciate the significance of place. "Vaguely" Ireland is not a problematic contention as long as we do not then also assume that Ireland is only vaguely significant.

It is often said of Joyce that he left Ireland the better to write about it, but this is not something that we commonly hear in relation to Beckett. In what follows I want to suggest that this statement is in fact relevant to Beckett's texts, and to try and link "the Beckett country" to a feature of memoirs written by expatriate Irish Protestants who left Ireland after the formation of the Irish Free State: a feature I have termed, somewhat clumsily, the topographical imaginary. This term is meant to distinguish Beckett's relationships to Ireland from the national imaginary that Benedict Anderson has theorised as forming the basis for an imagined community in the modern nation state (Anderson, 1983). One is an imagining of nation, the other an imagining of place.

In the early years of Irish independence the national imaginary tried to claim a monopoly on how Irishness was constructed at the same time as it claimed hegemony over a place corresponding to a nation defined as Irish. And at least some of the impetus behind Beckett's decision to leave Ireland was provided by his unwillingness, perhaps even his inability, to participate in such acts of imagining. Beckett never felt, with any conviction, that he belonged to the Irish Free State. He confided in interview (Driver, 1979: 220-21) that the entire agenda for cultural exclusivism being pursued in the early years of independence was a major disincentive to remain in "that whoreless rip of a country", which he felt was predicated on an "official, Gaelic, loutish complacency".[1] That said, Beckett retained affection for the Irish countryside and references to Ireland persisted throughout his entire oeuvre. There is an important sense in which he longed for the landscapes of his youth and felt a close personal bond to the area in which he grew up.

These are the terms that I want to examine with reference to Beckett's relationship with Ireland, belonging and longing: belonging in the sense of feeling affiliated to its national imaginary, and longing, a sense of emotional attachment to place present only in memory. Longing implies a residual affiliation to place, but cannot affiliate to the acts of national imagining that have consolidated their claim on that place, and this gives way to the experience of nostalgia. Many thousands of Irish Protestants found themselves in this position after 1923 and, reading Beckett's brief *Texts for Nothing*, originally published in French in 1954, I want to examine his relationship with his native place in the context of Irish Protestant nostalgia in exile.

We would do well, however, to first establish a distinction between exile and self-exile. According to Ahmad, the exile writes

---

[1] Beckett in a letter to Thomas MacGreevy, dated 28 September 1937 (TCDMS10402: 137).

primarily for a readership that is materially absent and is therefore "all the more vividly and excruciatingly present in the
writer's imagination". The self-exile, by contrast, "has no such ir-
revocable bond; he is free to choose the degree of elasticity of that
bonding, and [works in] a much more accountable relation with
the readership which is materially present within the milieu of his
productive work" (Ahmad, 1992: 131-32). Self-exile thus entails a
greater degree of choice regarding material and audience. Peter
Hart has done important work on the Protestant experience during the Irish revolution, with a strong emphasis on regional variations, and claims that "Protestant experiences of the revolution in
southern Ireland ranged from massacre and flight to occasional
inconvenience and indifference, from outraged opposition to enthusiastic engagement" (Hart, 1996: 81). In this context, it is fair to
say that Beckett, a member of the relatively secure Protestant
business community in Dublin, was a self-exile from Ireland, in
contrast to many Anglo-Irish men and women from Cork, for example, who can properly be called exiles. Although Ahmad does
not mention, I think he fits with that body of writers he describes
under the rubric modernism, itself framed

> so very largely by self-exiles and émigrés [...] who
> experienced 'suffocation' in their own spaces of this globe,
> and [created] the predominant image of the modern artist
> who lives as a literal stranger in a foreign [...] city and who,
> on the one hand, uses the condition of exile as the basic
> metaphor for modernity and even for the human condition
> itself, while on the other, writing obsessively, copiously, of
> that very land which had been declared 'suffocating'.
> (Ahmad, 1992: 134)

There is little doubt that Beckett felt suffocated in Ireland: he
once likened himself in Foxrock to an amphibian detained on dry
land.[2] The point is that, as a self-exile, without that excruciating

---

[2] Beckett in a letter to Thomas MacGreevy, dated 5 August 1938 (TCDMS10402:
166).

bond described by Ahmad, he still chose to write about Ireland for much of the remainder of his life, and the significance of that choice remains to be fully apprehended. There was no progressive falling away from Ireland into the "whey of words". Ireland remained central for Beckett, albeit in abstracted form, and abstraction succeeded only in obscuring the country's presence rather than exorcising its significance.

So, Beckett was a self-exile from Ireland who longed for the Irish countryside but could not feel that he belonged to the Irish Free State. In this, he was in good company among the various members of the Protestant minorities after independence. Indeed, the distinction structured the response to events among those Protestants who stayed on: remain in Ireland, ignore the state. Writing of the Anglo-Irish in 1952, Brian Fitzgerald identified this important fissure exactly: "It has been said that though they resided in Ireland, Ireland was their *country*; it never really became their *nation*" (Fitzgerald, 1952: 12, original emphasis). This is the distinction that I have tried to characterise in terms of imagining nation and imagining place: one could long for the place and reject the nation, even though they occupied the same territory. Some chose, some were compelled, to leave the nation, but almost all retained a strong affection for the place. Page Dickinson, who published his memoirs in London in 1929, was typical:

> I love Ireland. There is hardly a mile of its coastline or hills that I have not walked. There is not a thought in me that does not want well-being for the land of my birth, yet there is no room to-day in their own land for thousands of Irishmen of similar views. (Dickinson, 1929: 2)

Dickinson is careful to assert a purely topographical relationship with the land of Ireland, restricting his claim of Irishness to a sense of affinity with the Irish soil, thereby eschewing any claim to participation in the national imaginary of the Free State. Indeed, it was precisely the various imagined communities of Irish nationalism that had occasioned his departure, leaving the topographical imaginary of the island of Ireland as the most fertile source of belonging for an uprooted Anglo-Irishman.

Unsurprisingly, a sense of nostalgia pervades expatriate Protestant memoirs of this period. According to James Philips, nostalgia only proliferates when a past age is viewed in the light of subsequent events: "The 'I was' of recall is always accompanied by an 'and I was to become'" (Philips, 1985: 65-66). And, to the extent that the past is deemed more pleasurable than the present, one is vulnerable to a sense of nostalgic longing for that remembered past: "the only true Paradise is the Paradise that has been lost" (Beckett, 1965: 26). The former ascendancy had been uprooted at an extraordinary pace and, in the 1920s and 1930s, was still reeling from the effects of recent events. Peter Hart describes a "sudden massive upheaval" in the Protestant population that left 40 per cent of them in exile or self-exile after 1926 (Hart, 1996: 93) and it was this accelerated experience of dispossession that left them particularly vulnerable to nostalgia. What I want to do briefly is to examine Beckett's *Texts for Nothing* in the context of nostalgia for the island of Ireland among Protestant expatriates. This may seem incongruous, since many Beckett scholars situate the voices that speak these texts "de l'outre tombe" (Fletcher, 1964: 108) or in "the spectral now of the unborn dead" (Moorjani, 1996: 87). However, this kind of emphasis obscures the fact that many of these voices have much to say about viable social lives.

Many of the texts return to the time of Beckett's self-exile from Ireland and evoke the Beckett country: "I must have heard tell of the view", says N, the narrator of *Text for Nothing I*, "the distant sea in hammered lead, the so-called golden vale so often sung [...] the city in its haze" (Beckett, 1996: 101). In *Text for Nothing 7* N sees himself sitting at the South-Eastern Railway Terminus at Harcourt Street preparing to depart. He asks himself if he did not, in some sense, come to a standstill there: "Is it there I came to a stop, is that me still waiting there, stiff and straight on the edge of the seat, knowing the dangers of laissez-aller [...], waiting [...] for a train that will never come, never go?" (Beckett, 1996: 129). This sense of living in suspended animation after leaving Ireland is a common thread in expatriate memoirs. Elizabeth Hamilton described it as a feeling of "being torn from one's roots, lifted out of one's milieu, suspended in nothingness" (Hamilton, 1963: 75). The resonance with *Godot*, and the floating heads in Beckett's late drama, is difficult to ignore.

Returning to Ireland is another common theme of expatriate memoirs, and in *Text for Nothing 3*, N fantasises about the possibility of a return to the land where "all went out":

> this time it's I must go. I know how I'll do it, I'll be a man [...] a kind of old tot, I'll have a nanny, I'll be her sweet pet, she'll give me her hand, to cross over, she'll let me loose in the Green, I'll be good, I'll sit quiet as a mouse in a corner and comb my beard [...] her name will be Bibby, I'll call her Bibby, if only it could be like that. (Beckett, 1996: 110)

Bibby is the name given to Belacqua Shuah's family maid in Beckett's early fiction, and it was also the name of Beckett's own maid in Foxrock. The French original suggests that her name will be "Nanny" and that she will let him loose "dans les squares" (Beckett, 1958: 145-46), but the insertion of Bibby and the Green in translation evoke an Irish setting, one familiar to Beckett himself. N imagines himself with "an old crony" who has "served in the navy, perhaps under Jellicoe".[3] And both men claim to have "deserved well of our motherland" and trust that she'll "get us into the Incurables before we die" (Beckett, 1996: 111). N is here remembering the Royal Hospital for Incurables in Donnybrook, founded in 1743 and still providing care for the elderly today. Given these details, an Irish setting seems likely.

Even more suggestive is a passage in which N says of himself and his friend:

> The sport of kings is our passion, the dogs too, we have no political opinions, simply limply republican. But we also

---

[3] Sir John Jellicoe (1859-1935) was an admiral in the British Navy during World War One.

have a soft spot for the Windsors, the Hanoverians, I forget,
the Hohenzollerns is it. (Beckett, 1996: 112)

The rather confused, residual attachment to the British monarchy
suggests a Protestant background. This would make sense in
terms of their passion for horse-racing, the sport of kings, since
the Dublin Horse Show and Punchestown remained bastions of
loyalism well into the 1930s and beyond. In this context, the reference to an essentially apolitical disposition, a limp republicanism,
suggests the former ascendancy's unenthusiastic alliance with the
pro-Treaty nationalism of the Cumann na nGaedhael Party, particularly as it was caricatured by de Valera's more robustly republican Fianna Fáil Party.

Such memories do not belong to one living in the domain of
the unborn dead, but they do make sense in the context of the
Protestant experience of exile and nostalgia. As indicated by N's
current situation, in an "inextricable place, far from the days, the
far days" (Beckett, 1996: 109-10), the impulse behind *Text for Nothing 3* is the indignity of N's present circumstances: the "I was"
gaining poignancy from the "and I was to become", which Philips
claims is a prerequisite for nostalgia. This old crony demonstrates
the same hankering for a prelapsarian Ireland that was so common in Protestant memoir; Hamilton, for example, describes Ireland as a "lost paradise at the entrance to which stood an angel
barring the way with a flaming sword" (Hamilton, 1963: 28). N
imagines meeting an old friend, "arriving in sheets of rain, with
the brave involuntary swagger of the old tar", but recoils from
investing too heavily in the memory: "no, that's all memories, last
shifts older than the flood. See what's happening here, where
there's no one, where nothing happens, get something to happen
here, then put an end to it, have silence" (Beckett, 1996: 113). The
need for silence here is not a flight from some abstract Babel, the
prison house of language, but from memories of a time when the
speaker felt a keener sense of belonging than at present: a past
situated in Ireland. To be sure, it is an idealised past, nostalgia
masquerading as memory, but this does not rob it of its emotive

charge. For this reason, I think that *Texts for Nothing* can be usefully read in the context I have described, as that particularly poignant longing for belonging that is the expatriate Protestant's experience of nostalgia occasioned by displacement.

Nostalgia is not commonly discussed in the context of Beckett's relationship with Ireland, and far less emphasis is placed on these passages that seem to long for a return to Ireland than on those describing his famous obligation to express the nothing there is to express. This is probably due to the dominance of postmodernism and poststructuralism in academia which has meant, as Ahmad points out, that "the idea of belonging is itself abandoned as antiquated false consciousness". As a result, the

> terrors of High Modernism at the prospect of inner fragmentation and social disconnection have now been stripped [...] of their tragic edge, pushing the experience of loss, instead, in a celebratory direction; the idea of belonging is itself seen now as bad faith, a mere 'myth of origins'. (Ahmad, 1992: 129)

In this academic climate, only recently in decline, the longing for belonging that is nostalgia is downplayed in order to celebrate the critique of a Western metaphysics of presence.

Of course, Beckett had much to say on this matter, but there is little sense of celebration attached to his work in this regard. A predisposition towards celebration obscures the sadness — not to mention the sentimentality — that pervades many of his musings on his own sense of loss. And so Beckett's nostalgia remains obscured by the emphasis placed on his scepticism regarding voices and origins. In time, a more vulnerable Beckett may re-emerge, for whom the personal experience of displacement from his homeland was a central and deeply troubling experience. I imagine that our readings of even the most austere of Beckett's texts will benefit from this development. "My past has thrown me out", says the narrator of *Text for Nothing 8*. "Ever since nothing but fantasies and hope of a story for me somehow, of having come from somewhere and of being able to go back, or on" (Beckett, 1996: 132). For this more vulnerable Beckett, Ireland remained central. As the narrator of "The Calmative" reminds us: "There was never any city but the one" (Beckett, 1980: 51).

14

The Contemporary Appeal of Sophocles' *Philoctetes*

Loredana Salis

In his 1941 essay on the Philoctetes myth Edmund Wilson contemplates the modern appeal of Sophocles' *Philoctetes*, composed in the fifth century BCE. Quoting André Gide, who produced his own *Philoctete* in 1899, Wilson identifies the Greek hero as "a literary man: at once a moralist and an artist, whose genius becomes purer and deeper in relation to his isolation and outlawry" (Wilson, 1941: 244). In a similar way, the poet James K. Baxter observes that the situation of the main character in the play "mirrored so exactly the predicament of the modern intellectual" (Baxter, 1971: vii). For Baxter, whose "strongly metaphoric prose" version of the play, *The Sore Footed Man*, was first produced in 1967, Philoctetes was ultimately a victim of his own "intellectual roundabout" (Baxter, 1971: viii). These references to the modern reader and the modern intellectual fit their contemporary moment — Wilson's to the 1940s and Baxter's to the 1960s — and they remain unchallenged. What, though, of the later twentieth century? Can we talk of the *postmodern appeal* of the Philoctetes myth? And if so, in what terms?

I wish to consider the emergence of the Philoctetes myth in contemporary Irish theatre with a particular emphasis on versions

of Sophocles's play by Sydney Bernard Smith (b.1936) and Seamus Heaney (b.1939). A comparative reading of Smith's *Sherca*
(1976) with Heaney's *The Cure at Troy* (1990), focusing on each
play's treatment of time and space, is attempted here. I wish to
demonstrate how insularity discourse — a dense network of references to boundaries and edges, the literal and metaphorical images of the island — facilitates a postmodern approach to the
play, an approach no longer centred on its mythic hero. I will conclude my observations by highlighting the self-referential mode of
these texts, both of which are ultimately concerned with the process of their own making.

An island is by definition an isolated place, a portion of land
surrounded by water — isolation and boundedness being "two
factors that make islands special" (Royle, 2001: 11). However, an
island is never totally or permanently isolated from the outside
world, not even when it is depopulated or far removed from the
mainland. Where the metaphorical dimension of Smith's and
Heaney's islands is concerned, it is worth keeping in mind Thomas Hylland Eriksen's remark that "No society is entirely closed;
no society is entirely open either, since it then ceases to be a society. A society must have boundaries in order to be a society"
(Hylland Eriksen, 1993). Isolation and boundedness are constantly
at work in the insular context: their ambivalence is what defines
an island's insularity.

In their qualities of relativity and mutability, both literal and
metaphorical notions of insularity appeal to what might be called
the postmodern imagination. Islands are often deployed as metaphors for society at large, as well as being projections of individual yearnings for solitude. Islands can be a "refuge for the soul"
(as is Yeats's Innisfree[1]), and home to hermits, exiles, nomads or
poets. On a more negative note, islands may be prisons and places
for the outcast. However literal, romanticising or metaphorical the

---

[1] As Royle (2001: 12) observes, "whether Innisfree is a real island or an imaginary
refuge for the soul is of no consequence at all, so far as the spiritual significance
of the poem is concerned".

notion, an island is characteristically associated with the ideas of transience, temporality, finiteness, unreliability, instability; as Smith himself puts it, an island is a kind of "bus stop in the sea" (Smith, 1979: 6).

"Did sea define the land or land the sea?", asks Heaney in an early poem. "Each drew new meaning from the waves' collision. / Sea broke on land to full identity" (Heaney, 1966: 47). There is no fixed land-sea signification. Likewise there are no "cultural islands", that is, one cannot think of the contemporary world as made up of islands of culture wholly insulated from each other and from their shared marine environment. As Hylland Eriksen writes, "Insularity is a question of perspective", like "isolation proper", and the contemporary world "def[ies] boundaries and create[s] uniformity as well as self-conscious difference where there were formerly unexplored and unknown differences" (Hylland Eriksen, 1993).

The concept of insularity and insularity discourse can help articulate the problem of the past and the way we relate to it. If it is true that cultural islands do not exist, it is also true that we do not live in a temporal vacuum — however problematic our postmodern condition, the past is something we simply cannot elude. The question of "the past" is explicitly raised in both plays. Philoctetes' inability to forgive and forget is aptly visualised in the gangrenous wound in Heaney's play: "Your wound is what you feed on, Philoctetes. / [...] / stop eating yourself up with hate and come with us" (Heaney, 1990: 61). Philoctetes is thus entrapped in his own past: "The past is bearable, / the past's only a scar, but the future — *Never. Never again*" (Heaney, 1990: 73, emphasis added).

The transition from the temporal to the spatial in both plays reflects what Frederic Jameson calls the postmodern dissolution of time in space (Jameson, 1991). This is signalled in Smith's title, *Sherca*, taken from the actual Inis Sherca, an island "off the west coast of Ireland, formerly inhabited, but abandoned for some years before Phil came to live in it" (Smith, 1979: 4). It is a make-believe island, its Hiberno-English name shadowed by *searc*, a Gaelic word for love: "Leo: The island of love, something like that.

[...] Phil: Something like that. Untranslatable love" (Smith, 1979: 21). Untranslatable love is a love that cannot be rendered into another language: by definition it remains only partially accessible. There is a permanent gap between the source and the target language — no translation will ever be satisfactory and so this "love" is bound to remain to some extent unknowable. The very title of the play, then, reflects the perennial tension between two entities of which the English and the Gaelic idioms are metonyms, and between the fifth-century Greek original and this particular twentieth-century Irish version.

Untranslatable love is also a love that cannot be transferred, or displaced. Thus, love is bound to remain on the island, it *is* the island itself and therefore it is defined by its own boundedness and isolation. Boundedness and isolation are not absolutes, however, and love is consequently subject to change — hence Phil's decision to leave the island. There is yet another way in which we can read Phil's "untranslatable love". In its "untranslatability", Sherca is a signifier with no signified; in other words, it is an abstraction. Like hyperspace, Sherca — the name, and even to a degree perhaps the island itself — is one of Jameson's "images divorced from their referents" (Jameson, 1991: 11-12, 22).

Heaney entitled his version of the play *The Cure at Troy*, a title that similarly indicates a shift of emphasis away from the central hero. The focus is on the wound and the idea of healing as suggested by the word "cure". That the cure is at Troy reminds us of the play's happy ending — Philoctetes is cured, and the Greeks win the war. Moreover, the fact that we already know the ending means that our attention is less focused on the unfolding events and more on the way in which, through the characters' continuous change of heart, the end is achieved. To put it differently, what really matters is what happens *in between*. The focus of interest in both plays, then, is not Philoctetes *per se*, nor what happens to him in the end, but rather the circumstances and significance of the extreme condition epitomised by his wound and isolation. The play represents the here-and-now of the hero's existence between an indelible past and an uncertain future. Philoctetes does not "act in a vacuum", nor is he "isolated from past and future, from time and space, from society at large" (Sophocles, 1998: 6), quite the contrary in fact. His wound is the ever-present reminder of this.

The wound in Heaney is like isolation in Smith; both are manifestations of social malaise as well as of uncertainty and in-betweenness. Smith's Phil, however, bears no evident wound. He suffers no physical pain. Unlike Philoctetes, he is on the island by choice. *Sherca* tells the story of a self-exiled man of 55, a former member of the Communist Party who finds himself in deep disagreement with his comrades and decides to leave. His wound is of a different kind: it is his inadequacy and inability to fit into the big picture (society, the party, his own body even). This is reflected in his speech; when Leo asks "what happened to you?" Phil is unable to give a precise answer: "Did I leave the party, or did the party leave me?" (Smith, 1979: 15). When asked about his interests he replies "Spooks and spells. Time. Energy. Mind-reading. Prophecy", all of them "things" for which there may or may not be evidence; "it depends on your point of view" (Smith, 1979: 15).

Inadequacy, fragmentation and in-betweenness are reflected in the characters' shortened names: Odysseus becomes O'Dea, Neoptolemus is Leo and Philoctetes simply Phil. Smith adopts Hibernicised and truncated versions of the original names, thereby underlining the fragmented and conflicting nature of the characters themselves. Furthermore, discourses of insularity shape each play's self-reflexive mode. Each is ultimately about itself and about the politics of its own representation. *The Cure at Troy* opens with a Choral ode in which images of in-betweenness predominate. The Chorus is at once caught in between and is itself "more or less a borderline":

> Between
> The you and the me and the it of it.
> Between
> The gods' and human beings' sense of things.

> And that's the borderline that poetry
> Operates on too, always in between
> What you would like to happen and what will —
> Whether you like it or not. (Heaney, 1990: 2)

The quatrain articulates the tension that accompanies the act of writing that is about to start. Thus, the opening of the play co-incides with the beginning of the creative process itself (the re-presentation of the Philoctetes story). In the staged performance, this is suggested by the predominantly white scene — a plain space, like a white sheet of paper on which a story is to be in-scribed: "As the play opens, the white sheet covering everything on the stage billows up to suggest a blank desert waste, and is then withdrawn to reveal two white staircases flanking the set which provide exits and vantage points and which are joined at the back by a white wall" (Meir, 1990: 12). The narrative voice asks the audience to trust him as Philoctetes trusted the god who similarly spoke through poetry:

> Poetry
> Allowed the god to speak. It was the voice
> Of reality and justice. The voice of Hercules
> That Philoctetes is going to have to hear
> [...] but we'll come to that. (Heaney, 1990: 2)

The perspective of a trustworthy narrative, albeit almost unno-ticeable at this stage, is obliquely undermined from the outset. As one reviewer observed, "the shattered head of a giant white Greek sculpture lies against a white wall symbolizing broken Greek trust" (Meir, 1990: 12).

The "writing" begins with Odysseus instructing the young Neoptolemus so that he may win Philoctetes back: "All you'll need to do is listen / and do the things I tell you." Odysseus only knows one idiom and this he wants Neoptolemus to learn: "You are going to have to work out some way / of deceiving Philoctetes with a story." Neoptolemus' task is, therefore, to write a story. From the start he resists Odysseus's "policy of lies": "Why could we not / go at him, man to man?" (Heaney, 1990: 4-8). Deceit is not Neoptolemus' idiom. Thus, when he approaches Philoctetes he fails; Philoctetes inevitably detects the trick. The play abounds with references to "double talk", "reading between the lines", "turncoat talk", "sweet talk". Neoptolemus' first story — his attempt to sweet talk Philoctetes — makes no sense, and the young boy decides to come clean — "The real story is this" and "There is a meaning to it" (Heaney, 1990: 50). Neoptolemus' story is not, however, *his* story: it is Odysseus's and, ultimately, the story of Philoctetes. Neoptolemus cannot and will not produce an original narrative. Like *The Cure at Troy* itself, his story is a copy, a version. There is no prototype for postmodern culture; "the first copy is the original" and "modernist styles become postmodern codes" (Jameson, 1991: 17).

As the play progresses, and events unfold with twists and turns, so does the writing prove to be a difficult task: the Chorus is "in a maze": "Clear one minute. Next minute haze" (Heaney, 1990: 12). Though concerned "keep things moving on", the Chorus takes a decisive stance when faced with Philoctetes' unbending hatred and pride, and a rift develops. For the first time in the play it reprimands Philoctetes, saying: "You walked yourself into it", a statement reminiscent of the Chorus in Tom Paulin's 1985 version of *Antigone* in the scene which precedes her death. The story has to be written anyhow, and so the voice of the god (poetry itself?) intercedes to open "the closed road", so that the Chorus may finish its work, "to make the right road for you" (Heaney, 1990: 78). When they do — "Now, it's high watermark / [...] / What's left to say?" — they put down their last word, the half-rhyme, "love" (Heaney, 1990: 81).

Heaney makes "love" half-rhyme with "believe", which brings us back to the initial reference to trust. From the start there is a tension between a demanded trust and the awareness that "any kind of trust is a mistake" (Heaney, 1990: 52). He plays with the believe/suspect and trust/sweet talk antinomies all through in a manner that highlights the question of poetry and the relation between author and society. The apologetic lines — "No poem or play or song / Can fully right a wrong / Inflicted and endured (Heaney, 1990: 77) — reiterate Heaney's preoccupation with the necessary limits of poetic expression, a preoccupation also manifested in his criticism. One of his critical observations about the "place" of poetry is pertinent here:

> Poetry [...] does not propose to be instrumental or effective. Instead, in the rift between what is going to happen and whatever we would wish to happen, poetry holds attention for a space, functions not as a distraction but as pure concentration, a focus where our power to concentrate is concentrated back on ourselves. This is what gives poetry its governing power. [...] Poetry is more a threshold than a path, one constantly approached and constantly departed from, at which reader and writer undergo in their different ways the experience of being at the same time summoned and released. (Heaney, 1989: 108)

Likewise, the poet "is credited with the power to open unexpected and unedited communications *between our nature and the nature of the reality we inhabit*" (Heaney, 1989: 93, emphasis added).

A similar concern underlies Smith's play. *Sherca* is equally about the act of writing, the self-referential mode being largely mediated through the play's treatment of Phil's psychic powers. A metaphor for the original bow, Phil's power of the mind is like a laser:

> It concentrates light, in a ruby of all things, until the tension reaches an enormous level, and then, *phting*! Out it bursts, a tiny narrow stream of light, like a bullet. It'll go through anything, steel or whatever. (Smith, 1979: 10)

The passage articulates the before, during and after of a creative moment's actualisation. Phil's laser is not different from Heaney's power to bridge the gap between "nature and the nature of the reality we inhabit". The implication is that in its power to function as "pure concentration", poetry (and perhaps creativity more generally) functions as "a governing power". Phil is expelled from the party for the same reason he is wanted back (Smith, 1979: 9-10).

Sherca explores the stages of Phil's (artistic) maturation — that is, of his becoming aware of his psychic powers. Phil's first act of writing occurs when he "puts the words in [O'Dea's] mouth": "I made him. With my mind. [...] I can do this. If the signs are right" (Smith, 1979: 15). As the play proceeds, references to the writing process proliferate: "There's a future in rhyme", Leo tells Phil (Smith, 1979: 21). Phil's change of heart occurs under the influence of the *deus ex machina*, in a scene in which his posters of Che Guevara and Leonardo's Annunciation flame up. The scene bears a sexual connotation (the merging of the male and the female icons in the blaze) which is fulfilled in the Virgin's conception — the Word becomes flesh, and so speech is finally actualised. The scene concludes with a vision of purity, and as with *The Cure at Troy*, the protagonist's decisive speech can be read in terms of an authorial apologia:

> *I know the running sore in my mind.* Should I vent my own inadequacies, tearing down for the sake of tearing down, out of the purest self-abandon [...]. All iconoclasts are the same iconoclast [...] Yet in my head a world, how many worlds, of hands and souls and seeds and stars and suns, all mankind coming with a life to come. (Smith, 1979: 36, emphasis added)

The passage brings to the fore the dilemma of writers of all ages, figured in the postmodern era by the necessity to "redress the balance" or "even out the scales", as Heaney's Neoptolemus says (Heaney, 1990: 45). There is, as Terence Brown has observed, a paradox in the tension in Ireland between writers' inability to "fulfill clearly defined social and national roles" and the "demand that they do so" (Brown, 1985: 321-22). Both plays bear testimony to art's impulse to acknowledge at once the importance and the shifting, indeterminate status of the boundaries between individual and society, reminding us in the process of Linda Hutcheon's claim that a plot "is always a totalising representation that integrates multiple and scattered events into the unified story. But the simultaneous desire for and suspicion of such representations are both part of the postmodern contradictory response to emplotment" (Hutcheon, 1988: 68).

In conclusion, the Philoctetes play has not only a modern appeal but a postmodern one. Both Smith and Heaney deploy insularity discourse in order to articulate the condition of in-betweenness of which Philoctetes, as both character and play, is the referent. Space becomes the locus of personal experience, the site of Philoctetes' self-cognition in Smith and of his healing in Heaney, the blank page upon which his temporally fractured story is reinscribed and re-integrated. Both plays register the process of their own coming into existence, in a self-referential mode which testifies to their characteristically postmodern condition of in-betweenness.

Part 3

Negotiating Migrant and Diaspora Spaces

15

Exploring Diaspora Space:
Entangled Irish/English Genealogies

Bronwen Walter

In the summer of 2003 the English media was saturated with dis-tinctive names challenging, and in some cases defending, the British Labour Government in a charge of grave political mis-judgement, if not deliberate lying, about the necessity to invade Iraq.[1] At the heart of the furore were Andrew Gilligan, the BBC journalist who suggested that the document which had persuaded the House of Commons to vote in favour of going to war had been "sexed up", and Dr David Kelly, the Iraq weapons expert with private doubts about the existence of weapons of mass destruc-tion, who committed suicide as a consequence of the political backlash. Also prominent was Tom Kelly, the Northern Irish-born Downing Street official spokesman who provided justifications for the Government's role in the affair to the press. The fact that these are Irish names did not receive attention, even from the *Irish Post* newspaper which is usually quick to claim anyone in the

---

[1] I would like to thank Joe Bradley, Sarah Morgan and Patrick O'Sullivan for their helpful comments on this paper.

public eye who has Irish connections.[2] However, an academic website managed to unearth the information that Andrew Gilligan was third-generation Irish from Scotland and David Kelly third-generation Irish from Wales.[3]

What this tells us is probably not that there is an ongoing anti-establishment trait amongst those of Irish descent, however distant, but that Irish names have become entwined in British genealogies and are found at all levels of the social hierarchy. They are of course only symbolic of a long-established Irish presence, the accidental residue of a male-to-male line which forms a rapidly diminishing proportion of the totality of people with Irish ancestry. For example, it is estimated that 52.1 per cent of Irish-descended Catholic males in Scotland have Irish surnames (Williams, 1993: 310). In England, where religious divisions have much lower intensity, rates of outmarriage have been far higher, especially in regions with small Irish-born populations (Hickman *et al.*, 2001: 13-17). It must also be remembered that many Irish surnames are identical to English ones, reflecting much earlier Norman and English immigration into Ireland. When the additional loss of Irish names by many women on marriage is included, the pool of distinctive Irish surnames still attached to those of Irish descent will be very low relative to the number of people with similar "blood" ties.

In this paper I want to explore in more detail a concept which allows us to re-imagine the notion of England as constituted by a very longstanding hybridity of which an Irish cultural background has been a major element. This is the notion of "diaspora space", Avtar Brah's innovative and imaginative contribution to diaspora theorising which describes specific sites of cultural intermixing as a consequence of migration. She argues that

> diaspora space as a conceptual category is 'inhabited' not only by those who have migrated and their descendants

[2] The *Irish Post* is a weekly newspaper, sold widely, which describes itself as "the voice of the Irish in Britain". See website www.irishpost.co.uk.

[3] See the Irish-Diaspora list website at http://www.irishdiaspora.net/

> but equally by those who are constructed and represented
> as indigenous. In other words, the concept of *diaspora space*
> (as opposed to that of diaspora) includes the entanglement
> of genealogies of dispersion with those of "staying put".
> (Brah, 1996: 181, original emphasis)

The key contribution of this concept is to decentre those who are conventionally regarded as the mainstream indigenous population and emphasise their inextricable involvement in the process of diaspora. The discourse of diaspora space thus replaces the language of majority and minority by including all inhabitants equally and indissolubly within the same project.

The need to acknowledge the centrality of entanglements within national spaces chimes closely with Jan Nederveen Pieterse's thinking on hybridity. He points out that, in addition to new hybrid forms which now attract considerable attention both inside and outside the academy,

> hybridity thinking also concerns existing, or, so to speak,
> old hybridity, and thus involves different ways of looking
> at historical and existing cultural and institutional
> arrangements. This is a more radical and penetrating angle
> that suggests not only that things are no longer they way
> they used to be, but never really were the way they used to
> be or used to be viewed. (Pieterse, 2001: 221)

To him, "That history should not be seen in this way and hybridity somehow viewed as extraordinary or unusual is baffling" (Pieterse, 2001: 221). Pieterse argues that hybridity, the product of entanglement, has been treated as extraordinary because of boundary fetishism, whose latest form is "ethnicity". Constructing boundaries around groups, instead of focusing attention on crossovers, allows power hierarchies based on "purity" to be strengthened and legitimised. He also highlights the significance of the choice of "hybridity", with its biological and hence racial overtones, as a term to describe cultural diversity of individual backgrounds, in preference to words such as mixing, blending, melding or merging.

At present diaspora space is widely used at the conceptual level as a descriptive tool. It has quickly entered into academic discourse as a useful shorthand for the arena in which encounters take place between people of different "origins". However, I would argue that there is still work to do on elaborating and grounding the notion, especially if it is to gain the political purchase which it promises. In many ways this is a much larger task than the grounding of specific diasporas which is urged by many writers. I want to use the notion of genealogies to explore this multi-generational long view, both in the Foucauldian sense of Brah's understanding of diaspora as "an ensemble of investigative technologies that historicise trajectories of different diasporas and analyse their relationality across fields of social relations, subjectivity and identity" (Brah, 1996: 180), and in the different but related meanings of genealogy as connected family relationships over generations. This "popular and more mundane practice of doing family trees" is of course itself far from simple in its political implications, as Catherine Nash demonstrates (Nash, 2002: 28). Linking bodies, and their representations, over time and space begins to unearth long-sedimented evidence of the importance of English-Irish mixing within the national space of England.

In this paper I explore three areas which repay more extensive theoretical and empirical investigation. The first is the process of rethinking natives as diasporians which requires elucidation and illustration. Secondly, geographical unevenness within a particular national diaspora space can be investigated at many interlinking scales and provides spatial specificity to the processes at work. Thirdly, the body itself is often the most public site of identification, as the personal naming process mentioned above suggests. Moreover, the hybridity of bodies, constructed as discordant in "mixed race" crossings between the binary categories of indigenous and diasporic, is often overlooked when it reflects relationships *between* subordinated groups.

Entanglements of Natives and Diasporians

The very complex issue of the ways in which the indigenous population has been thoroughly changed by encounters with the Irish diaspora, so that it cannot be imagined outside of these entanglements, is illustrated by the place of Irish female domestic servants in the diaspora space of England. Writing about domestic servants in English households in the later nineteenth century, Anne McClintock describes "a cordon sanitaire of racial degeneration thrown round those who did work publicly and visibly for money" (McClintock, 1995: 216). In my book *Outsiders Inside: Whiteness, Place and Irish Women* I follow McClintock and Leonore Davidoff (1974, 1995) in arguing that domestic servants in the late nineteenth century were racialised as "other" because of their working-class status, but extend this theorisation to argue that othering was given added impetus and weight by the racialised Irish origins of increasing numbers of servants (Walter, 2001: 98-105).

This links with the idea of the geographical unevenness of diaspora space by focusing not only on specific regions and neighbourhoods where middle-class English households employed domestic servants, but on the household level where they were literally outsiders *inside*. My argument is that not only did servants perform the symbolic function of highlighting the boundaries of white, middle-class masculinity, but that they also interacted in a close personal way with the children of the householders. This meant that the next generation had a knowledge of Irish culture which would remain with them throughout their lives, even when its source had been forgotten. In the case of Irish servants there would be the added, and politically threatening, difference of a Catholic content, which would clash strongly with Protestant Englishness. Drawing on a range of Victorian texts, including the works of Sigmund Freud and Arthur Munby, McClintock suggests that both the presence and activities of servants could have a powerful effect, especially on sons. Her writing seems to resonate with a distinctively "Irish" tinge through its references to oral culture and the supernatural:

Can we not, however, more properly see this doubled image of women that haunts the glassy surfaces of male Victorian texts as arising less from any archetypal doubling in the male unconscious, than from the contradictory (and no less patriarchal) doubling of class that was a daily reality in the households and infancies of these upper-middle-class men? The goblins and faeries that populate male texts might more properly be seen to stream up not from a universal male unconscious but rather from the historical memory of the female working-class kitchens and back passages, from the laps of the *working-class nurses and maids who brought the echoing whispers of faery into the middle-class nursery*. The images of monsters and mermaids are remnants of an oral tradition borne by working-class women. These images are indeed images of female power, but they are specifically memories of female working-class power and are rooted in class divisions and historical mutability. (McClintock, 1995: 95-96, emphasis added)

Empirical data to support or flesh out this hypothesis is inevitably elusive or entirely missing. The activities themselves are small moments of everyday intimacy and the participants in such shared activities — servants and children — are amongst the least likely to leave records. The time period, now more than three generations ago, is beyond the reach of oral histories. And although we can use nineteenth-century censuses to calculate statistics about the numbers of Irish-born servants present in middle-class English households where there were young children, these cannot be used as "proof" that such exchanges took place (Walter, 2004b: 435-36).

However, a recent novel uncannily echoes key elements of McClintock's thesis and adds the crucial detail of a domestic servant's Irish origins. Helen Dunmore's *A Spell of Winter* (1995) describes the centrality of Kate, who grew up in Dublin, to the upbringing of two young upper-middle-class children in an English country house. The historical and geographical contexts are not clearly spelled out, but the book is set around the turn of the

twentieth century in an unspecified part of rural England, probably in the south. The story concerns a family living in a large
country house with a number of servants. The household is
headed by the grandfather, whose daughter has disappeared to
France leaving behind her two young children, Rob and Cathy,
and her husband, their father. The children's father, never closely
involved in the household, suffers a mental breakdown and dies
soon after entering an institution, leaving the children to be cared
for by servants.

The book opens with Kate telling the children a frightening
but fascinating story about her own grandmother in Dublin, who
was extremely religious and superstitious. When a son died in his
twenties she was overcome by grief and refused to bury him.
Eventually the body was brought down the narrow stairs and because of its decayed state an arm fell off in the process. This is one
of many stories about her family Kate tells the children, which
contrasts strongly with their own lives in terms of religion, culture
and class. Kate is a mother substitute for the children and they
rely on her completely. She deals sympathetically with many
problems for them, including Cathy's abortion after her incestu-
ous relationship with Rob. But when they are young adults, Kate
suddenly announces she is leaving to go back to Ireland. They are
devastated but she reminds them that it is only a job for her and
that she always intended to go. Then, unexpectedly to Cathy, it
appears that Kate is leaving to emigrate to Canada with Rob.

The story resonates with many of the theoretical ideas outlined
above. It concerns the unacknowledged importance of servants in
the lives of young upper-middle-class children in England. It also
illustrates the differential impact on boys and girls. Boys are significant because they are the next generation of white, middle-class
males; girls, on the other hand, identify both with and against servants. In the novel Cathy closely identifies with Kate, and almost
shares her name, but is also separated by the gulf of class, of which
Kate's sudden departure is a harsh reminder. Moreover, notions of
genealogy run through the story. Kate is a surrogate mother but
also potentially a sexual partner for the son. This raises questions

about the ambiguous place of adoptive and birth parents in people's family trees and the forms of identity they engender. Whereas
genealogical ties are recorded biologically, reinforcing the racialised notions of "blood ties", parenting roles, by which culture is
imparted, may be carried out by "others".

There is, however, an extra Irish twist to this story which
might alter its relationship to these themes. It is likely, though
never stated, that the grandfather himself came from Ireland.
There are a small number of clues, which would probably fail to
register with many readers as they are not central to the narrative.
He is described as "the man from nowhere" (Dunmore, 1996: 14)
who bought the house when his daughter was a baby, after his
own wife died. Cathy herself says: "I ought to have made sure I
knew more. He'd had a past, a geography of silence. None of us
had ever mapped it" (Dunmore, 1996: 14). She also says that he
"had given my mother everything, even the fine, slender upright
Englishness of father" (Dunmore, 1996: 42), implying that this was
a calculated move to secure the "outsider" family a position in
English society. Cathy's mother and she herself are said to have
"Irish hair" (Dunmore, 1996: 19), and the grandfather's name is
mentioned as Quinn at the end of the book. Another Irish name is
given to the part-time governess, Miss Gallagher, who nevertheless rails against Irish people at one point, perhaps to disavow
origins of which she is ashamed (Dunmore, 1996: 74).

So what can we make of this? What kind of evidence is offered
by fiction, when it so closely fits with themes which are hard to
recover elsewhere? One possibility is to explore the context in
which the novel was written. Did the author research this theme
or does she have an unexamined understanding that English society works like this? I contacted Helen Dunmore to pursue these
questions and her response was revealing:

> It's always hard to say where material for a novel comes
> from — it is such a mixture of reading, research and
> personal experience. I used some family material — Kate's
> story of the arm falling off the dead man was first told to
> me by my grandfather, and was a childhood experience of

his, he said (but it was a leg, not an arm). Again, the name
Quinn is the maiden name of my maternal grandmother;
when I think it over, there are many family stories in *A
Spell of Winter*, but they are changed and rearranged.[4]

The circulation of stories within families which have an Irish connection several generations back reinforces the notion of taken-
for-granted entanglements which re-emerge in imaginative narratives. That the story appears plausible to the author and presumably to readers suggests that it resonates with their understandings
of English society just beyond historic memory. Far from being a
flimsy basis on which to draw support for the thesis of Irish servants' influence on children in English households, it may draw
together a range of processes operating at an unconscious, but
deeply significant, level.

Uneven Contours of Diaspora Space

At present the concept of diaspora space is usually applied at the
national scale, which is where Brah herself primarily located it.
But since, by focusing on cross-cutting links, it de-emphasises national boundaries, this is not the only scale at which this concept
can be applied. Within national boundaries, regional differences
may be very important, whilst much everyday experience of diaspora space is at the much smaller neighbourhood scale. Even
more locally, households are in many senses at the cutting edge of
where differences are negotiated and close entanglements performed, as the discussion of *A Spell of Winter* illustrates. National
spaces are therefore far from homogenous internally. Moreover,
diasporas by definition flow across national boundaries in ways
which identify them as barriers only in specific and limited ways.

In this section I examine two illustrations of this unevenness
which draw out the significance of *places* as a richly detailed
grounding to the imaginative potential of *space* (Massey, 1994:
168). There are already some very productive examples of un-

---

[4] Personal communication, 23 April 2004.

earthing hidden hybridities at specific locations within national diaspora spaces. In his detailed interpretation of John Walsh's *The Falling Angels* (2000), Liam Harte describes Walsh's pleasure at discovering that significant English settlement took place on the Aran Islands in the seventeenth and eighteenth centuries, which means that "a place that once symbolised 'authentic' Irishness is transformed into a glowing metaphor of heterogeneity and hybridity, one that proves the dialogic, contestatory nature of all national identity formations and suggests the hybrid is the true native" (Harte, 2003b: 303). There is a parallel postscript to add to my own biography which I used in *Outsiders Inside* to illustrate the small Irish presence in my very "English" home town of Poole in Dorset (Walter, 2001: 28-29). Like one part of Harte's categorisation of the Aran Islands as the locus of "authentic Irishness", I presented Poole as a place almost entirely untouched by Irish presence because of its peripheral location on the south coast of England. By implication, this was a space of "authentic Englishness". But — in a striking similarity to with openness of the Aran Islands — Poole's coastal location entirely overturns that apparent homogeneity.

After my book was published, I visited Waterford on the south coast of Ireland and suddenly realised that its strong connection with the Newfoundland cod fishing trade exactly mirrored the stories I had often heard about Poole. I quickly found that Poole was indeed the port of origin of the ships which took on labour and provisions in Waterford before sailing west (Handcock, 1989: 185-201). Once in Newfoundland, Waterford and Poole people settled side by side in adjacent townships. My personal genealogy was entangled much more deeply than I had realised when I reflected on the small number of Irish people I had met in Poole as a child, or who had lived in the same neighbourhoods as my paternal ancestors. My maternal ancestors were merchants in Poole in the eighteenth and nineteenth centuries and I found their names in records of ships sailing to Waterford and travelling on to Newfoundland. Far from being at the fringes of the diaspora space of England, Poole was central to English/Irish interactions in Newfoundland, in which my "English" family genealogy was intimately involved.

A second example of internal geographical variation in the diaspora space of Britain is provided by the findings of the *Irish 2 Project*, which aimed to compare the senses of identity and social positionings of people with at least one Irish-born parent (or grandparent in the case of participants in Scotland) living in contrasting British locations.[5] Significant differences between Scotland and England illustrate the notion of unevenness at a national level in the constituent nations of Britain, and contextualise the English case study. In Scotland, for example, third-generation Irish people could feel as strong or even stronger than the second generation about their Irish identities. One third-generation interviewee, who had never set foot in Ireland, was one of the strongest identifiers with Irishness and considered himself "Irish". Most second- and third-generation participants in Scotland could relate stories of anti-Catholic sectarianism in the workplace, whereas very few mentioned this in England. Indeed, few interviewees in Scotland did *not* mention discrimination in the workplace. Many could relate stories about this, while a significant number re-told experiences of feelings of sectarianism against themselves and their community.

Celtic Football Club was recognised as an important focus for celebrating Irish heritage, culture and identity in Scotland and again there was no comparable focus in England. Indeed, Bradley has argued that the foundation and development of the club in Scotland has given it a unique sporting position within the worldwide Irish diaspora (Bradley, 1998). People in Scotland often mentioned that they were challenged about their Irish identities, even by people of similar descent. As a consequence they were

---

[5] The *Irish 2 Project* (2000-02) was funded by a research grant from the Economic and Social Research Council. The co-applicants were Bronwen Walter, Anglia Polytechnic University, Mary J. Hickman, London Metropolitan University and Joseph M. Bradley, University of Stirling. Sarah Morgan was Research Fellow. The website, which includes newsletters and a discussion of the methodology, can be accessed at http://web.apu.ac.uk/geography/progress/irish2/

wary about where they discussed their Irishness, keeping it within family and friendly circles. Almost all interviewees who esteemed their Irishness could relate stories of the contestation that they had experienced regarding their Irish identities and the subsequent privatisation of this. Again, it was in the Celtic club environment that many of these people felt most at ease with their Irishness, it being often the one public space in which they felt able to express this (Bradley, 2004: 43-44).

These contrasts with England were brought out vividly in the feedback sessions we held with participants to discuss the project's findings. A group of Manchester participants were fascinated and also horrified by some of the reports emanating from our project in Scotland. In turn, the member of the research team who had interviewed participants in Scotland found it hard to believe that Irishness was such an uncontested identity in Manchester and could be freely expressed. Our project was therefore actively constructing people's perceptions of the unevenness of experiences of being of Irish descent in Britain.

There was also considerable variation in the experiences of being second-generation Irish in England between the four places we had selected — Manchester, London, Coventry and Banbury. Banbury was the location where Irish identities had been most thoroughly intertwined with English ones. Again, we contributed to local people's sense of unpicking and acknowledging cultural differences in their own lives by publishing an account of the project and its aims in our recruitment strategies. It was a measure of the strangeness of the notion that Irish identification could be part of Banbury residents' lives that the local newspaper responded with great interest to our approach (Walter *et al.*, 2002). The journalist chose two young men with very Irish-sounding names — Kieran Sullivan and Eddie Quinn — to illustrate our point to her readers. Kieran said he had Irish-born parents but felt English, whereas Eddie said he was Irish: "I don't know why because it wasn't taught to me but when I was younger I was always going to Ireland."

Over 30 people responded to the newspaper article, all very keen to participate and talk about their Irish and part-Irish backgrounds. Particularly striking was the wide range of backgrounds of those who contacted us. Unlike the situation in other locations in England, where it was often extremely difficult to locate people who were not already engaged in Irish activities, in Banbury a very varied cross-section of the population responded. They included "low identifiers" who saw themselves as mainly English, and Protestants from both the north and south of Ireland, another group which was very hard to trace elsewhere. There was also a wide age range, markedly different social class positionings and people with complex migration histories within England, which included living in small towns and rural areas as well as large cities. The strength of the response could be seen as an indication both of the importance people attached to the acknowledgement of their Irish cultural heritage and of the ways in which it had been submerged in the dominant "white" English culture in which they lived.

Such experiences and responses offer parallels and contrasts with those of the participants in the project who make up the final section of my paper. This is concerned with a particularly under-explored aspect of the diaspora space of England, that of "mixed race" crossings between subordinated groups, rather than within the so-called "white" population, which is where Irish/English mixed parentage is usually located.

Mixed-race Crossings

An important facet of the notion of diaspora space which Brah sets out in her theorisation is the entanglements between different diasporas which do not include the dominant group:

> What I am proposing here is that border crossings do not occur only across the dominant/dominated dichotomy, but that, equally, there is traffic within cultural formations of the subordinated groups, and that these journeys are not *always* mediated through the dominant culture(s). In my

schema such cultural ensembles as British Asian-ness,
British Caribbean-ness, or British Cypriot-ness are cross-
cutting rather than mutually exclusive configurations. The
interesting question, then, is how these British identities
take shape; how they are internally differentiated; how
they interrelate with one another and with other British
identities; and how they mutually reconfigure and decentre
received notions of Englishness, Scottishness, Welshness, or
Britishness. *My argument is that they are not 'minority'
identities, nor are they at the periphery of something that sees
itself as located at the centre, although they may be represented as
such.* (Brah, 1996: 209-10, original emphasis)

Four mixed-race people with an Irish parent were interviewed
for the *Irish 2 Project*. All were born in the 1960s, placing them in
the peak years of the second-generation population profile and
allowing them to reflect on a 30 to 40-year lifespan including
childhood, adolescence, entry to and movement within the work-
force and, in two cases, parenthood. We made strong efforts to
recruit people of mixed race, but impersonal calls for volunteers
produced very few results. In three of the four cases, recruitment
was by "snowballing", usually through recommendations from
colleagues working in associated professional fields.[6] The four
now work professionally in the areas of education, social work,
mental health and international development, all careers which
directly relate to their cultural backgrounds. In three cases this
had involved substantial upward social mobility, which contributed to the class breadth of participants' reflective approach to
discussions of the issues. The recruits were two women — Gail,
who had an Irish mother and African Caribbean father, and Yasmeen, whose mother was Irish and father Pakistani — and two
men: Rick, with an Irish mother and Nigerian father, and Tariq,
who had an Irish mother and Pakistani father.[7] They had been

---

[6] One person responded to a notice in *Connections*, an in-house magazine published by the Commission for Racial Equality

[7] All participants were given pseudonyms.

born and raised in different parts of England, Yasmeen and Tariq in London, Gail in Birmingham (now living near Coventry) and Rick in Manchester. Two, Yasmeen and Rick, had spent substantial periods of their childhood in care.

The most striking shared characteristic of this sample was that they all had Irish mothers. The greater likelihood of Irish women having partnerships across the black/white divide in Britain has already been recorded (Walter, 1988: 22). Gail commented that she would instantly assume that a stranger of her age, mixed parentage and urban background had an Irish mother. This gendering has significant consequences for such children's experiences and senses of identity. Two of the most obvious are those of surnames, traditionally inherited through the male line, and the intimate, mundane routines of childhood which are usually carried out by mothers, particularly in the cultures represented here. Such assumptions about interpreting genealogies through the male line took on a more complex aspect in the case of this sample, however. Rick had been given his unmarried mother's surname (not distinctively Irish to English ears), and Gail's African Caribbean father had a strongly Irish surname himself, probably reflecting his distant descent from planters or indentured servants in the sixteenth and seventeenth centuries (McGinn, 2003). Thus, mixed-race entanglements, which had also involved Irish people in British colonies, were being repeated several centuries later as labour flowed back into the former imperial centre.

The "Irish" input into the early lives of these mixed-race individuals varied markedly. The two people with Pakistani fathers, both from London, had extremely contrasting senses of identity. Tariq, whose parents had lower professional occupations, said he felt mainly Pakistani. His Irish-born mother had converted to Islam and taken a Muslim name. There might appear to be parallels here with Blake Morrison's account in his memoir *Things my mother never told me* (2003) of how his Irish mother gave up Catholicism on marriage at the insistence of her husband's English Protestant family, and also changed her name (from Agnes to Kim). Both were well-educated women who had grown up in the

west of Ireland. But in Tariq's mother's case, this had been a voluntary change and she felt free to retain her Irish identity alongside her Islamic one. Tariq described himself as "Irish Pakistani",
an identity which could easily be expressed in the south London
borough where he grew up. However, he was made uncomforta-
bly aware of the unevenness of English diaspora space when he
started a degree at Exeter University, where his "blackness" singled him out. After a year he transferred to Sussex University near
Brighton, which he described as cosmopolitan, like the London he
had known as a child.

A very different childhood was described by Yasmeen, whose
parents were manual workers. She experienced violent sexual
abuse at home and was taken into care between the ages of eleven
and sixteen. As a person of mixed race, she felt she was not accepted by either the Pakistani or English communities. At school
she was labelled a "dirty Irish Paki". Her Irish Protestant mother
was very socially isolated. Yasmeen said she had found it very
difficult to find an identity. She had very light-coloured skin and
could easily have "passed" as "white", but she felt she was simply
"mixed race":

> it is hard when you can't be whole in something. It is like
> making a curry but not adding the chicken, that is what it
> feels like. It is a bit of this and that, you put them together
> but it doesn't make a whole, it makes a mixture of stuff,
> which doesn't feel whole.

In a very different account Gail, who grew up in a predominantly
white working-class area of Birmingham, felt strongly Irish:

> I had a very strong Irish identity when we were children,
> my mother was one of nine children, I hardly knew my
> black grandparents. We had a black grandmother who
> lived with us for a while. We called her black nana, we
> called our Irish nan, nan. So Irish was the default if you
> like, whereas black was black nana, or black cousins, but
> Irish was normal. My father was mostly an absent father,
> he was around but a very remote man, whereas my Irish

mother, Irish cousins and family, were very vocal, very noisy, very "there". So I had a strong sense of being Irish, that is my sense of identity first, although I look African Caribbean so people don't think there is an Irish person, they think there goes an African Caribbean woman. That is not how I see myself.

But Gail said that her Irish identity was not accepted by most Irish people and that she was treated with incomprehension when she attended Irish functions.

Finally Rick, who had lived in Manchester all his life, also felt that his visibility as a black man overwhelmed his Irish identity. However, unlike Gail, who could separate her own strong feelings of an Irish identity from ways in which others saw her, Rick's experiences had made him prioritise the African element of his ethnicity. Nevertheless, as an adult he had begun to rediscover his Irish cultural background and now found it a source of private pleasure and satisfaction:

> If I wasn't black, which would make me somebody else, I would have a more outraged sense of the mistreatment and lack of recognition of the Irish. Compared to the issues it has brought me in terms of colour and identity, it is so far down on the list. I can happily say, almost with a shock value or interest value, that I see it very positively. Because the Africanness comes very glaringly in terms of my treatment, and how people have treated me, and how I set myself up to be treated by people.

None of the four participants described themselves simply as "Irish", whereas this was an identity chosen by about a quarter of the "white" second-generation people in the study, including a number with one Irish-born parent. Although in genealogical terms there was no difference in the "Irish" proportion of their family trees, this became lost when translated into a claimed identity. Its absence was mirrored by the wording of the 2001 Census which invited people to answer the question "What is your ethnic group?" in two stages. The first, prioritised stage was self-identification by "race" (White, Mixed, Asian, Black, Chinese, Other) followed by a second, subordinate stage indicating "cultural background", where the option to tick "Irish" was provided only in the section labelled "White" (Walter, 2004a: 185-86). For those with a "black" parent, therefore, the only possibility was Mixed ("race" implied, but not stated) then four separate options: "White and Black Caribbean", "White and Black African", "White and Asian" or "Any other mixed background. Please describe" (followed by a blank line). Whereas under "White" the Irish were allowed to form a separate grouping, under the "Mixed" category people with a white Irish parent would be scattered across all categories, denying any commonality on the basis of an Irish background. The single "White" category suggested no real difference between groups defined as such. In fact, as the participants explained, having an Irish parent placed them very differently in relation to Englishness. Tariq spelled this out clearly:

> I guess for me my mum has never been white in the sense, not that she is not white in colour, but she is not British, she has never been white in any kind of way of identifying herself. For me I had a notion of what the implication was to be white on that form, there was almost this "them" and "us" feeling about it, "inside" or "outside" feeling about it. My mum is Irish she has the same attitude towards Britishness, more so than I do. English, no way.

Conclusions

Mixed-race children with an Irish parent throw particularly revealing light on Irish dimensions of diaspora space. They draw attention to shared locations of outsideness which are often denied to those categorised as Irish because of their "'whiteness'". In doing so, they challenge the discourse of assimilation of second-generation Irish people whose difference is denied when their parents are of "white" Irish and British background. Identifying the common and dissonant experiences of mixed-race and mixed-white heritage second-generation Irish people reveals disjunctures for the latter which are often papered over by powerful assumptions deriving from "white" skin colour. There are clear parallels with "white" second-generation Irish people who are "not allowed" to be Irish because their birthplace and — above all — their accent places them as "English" (Hickman *et al.*, 2005: 174-75).

The focus on "looks" — being either not white enough to be the same or too white to be different — forcibly excludes and includes people of Irish descent within the English *national* space. Re-imagining it as *diaspora* space shifts attention from these racialised boundaries and focuses instead on the myriad of crosscuttings ties between people occupying this shared territory. Brah describes the text in which she elaborates this notion as "a cartography of the politics of intersectionality" (Brah, 1996: 16). This means that "race" is only part of a much larger array of positionalities including gender, class, religion, age, generation and ability, which produce the "differentiated, heterogenous, contested spaces" (Brah, 1996: 184) where we all live. Tracing the everyday genealogies of Irishness in England, both bodily and cultural, illustrates its deep embeddedness in "ordinary" life.

16

An Eighteenth-Century Version
of Diasporic Irish Identity

Thomas Byrne

In this paper I would like to look at two contrasting examples of Irish identity in the long eighteenth century.[1] The port of Amsterdam provides an appropriate point of entry for our first example, since it was there in June 1685 that a young man boarded one of three ships bound for an attempted invasion of England. The ships riding at anchor in Amsterdam bore the Protestant Duke of Monmouth and his small, but loyal, party of followers. This expedition was intended as a final and most extreme attempt to carry forward the aims of the Whig Party in England (Zook, 1999: 29). From the early years of the 1670s this growing faction in English politics had increasingly taken issue with the prospective succession of a Catholic, James, Duke of York and brother of Charles II, to the thrones of England, Ireland and Scotland. Divisions within the English political nation had descended into extreme hostility and bitterness, giving rise to the hysteria surrounding the fictitious popish plot of 1678. As one scholar puts it:

[1] I would like to acknowledge the support of the Irish Research Council for the Humanities and Social Sciences in funding the research upon which this paper is based.

"The corruption of the Stuart polity by Catholicism was equated with the destruction of laws and liberties, parliaments and Protestantism" (Doyle, 2004: 35). A faction led by the Earl of Shaftesbury manipulated the panic caused by the plot to demand, in three successive but short-lived parliaments, the exclusion of James from the succession. The most viable of a number of alternatives proposed by James's enemies was adjudged to be the replacement of James in the line of succession by Charles's illegitimate son James Scott, Duke of Monmouth.

Charles II was equally adamant that the divinely ordained principle of hereditary succession should not and would not be challenged. This poisoned state of affairs culminated in a royal backlash in 1683, in the wake of an alleged assassination conspiracy against the royal brothers (the Rye House plot) and the flight of many of the most ardent Whigs into exile in Holland. There, they planned, plotted and schemed, seeking ways to undo the Stuarts (Walker, 1948). One of their means of attack was an avalanche of hostile pamphlets disseminated throughout the three kingdoms designed to evoke public sympathy for their cause.[2] The second element of their plan was an armed intervention with the aim of triggering widespread revolt against the prevailing monarchy and the installation of the Duke of Monmouth as king. In February 1685 Charles II died and his brother James II succeeded without hindrance to the thrones of England, Ireland and Scotland. For the exiled Whigs the time had come to put their plans into action.

The young man who boarded the ship on the day of departure was there in his role of personal chaplain to the Duke of Monmouth. He was deeply committed to the righteousness of the Whig cause, a fact attested to in a letter he wrote in which he said: "I am ready to shed my blood in the defence of [my religion] &

---

[2] Two pamphlets published in 1684 are of particular note: Henry Danver's *Murder will out; or a clear and full discovery that the earl of Essex did not murder himself, but was murdered by others* and Robert Ferguson's *Enquiry into and detection of the barbarous murder of the late earl of Essex*.

my country's rights against all deceivers who would corrupt the one, & usurpers who invade the other."[3] While such views were to be expected, what was unusual about this young gentleman, barely twenty-one, was the fact that, unlike the vast majority of the other members of the expedition, he was not English.

The exact nature of his identity is difficult to determine. He was born in 1664 in a small village near Drogheda in County Louth.[4] This would, in terms of place of birth (*jus soli*), make him quite discernibly Irish. However, his family, successful merchants in Dublin, were quite recent English settlers in the Irish capital. Ethnically (*jus sanguine*), then, our young gentleman is, in historical terms, New English, or New Protestant. His grandfather had integrated himself, to some extent, into the commercial life of the capital by the early 1640s (Barnard, 1975: 82). However, his real rise to prominence comes in the wake of the Cromwellian invasion and subsequent period of Parliamentary rule. By subscribing money and supplies to the Parliamentary cause, and becoming a leading member of a religious sect heavily supported by the army, he improved his position in city politics, eventually becoming Mayor of Dublin in 1654 (Dunlop, 1913). His ability and reliability saw him deeply involved in the Cromwellian administration, including the transplantation to Connacht of those adjudged guilty of rebellion (Hardinge, 1862: 67).

This family involvement in the Cromwellian regime, combined with strong Protestant beliefs, deeply influenced the outlook and world view of our young Irish rebel. While attending Sidney Sussex College, Cambridge (Oliver Cromwell's alma mater) he became ever more deeply involved with radical politics and the various machinations of the Whig Party (Zook, 1999: 29). Eventually he became so deeply immersed within this shadowy underworld that he was forced to seek refuge in Holland, where he established himself in the Duke of Monmouth's household,

---

[3] British Library Additional Manuscript 41817 f. 86, Nathaniel Hooke to Fr. Ambrose Grymes, Brussels, 3 June 1685.

[4] B.L. Add. Ms. 72873 (A).

and became energetically involved in preparations for the invasion of England.[5] Despite his commitment and hard work, however, the Monmouth invasion of south-west England was a short-lived affair, eventually crushed by a military force that included John Churchill, the future Duke of Marlborough and Patrick Sarsfield, later to be Earl of Lucan (Earle, 1977; Clifton, 1984). Our young Anglo-Irishman was lucky to escape the tender mercies of "Hanging Judge" Jeffries in the bloody aftermath of the rebellion, managing to flee back to safety, renewed exile in Holland and life as a fugitive from English justice (Greaves, 1992: 309). Our first example of Irish diasporic identity, then, is that of a Protestant, New English, Whig commoner.

Our second, contrasting, example of Irish diasporic identity in the long eighteenth century died in Paris in 1738 having reached the rank of major general in the French army. He had, like many others, arrived in France as part of the migration of defeated Jacobites after the signing of the Treaty of Limerick in 1691. In subsequent years he fought as part of the Irish regiments on battlefields throughout Europe. In a natural progression from, and in addition to, his role as a soldier he became involved in the closely aligned fields of espionage and diplomacy. In fact, he was so successful in fulfilling this position that he transferred to direct French service in 1701, although he continued to retain close links with the exiled Jacobite court located at St Germains.

This was an exceptionally intense period in the history of European diplomacy. Both prior to and after the outbreak of the War of Spanish Succession in 1702 overt and covert diplomatic initiatives were pursued actively and vigorously (Bély, 1990). These efforts went hand in hand with continuing military endeavours. As the fortunes of war increasingly saw France hard pressed on three fronts in Europe, Louis XIV and his ministers sought some means of removing or at least grievously weakening one of the Allies ranged against them, either the United Provinces, Britain or the Habsburg Empire. Of the three, Britain seemed the

---

[5] B.L. Add. Ms. 41817 ff. 13, 49, 56, 64, 199-200.

most vulnerable candidate. After all, the rival claimant to the British throne James Francis Edward Stuart, James VIII of Scotland and III of England, was resident on French soil and to a large extent therefore dependent on French aide.

Our Irishman — at this stage a colonel in the French army but still a committed Jacobite — was entrusted with the task of secretly visiting Scotland to assess support and recommend a plan of action to Louis XIV and the French Council of State. On the basis of his submission a full-scale attempt was made to send a fleet of 30 ships, carrying 6,000 men, mainly Irish, to land in Scotland and restore James VIII to the throne (Hooke, 1760: 131-36). This attempt would, at the very least, divert British troops from the continent, thereby relieving pressure on the French armies. The attempt was launched in March 1708, successfully evaded the English navy and reached the coast of Scotland. However, due to circumstances never quite satisfactorily explained, no landing was made and the endeavour ended in failure (Hooke, 1760: 147-65). Not only did our Irish colonel escape the blame for this military fiasco, he was promoted to brigadier and raised to the peerage as a baron of Ireland by James III. He went on to have a successful diplomatic career in France, where his application for naturalisation was confirmed in 1720. In 1728 his career was crowned by investiture into the prestigious Royal and Military Order of St Louis as one of only 52 living Knight Commanders. On 25 October 1738 our second example of Irish diasporic identity died as a Catholic, Irish, Jacobite noble.

The strange and intriguing fact about these two contrasting versions of identity, polar opposites in terms of religion, politics, social status and nationality (using that term advisedly in the context of its limitations in the period under discussion), is that we are actually speaking of the same person. The Protestant, New English, Whig commoner and the Catholic, Irish, Jacobite noble are both versions of identity embodied in one man: Nathaniel Hooke.

The missing element in this surprising tale of identity formation and reformation emerges in the wake of Hooke's return to

Holland in 1685 after the failure of Monmouth's rebellion. He spent three years on the run during this period, constantly in danger of being apprehended by English agents or even of being dispatched on the spot, such was James II desire to apprehend those mixed up in rebellion (Miller, 1984: 197). Reduced to a state of near psychological despair by the summer of 1688, Hooke took his life in his hands. Declaring that in his present state "life itself was not worth living", he returned to London, surrendered to James II and requested pardon or death (Ellis, 1829: 103). His audacity paid off. James II was impressed by his sincerity and bravery and granted the young Irish rebel a full pardon. Hooke in turn was so grateful for this display of mercy from his former, much demonised enemy that he entered James's service and converted to Catholicism. Thereafter he remained loyal in the wake Prince William of Orange's invasion of England in November 1688, despite enticements then and later to defect.

Curiosity about Hooke's complicated identity is not only a modern phenomenon. His contemporaries were also aware that there was more to him than initial impressions suggested. Rarely, I suspect, has the question of identity been discussed at such exalted levels. At the centre of power in early eighteenth-century Europe lay the court of Versailles. No less a person than Louis XIV himself, France's renowned Sun King and the most powerful sovereign in Europe, was moved by curiosity to enquire about Hooke's origins (Masson, 1884: 109). In his response to Louis's query his foreign minister, Jean Baptiste Colbert, Marquis de Torcy, gives a glimpse of another enduring facet of Irish identity: begrudgery. He recounted details regarding Hooke that he had gleaned from conversations with an Irish monk. The good friar, obviously unimpressed by Hooke's achievements, rank and titles filled in some of the man's family background, including the fact that "his father was Irish and nothing more than a man from the common people" (Masson, 1884: 109). In other words, there was no reason for Colonel Hooke to be aspiring to ideas above his station! Furthermore, de Torcy explained why Hooke had a number of enemies at the Jacobite court at St Germains. His change in religious and political identity aroused suspicion, leading to charges of espionage, treachery and irreligion. For his part, Hooke was so disgusted at the constant internal bickering and internecine fractiousness in Jacobite circles that he refused to be involved in later efforts to resurrect the Scottish enterprise (Masson, 1884: 95).

Having such a shifting, convoluted identity caused problems for many contemporaries accustomed to assigning individuals to black and white categories. Difficult questions arose. What to make of a man who was once Protestant and was now apparently Catholic, who previously espoused Whig principles but now seemingly supported the Stuart cause, and who could variously be described as Irish, English and/or French? How is it possible to tell if he is really one of us, if he is our sort of person, when we cannot tell what exactly he is? This uneasiness with Hooke's multi-dimensional identity remained a factor in later representations of him. For an Irishman who was one of the very few to initiate, plan, organise and participate in an invasion of Britain, he has attracted surprisingly little attention. In fact, he has been quite neglected in Irish history. In works where references to him might well be expected he does not feature; in those in which he does, the question of his ambiguous identity still seems to cause problems.

For example, in J.C. O'Callaghan's *History of the Irish Brigades in the Service of France* allusions to Hooke's Protestant New English past are entirely absent (O'Callaghan, 1870). Regarding his family background, O'Callaghan states that Nathaniel Hooke was an offshoot of an old line of that name expelled from their lands in Westmeath by the Cromwellians. As we have seen, however, the Hooke family had been Cromwellians themselves, and far from being victims of confiscation were much more likely to have been the perpetrators. Thomas, Nathaniel's grandfather and family patriarch during the Interregnum, had actually gained land and fortune through his connections and service in the Cromwellian administration. O'Callaghan also refers to Hooke coming to France with King James's Guards but there is no information on his activities prior to this. We can perhaps excuse O'Callaghan because his work was published in 1870, the same year that also saw the publication of *Correspondence of Colonel Nathaniel Hooke, Agent from the Court of France to the Scottish Jacobites, in [...] 1703-1707*, edited by W. D. Macray. The preface included a long, detailed and largely accurate history of the Hooke family in Ireland, including their Puritan beliefs and intimate involvement with the Cromwellian regime. This rather in-depth treatment of the Hookes' politics may be explained by the fact that Macray, an Oxford scholar and Bodleian librarian, would have viewed the family's Cromwellian associations more benignly than many in Ireland at this time, when the demonisation of Cromwell and his outrages became fixed in the public mind.

The section on Hooke in Richard Hayes's *A Biographical Dictionary of Irishmen in France* (1949) again presents an edited version of his identity, with only the briefest mention of the underlying complexities: "Born at Corballis, Co. Meath in 1664. Entered Trinity College in July 1679, left soon afterwards, became an enthusiastic Jacobite and reverted to Catholicism, the religion of his immediate forbears" (Hayes, 1949: 127). The use of "reverted" here presents a problem. None of Hooke's immediate ancestors were in fact Catholic. Hayes may have been following O'Callaghan's account for some of his extract, but there is no mention of Hooke's attendance at Trinity College in that passage. Quite possibly the *Dictionary of National Biography* (1885-1900) was also used, but this again raises problems as it mentions Hooke's attendance at Glasgow and Cambridge as well as Trinity, his Puritanism and his active participation in Monmouth's rebellion. In addition to the *DNB*, Hooke's correspondence had been in publication for almost eighty years by the time Hayes was writing.

Given the availability of these sources, which reveal the actual history of the Hooke family rather than the romanticised version, we might be justified in concluding that while an Irish Catholic Jacobite officer and gentleman could be accepted in Irish historiography in 1949, a more ambiguously identified Irish/English, Catholic/Protestant, Jacobite/Whig with strong connections to the infamous *bête noire* of Irish history, Oliver Cromwell, could be less readily accommodated. *When in doubt leave him out*, may have been the guiding motto, with the simplified picture fitting much more easily into the homogenised spirit and outlook of the times. Over a half-century later, it is to be hoped that historians might be more willing to explore the factors which shaped such a heterogeneous identity. Nathaniel Hooke's *volte face* of 1688, while regrettable in terms of the human suffering and mental anguish that preceded and precipitated it, provides for us today an opportunity to gain a unique historical insight into different constructions of political, religious, social and ethnic elements of identity, sharply focused through the experiences of one man.

17

Forging an Irish Identity in Nineteenth-Century Quebec

Aidan McQuillan

Quebec, or Lower Canada as it was known through much of the first half of the nineteenth century, represented a unique milieu for new immigrants in North America. It represented a large corner of the continent, centred on the St. Lawrence River, one of the major routes to the heart of the great landmass, and it had been colonised by the French from the beginning of the seventeenth century. When Irish immigrants began arriving more than two hundred years later they found a large, rapidly growing French community with a very distinctive culture. Although Britain had conquered the colony in 1763, *Canadiens* had retained their language, their Roman Catholic faith, and their seigneurial system of land survey and land tenure that had created a unique landscape. They occupied the lowlands on either side of the St. Lawrence and had a powerful sense of their distinctive identity in the largely Anglophone world of North America. Many of them aspired to independence from their British colonial masters but were wary of joining the revolutionary former colonies which had created the United States to the south. Thus, it is an understatement to say that Lower Canada was different from the other British colonies in North America.

Irish migration to the Canadas began after the end of Napoleonic Wars and reached a crescendo in the 1830s but began to decline during the 1840s. Few of the Famine refugees of the late 1840s remained in Canada despite the fact that Quebec City was a major port of entry; most of them proceeded southwards to the United States. Consequently the number of Irish immigrants who made Canada their transatlantic home dropped steadily for the remainder of the century, except for a small resurgence during the 1880s. When the Irish began arriving in large numbers during the 1820s the best agricultural lands along the St Lawrence Plain were already occupied. Consequently, Irish communities were established along the margins of the valley, on the fringes of the Canadian Shield to the north and in the low hills of the Appalachians to the south — an area that became known as the Eastern Townships. They formed a garland of colonies in the Laurentides to the north with names such as St Colomban, Kildare and Kilkenny; and in the Eastern Townships to the south with names such as Armagh, Coleraine and Ireland (Blanchard, 1947: 428-29). Many of the largest Irish communities did not have Irish place-names. They included Gore, Rawdon and Val Cartier to the north and the townships of Frampton, Leeds and Inverness to the south. These last two — Leeds and Inverness — were immediately adjacent to the parish of St Sylvestre in the old seigneurial lands, and together they formed a large contiguous settlement where serious conflicts occurred during the 1850s between Irish Catholics and Irish Protestants. There were also many Irish in the lowlands south of Montreal, along the US border, but they were interspersed with other Anglophone and *Canadien* settlers.

The Irish also settled in the two largest cities of Lower Canada, Montreal and Quebec City. By mid-century Montreal was much the larger of the two and the Irish Protestant component was clearly identified with the ruling British elite: indeed, some such as the McCord and Workman families had already made considerable fortunes in the city and were considered members of the commercial elite (Keep, 1950: 40; Nolte, 1975: 86). Although the middle class was expanding there was a sizeable working-class component in the Irish Protestant community. Irish Catholics, by contrast, were still heavily concentrated in the working class with the exception of a small number in the medical and legal professions. The Irish community in Quebec City was much smaller than in Montreal at mid-century, and more heavily Catholic than Protestant. In addition, the Catholic middle class, though small, was proportionally larger in Lower Canada's second city. The Irish Protestant community there was much smaller and more heavily represented within the working class than in Montreal.

The story of Irish Catholic immigrant adjustment to nineteenth-century Quebec can be roughly identified in three phases: (i) the 1830s when Irish Catholics were wooed by Joseph Papineau and his nationalist *Patriote* movement before the Rebellion of 1837; (ii) the 1850s, when riots and bitter struggles disrupted the traditional harmony between Catholics and Protestants and deepened sectarian divisions; (iii) the unifying vision of D'Arcy McGee and the overwhelming response to his assassination in 1868 that ensured the success of that vision. These were not sharply delineated, mutually exclusive periods but they may be considered major turning points in the history of Irish Catholics in this unique region of the North American continent.

Irish Catholics and the *Patriotes*

A growing desire for political independence in Quebec (Lower Canada) during the 1820s and 1830s offered French Canadians and Irish Catholics an opportunity to make common cause against their British colonial masters. To begin, there was much that united the two groups. Both were overwhelmingly poor, rural-based societies with a meagre resource base on which their populations had exploded during the last third of the eighteenth century. Their agricultural economies were restrained by imperial trading considerations and there was limited opportunity for the development of free trade based on a commercial wheat economy. The struggle for economic freedom was paralleled by a growing passion for political autonomy and the retention of their distinctive cultural identities.

Religion and language had both been important for French Canadians and Irish Catholics as they struggled to maintain their distinctive identities. The Catholic Church had played an important role in keeping alight the flame of nationalist culture in both Ireland and Quebec and it had acted for a time as a bulwark against the expansion of British imperial power until they had negotiated their own special concessions within the power structure of the state. Only in the matter of language was there a substantial difference between Ireland and Quebec. The Irish were in the throes of abandoning *their* national language in favour of English at the time of emigration, whereas French Canadians fiercely retained theirs as a fundamental factor in their identity.

In the political arena the *Patriotes* had begun as a reform movement seeking to broaden the powers of the Legislative Council and to curtail the influence of entrenched commercial interests. But during the 1830s their goals increased to include political autonomy. Papineau appealed directly for Irish Catholic votes on the basis of common interests. He was proud to be known as the "O'Connell of Canada" (Greer, 1993: 134) and his fundraising efforts were modelled directly on the O'Connell Tribute in Ireland. His appeals met with a very limited response among the Irish in Quebec City but he was temporarily successful in Montreal. The small rural community of St. Colomban north of Montreal also joined the *Patriote* cause but that may have had more to do with the geography of rebellion and the proximity of Orange lodges in the adjacent Ottawa Valley.

Irish Catholics were a key group in the constituency of the Upper Town in Quebec City in elections between 1827 and 1836; the margin of victory in 1827 had been only eleven votes. But Irish Catholics in Quebec City were not flocking to the *Patriote* banner in the 1830s. There are several factors that may explain this. First, the Irish Catholic community had split between those affiliated with the St. Patrick Society in the Upper Town — mostly middle-class businessmen who were Constitutionalists with strong Tory sympathies — and the Irish Reformers concentrated in the Lower Town who were led by Dr. E.B. O'Callaghan, a newspaper editor. Leadership of the Reform group, which identified closely with the *Patriotes*, was lost in 1832 when O'Callaghan moved to Montreal to take over a newspaper there. Second, the Constitutionalist candidate was the distinguished lawyer, Andrew Stuart, who had helped negotiate the purchase of land for the new St. Patrick's church and was so warmly regarded in both Irish communities that in "the by-election of 1836, despite the *Patriote* invocation of St. Patrick and Daniel O'Connell, Irish Catholics, like other Irish, voted en masse" for him (De Brou, 1991: 316, 324). Irish Catholics voted with the other Anglophones in the constituency to give Stuart 97 per cent of their votes. Whatever support had once existed for the *Patriotes* among Quebec City's Irish Catholics had clearly evaporated.

The scenario in Montreal played out somewhat differently during the 1830s. In 1832 a special by-election was called in the constituency of Montreal West to replace a member of the English party who was retiring on account of ill health. The contestants were Stanley Bragg, spokesman for the business elite in Montreal, and Daniel Tracey, leader of the Reform group. Tracey was an Irish doctor, who founded and edited the *Vindicator* newspaper that strongly supported the *Patriote* position. Bragg drew his support from amongst the British and American entrepreneurs who made up much of the Anglophone middle class in Montreal. Tracey's strength lay with the much poorer, working-class Irish Catholics and French Canadians who had the property qualifications to vote. Tracey emphasised opposition to massive immigration, to the monopoly of land by the London Company, and to the interference of the Imperial Government in the affairs of Lower Canada; all themes that appealed to *Patriotes* and French Canadians. He won by a narrow margin of four votes, 691 to 687. Tracey's triumph was short-lived; he died in the cholera epidemic of 1832 and O'Callaghan was called from Quebec City to take over at the *Vindicator*. *Patriote* influence with Irish Catholic voters seemed very strong.

That influence was even more apparent in the general election of 1834 in Montreal. The *Patriotes* were going from strength to strength and had sent off to Westminster their famous "Ninety-two Resolutions" for the reform of the Crown-appointed Legislative Council in Lower Canada. This became their platform in the election. Papineau himself became a candidate in the heavily Irish Catholic constituency of Montreal West. The Tories opposed him with an Irishman, John Donnellan, in an attempt to split the Irish Catholic vote. Papineau appealed directly for the Irish vote with warm references to O'Connell and the emancipation movement in Ireland. The parallels between O'Connell's and Papineau's aspirations were readily apparent and Papineau won easily. Irish Catholics in Montreal now seemed secure in the *Patriote* camp. The 1834 election, in retrospect, represented a high water mark in Irish/French Canadian alignment; thereafter, Irish Catholics in Lower Canada's largest city abandoned the *Patriote* cause.

Two factors probably contributed to this sudden change. First, the *Patriote* position became increasingly radicalised, with growing anti-clericalism and talk of open rebellion against the government; and second, Church authorities increasingly made clear their opposition to violent protest. Bishop Lartigue of Montreal issued a pastoral letter in 1837 declaring that no Catholic could join a revolt against a legally constituted government and this brought many Irish Catholics back into a Constitutionalist line. When the Rebellion broke in 1837 Irish Catholic support had evaporated, with the one notable exception of the rural parish of St Colomban, which was still being actively settled in the 1830s. Here, the Irish refused to be intimidated and voted for the *Patriotes*. Three years later, as tensions increased during the summer of 1837 and "rumours spread that the tough Orangemen of the Gore had promised to come down to the aid of the beleaguered anglophones of the south", the Irish in St. Colomban remained a hotbed of radicalism (Greer, 1993: 176, 183). Even after the Rebellion had failed and as the Constitutionalist forces sought retribution, St Colomban did not yield. An overwhelming majority of the Irish there refused to take the oath of allegiance to the Crown and so remained resolute in their support of the *Patriote* cause.

The Difficult 1850s

There can be little doubt that the Famine migrations of the late 1840s greatly changed the character of the Irish community in Lower Canada. The Famine immigrants were overwhelmingly Catholic, disease ridden, completely destitute, and without skills or resources to survive. The Irish communities in Lower Canada's two largest cities, both Catholic and Protestant, responded generously to their plight. The Montreal Famine Committee, largely composed of successful Irish Protestants in the city, provided help for the fever victims and assistance to the immigrants in making a start in the New World. One of the new arrivals, Fr O'Dowd, set out immediately in 1847 to collect funds to build a shelter for the immigrants and later the St. Patrick's Orphanage. With the help of the Grey Nuns, St. Bridget's Refuge for widows and young girls opened in 1847 and the nuns' care of fever victims led to the opening of St Patrick's Hospital in 1852. Despite the many acts of charity and cross-community cooperation in the face of this massive immigration, however, the Irish Catholic and Protestant communities began to drift apart. In 1856 Irish Protestants in Montreal withdrew from the St Patrick's Society, which had always been free of sectarian differentiation, to form their own Irish Protestant Benevolent Society. Although relations between the two organisations remained amicable (Cross, 1969: 157), there were small elements in both communities capable of inflaming old passions and these became increasingly active as the 1850s unfolded.

The Orange Order had always existed in Montreal although it had never been particularly robust. Historians differ on the number of Orange lodges in the city by 1860 but agree that membership was less than two hundred (Cross, 1969: 166; Keep, 1948: 114). The strength of the Order in Quebec City was even less than in Montreal but it had a counterpart in the Catholic community, the Ribbonmen. The Ribbonmen began in Ireland as a secret land protest movement in the early decades of the nineteenth century but on crossing the Atlantic morphed into a secret sectarian organisation, effectively becoming the Catholic equivalent of the Orange Order, though with a less formal structure. It was outlawed by the Catholic Church as were all secret societies. The Ribbonmen nevertheless existed in working-class districts of Quebec City but there was no evidence of their presence in Montreal. Though their numbers were small, the growing activity of the Orange Lodges and the Ribbonmen in the 1850s threatened the harmony that traditionally existed between the Irish Protestant and Catholic communities in both Montreal and Quebec City.

Two events highlighted the violent breakdown in intercommunity relations during the 1850s. The Gavazzi riots of 1853 in Quebec City and Montreal marked a low point for the Irish communities in both the cities; and the Corrigan murder in the rural parish of St Sylvestre in 1855 agitated not only a large rural area that included the townships of Leeds, Inverness and Ireland, but reverberated throughout Canada and contributed to the fall of the government. Both cases were driven by acute sectarian bitterness. The 1853 riots were provoked by the inflammatory anti-papal diatribes of Alessandro Gavazzi, a renegade Italian priest who claimed that the Pope and the Catholic Church were no longer true to the original ideals of Christianity. When one of his public talks in Quebec City was broken up by a Catholic mob in June 1853, the police opened fire, killing six people, all of them Protestant. The extreme passions roused by the Gavazzi riots had created deep wounds within the Irish community, including among moderates on both sides, that would take a long time to heal.

Barely eighteen months later an extraordinary murder occurred in the parish of St Sylvestre, located next to the townships of Leeds and Inverness. The victim was one Robert Corrigan, a newcomer and a farmer, who had boasted of his physical prowess and said that he could beat a Catholic farmer also known for his strength. Corrigan was Protestant although it was later discovered that he had been born Roman Catholic in Ireland. When, in October 1854, he was called upon to judge sheep at a local agricultural fair, his decision to favour the flock of an Irish Protestant farmer over those of an Irish Catholic led to him being set upon and beaten (Barlow, 1998). His death three days later led to months of near terror during which both the Ribbonmen and Orangemen of St Sylvestre claimed that they were in mortal danger of being burned from their homes or shot. The police appealed for information but a silence as total as any Sicilian *omertá* had descended on the Irish Catholic community. Eventually a secret deal was struck between a Justice of the Peace and the leader of the accused group, leading to a trial in Quebec City. The acquittal of the accused led to them being paraded through the Lower Town of Quebec; the Ribbonmen had murdered a Protestant farmer in broad daylight and snubbed their noses at the law. Upper and Lower Canada were stunned by the outcome, Orangemen everywhere were enraged, and the government, already a shaky parliamentary coalition, collapsed. The Corrigan Affair, as it became known, had reverberations throughout Canada and certainly poisoned relations between Protestants and Catholics far beyond the confines of St Sylvestre and the Eastern Townships.

The Unifying Vision of Thomas D'Arcy McGee

At this time a new figure appeared on the scene who would have a profound influence on the Irish in Canada. Thomas D'Arcy McGee emigrated from Ireland to Boston as a youth of seventeen and returned to Dublin three years later to become editor of a nationalist newspaper. A committed nationalist with powerful anti-British views, he joined the Young Ireland movement and when the organisation was outlawed escaped to the United States in 1848 via Scotland. Over the next nine years McGee lived in Boston and New York where, like many young radicals, he ran foul of the powerful Archbishop Hughes. He subsequently reconciled with the Church but his taste for American democracy turned sour. He saw clearly that the American political system, for all its high-blown rhetoric, simply exploited the Irish immigrant and deliv-

ered none of the promises of freedom and opportunity. In 1857 he
made a sudden decision to come to Canada to work for a Montreal newspaper but instead founded his own, the *New Era*, that
became his political mouthpiece. He moved quickly, being elected
to the Legislative Assembly in December 1857, mere months after
moving to Montreal (Clarke, 1868).

McGee's political views matured over the next decade and he
soon realised that British parliamentary democracy offered Irish
immigrants the opportunity and fairness he sought. Although his
party affiliations fluctuated he developed a vision of the Irish in
Canada. He envisioned Protestants and Catholics uniting to form
a bridge between the Protestant British and the Catholic French
Canadian, thereby creating a new, unified nation. He became
deeply committed to the movement to unite the British colonies in
a new state, and achieved considerable success in uniting the Irish
in Montreal. He urged the Irish Protestant Benevolent Association
to put aside religious controversy and join in the great project of
creating a new nation, and condemned the narrow sectarianism of
the Orange Order and the Fenian Brotherhood (McGee, 1865: 36-
37). John A. Macdonald, rising star in the Conservative Party (and
later Canada's first prime minister) soon recognised the political
acumen and oratorical skills of the young member from Montreal
West and had him campaign for Irish votes in Canada West (later
Ontario). McGee also developed a strong following among the
Irish in Nova Scotia and New Brunswick and would play a key
role in bringing the Maritime colonies into Confederation. But for
all of his far-flung influence, McGee had to secure his home base
in Montreal West with its heavy concentration of Irish Protestant
and Catholic constituents.

During the 1860s McGee encountered serious political challenges within his constituency, especially from the Fenian Brotherhood, which recruited among Irish Catholics in Toronto with
limited success and then turned its attention to Montreal (Nolte,
1975: 302). McGee, of course, was anathema to the Fenians because his political position had changed one hundred and eighty

degrees and he was now loyal to the British monarch. At the annual St Patrick Society's dinner on March 17 in 1866 he declared:

> I do not consider this magnificent demonstration as one of personal respect to myself. I accept it as evidence on your part of loyalty to our gracious Sovereign, and of attachment to the institutions of our land; and further as a protest on your part against the principles and designs of wicked men who would disgrace the name of Irishmen. (quoted in Keep, 1948: 122)

Some of those "wicked men" to whom McGee was alluding here had, from 1864, organised an alternative dinner in opposition to the official one patronised by McGee. Two years later the Fenians infiltrated St Patrick's Society, which in 1867 elected a new president, a man called Devlin who was a committed Fenian. The gauntlet had been thrown down and the Fenians now challenged McGee for leadership of the Irish Catholic community in Montreal.

In the first national elections of the newly confederated Canada in September 1867 McGee unexpectedly switched parties at the last minute from *rouge* to *bleu*, joining Macdonald's Conservatives. His former party colleagues were, quite naturally, incensed and although they maintained their distance from the Fenians, they ran Devlin against McGee in revenge. The ensuing campaign was marked by violence and threats of violence. Devlin's supporters broke up McGee's meetings and the Fenians, for their part, issued a death threat if McGee ran against Devlin in the election or if he published, as promised, an exposé of how Fenianism had taken hold in Montreal. McGee refused to yield and published his promised exposure. The election result was very close but McGee won by a slender 286 votes. He lost the Irish Catholic working-class ghetto of Griffintown, however, and owed his narrow victory to Irish Protestant, English and Scottish votes in Montreal West.

The Fenians had come very close to a stunning upset and their influence seemed in the ascendancy. In two short years they had manoeuvered McGee from leading light of the St. Patrick's Society to marginalised outcast. His future was far from secure. Then, on Good Friday, 7 April 1868, a Fenian assassinated McGee as he returned home from a late night parliamentary session (Nolte, 1975: 320). His funeral the following Monday was the largest outpouring of public grief ever witnessed in Canada. The impact of his death was at once profound and electrifying: massive crowds lined the streets of Montreal and huge demonstrations materialised in Ontario and across Canada (Goheen, 1999). McGee's vision of a unifying Canadian identity would now triumph and the Irish in Quebec, indeed across Canada, set out on a new course. From this point forward, Irish Catholics and Irish Protestants would become fervent Canadians within the British imperial family of nations, making McGee's integrated ideal a reality: "A Canadian nationality, not French-Canadian, nor British-Canadian, nor Irish-Canadian — patriotism rejects the prefix — is, in my opinion, what we should look forward to" (Keep, 1950: 42).

18

The Potency of Cheap Music: Ballads and Performance in Irish Cinema

Ruth Barton

A recurrent marker of Irishness in films made in and about Ireland has been the performance of ballads. These tend to be reproduced as part of the film's soundtrack and to underscore moments of intense emotion. One only has to think, for instance, of the closing moments of Neil Jordan's *Michael Collins* (1996) for one example amongst many. In it Sinéad O'Connor sings "She Moved Thru' the Fair" over a sequence in which Kitty Kiernan (Julia Roberts) tries on of her wedding dress. That scene is intercut with the assassination of Collins (Liam Neeson). The effect of the ballad is to heighten the sense of imminent tragedy for which the audience, either through its own historical knowledge or via the film's flashback structure, is already prepared. The use of this ballad is striking, not least because of the anomaly that exists between the version used in the movie and the more conventional form of the ballad. According to Padraic Colum's canonical version, the final verse is as follows:

> I dreamt it last night that my young love came in,
> So softly she entered, that her feet made no din;
> She came close beside me, and this she did say
> 'It will not be long, love, till our wedding day'.
>
> (Colum, 1932: 109)

The version sung by O'Connor, however, reverses the gender identity:

> Last night, I dreamed that my own love came in.
> He came so sweetly, his feet made no din.
> He stepped close beside me and this he did say:
> 'It will not be long love, till our wedding day'.

This gender reversal has not, to my knowledge, occasioned any comment, yet it is significant for a number of reasons. The ballad has historically been the domain of the male tenor voice, expressing a sense of loss that is associated with a departed female figure (often the mother) who is in turn metonymic for the land that has been left behind (Ireland). A greater happiness may be hinted at in a space and time beyond the grave. In terms of *Michael Collins*, the gender reversal makes sense in so far as it articulates and anticipates Collins' death and Kitty Kiernan's mourning. As sung by O'Connor, the lament sounds much more like the traditional *sean-nós* with which she was herself to be associated on her album *Sean Nós Nua* (2002). If we look back at the history of the ballad, and its association with film, we can better understand why this should be so unusual.

Very little academic attention has been paid to the place of ballads within Irish film. This genre of popular song has suffered over the years from a suspicion that it represents a debased, adulterated strand within the national cultural canon. Ballads tend to be compared unfavourably with *sean-nós* singing, which "involves the transmission of the pure spirit of an ancient and timeless cultural message" (O'Connor, 1991: 16). The fact that most of the surviving ballads are in the English language recalls a history of colonialism, even if many of those originally introduced by English settlers were adapted for local circumstances by the native Irish (Munnelly, 1986). Part of this suspicion may also stem from anxieties about the content and places of performance associated with the immensely popular Moore's *Melodies* of the mid-nineteenth century. As O'Boyle argues, Moore's songs "were far removed from the elemental beauty of the traditional singing in the Irish language which even in his day was the predominant vernacular in the whole western half of the country" (O'Boyle, 1976: 13). Moore's reputation has since been rescued from that of Regency drawing room entertainer by scholars such as Joep Leerssen who argue that beneath their veneer of light entertainment an often radical political message was being delivered. Leerssen's reading, however, is dependent on putting to one side the "sentimental poems about friendly meetings and partings, roses at the end of the summer, and similar trifles" (Leerssen, 1996: 82). It is precisely this sentimentality, particularly associated with loss, departure and return, that is most prominent in the ballads used in Irish cinema, whether those penned by Moore or by other nineteenth-century composers.

Such ballads, as Williams argues in his seminal study of American popular song lyrics of the late nineteenth and early twentieth centuries, chimed with the emotional needs of both immigrants and the dispossessed rural dwellers of newly urbanised America:

> For many Irish Americans, Ireland had become a mythical place, the Emerald Isle, an ideal within which various vaguely defined but deeply felt needs could be met [...]. A very different place, this imagined Ireland, from the gritty, crowded, multi-ethnic urban cities where most of Irish America lived. The Eden-like quality of this mythical Ireland of popular song was reinforced by the fact that this was a 'lost' land. Its beauties and joys, like the childhood of the singers, were gone, lost in time or inaccessible across the miles of the gray Atlantic. Thus, the Emerald Isle was drenched in nostalgic yearning for the unattainable. (Williams, 1996: 230)

These songs fulfilled a further function, however, which was to reconcile the wider community to native Irish culture. The use of the Irish tenor (a concoction of the commercial stage) rather than the traditional *sean-nós* singer, who was less acceptable to an uninitiated audience, is indicative of the films' ambitions in the mar-

ketplace (Williams, 1996: 215-16). The performance of cheap, sentimental numbers drawn from music-hall and variety repertoires
underlined the point that Irishness was a "safe" ethnicity and one
ripe for commodification, as it has remained. This is particularly
evident in cinema, where such Irish ballads performed the dual
function of appealing to Irish audiences and drawing on Irishness
as an "entertaining" ethnicity. With cinema gradually supplanting
music hall as the primary locus of working-class entertainment,
many filmmakers incorporated ballads into the soundtracks and
even the diegetic space of their productions. Just as Tin Pan Alley's espousal of the Irish ballad was motivated by their commercial prospects, we may argue that the reproduction in cinema of
these songs was both incremental to the storyline and judged to
increase audience numbers.

Ballad-singing in film seems to me to re-unify the fragments of
Irish popular culture that had become dispersed through generations of emigration. It appealed to the Irish at home and abroad
and allowed for a common emotive link with a culture of exile. I
would like to argue here that the performance of such ballads creates an Ireland that is an *exilic* space.[1] Examples from two films,
Old Mother Riley's New Venture (1949) and *Rio Grande* (1950), will
allow us to see how this concept is worked through. The first film
is one of a series to feature the popular music-hall duo of Arthur
Lucan and Kitty McShane in their roles of Irish washerwoman
and her daughter (Lucan performed in drag). Storylines were
nominal and the films moved from one set-piece to the next, in-
variably charting Old Mother Riley and his/her daughter's encounters with, and eventual triumphs over, an array of pompous,

---

[1] I am conscious of the problems surrounding terminology here. "Exilic" and
"diasporic" are fluid terms which authors and readers will interpret according to
their own inclination. Brah (1996) and Naficy (2001) would certainly prefer "diasporic" over "exilic", though both authors are more concerned with physical
and geographic location than I am here. By "exilic space" I mean more a state of
mind than an actual location. I am indebted to Bronwen Walter for guiding me
through this terminological maze at the "Ireland: Space, Text, Time" conference
that gave rise to this collection.

middle-class bureaucrats and authority figures. Lucan and McShane were celebrated music-hall acts, appearing primarily in northern England in the inter-war period but also travelling to Ireland where they were guaranteed a familiar audience (King, 1999). Like many music-hall performers, such as The Crazy Gang and George Formby, they were appropriated by British popular cinema in the 1930s and 1940s, appearing in a number of films that were little more than flimsy narratives constructed around a series of set-piece comic routines.

In *Old Mother Riley's New Venture* Lucan and McShane take over the running of an English hotel and entertain their guests with a St Patrick's Day cabaret. The hotel is decked out in gaudy decorations and the tenor, Willer Neal, performs the ballad "I'll Take You Home Kathleen" to a delighted audience, among them Old Mother Riley, a cut-away shot of whom reveals her clasping a beer keg and swaying, with deeply moved expression, in time to the melody. Although we cannot establish for certain the audience for such a film, its low-budget nature and demotic mode of address place it in the category of regional entertainment that would suggest a working-class and immigrant viewer. This was Lucan and McShane's constituency, their acts and films having little appeal to the middle-classes, and here Lucan performs on behalf of, as well as to, that audience.

By incorporating moments such as the St. Patrick's Day cabaret, the duo, I would argue, reach out to that immigrant Irish audience in a manner that is, to borrow a term from the analysis of melodrama, "excessive". That is, they provoke an emotional response that exceeds the "meaning" of the narrative and that cannot be contained within the text, achieved here through the audience's recognition of extra-textual cultural reference points. Just as in John Ford's *Rio Grande*, they connect with that audience through the performance of a ballad that carries strong Irish immigrant associations. *Rio Grande* also has little overt Irish content, other than establishing that the Maureen O'Hara character, Kathleen, comes from an Irish-American family whose property Lieutenant Colonel Kirby Yorke, her on-screen husband (John Wayne), has had to burn to the ground as part of a military strategy. Again, the forward momentum of the film — the working through of the "fabula" — is halted for an extended performance of Irish ballads. As Kirby and Kathleen are dining in his tent, the regimental players appear outside to serenade the couple, launching into a somewhat drawn-out rendition of "I'll Take You Home Kathleen". Kirby listens stiffly, Kathleen with a demeanour that suggests a gradual release of inner emotion, signalling the couple's eventual reconciliation. In a manner that echoes the otherwise completely contrasting British film, the scene starts with Kathleen fondling an object, in this case a music box, which also plays "I'll Take You Home Kathleen".

Home in each film is in fact England and America respectively. So when the chorus sings the ballad, they are invoking a space, Ireland, that none of these characters has expressed any desire to be in or is likely to return to at any point. Yet in each case the performance of the song is staged with a deep sense of promise, as well as a large dose of sentimentality. Ireland is doubly a point of origin and return; it is where Kathleen of the song was born and where she will now return to die, where her "heart will feel no pain" when "the fields are fresh and green". The song also allows for a high degree of male agency, emphasised through its inevitable performance by a male tenor.

In fact, "I'll Take You Home Kathleen" is not of Irish origin; it was written in 1876 by an American, Thomas Westendorf. As Williams records:

> The fact that there is no mention of Ireland in the lyrics made little difference to many Irish Americans then or since. The name of "Kathleen" in the title and the longing for the home over the sea was enough to make it Irish. [...] Westendorf was not the only songwriter to suggest an Irish theme in the title while avoiding a clear Irish identification in the lyrics. [...] It was a way of using an Irish hook while appealing to the largest possible audience. (Williams, 1996: 101-02)

Home in both productions, therefore, is an absent, imaginary space evoked through the ballad tradition. The fact that film, a visual medium, refuses to reify this image reflects Ireland's figurative absence in exilic discourse. This Ireland/home exists in "exilic" rather than "real" space. Exile can and has been defined in any number of ways; however, here I take it to mean a state of mind as much as a physical dislocation. By extension, Ireland too becomes a state of mind and the country as home may be said to be recreated, in Hamid Naficy's terminology, synecdochically. Naficy writes that an exilic sense of loss centres around "house" and "home":

> *House* is the literal object, the material place in which one lives, and it involves legal categories of rights, property, and possession and their opposites. *Home* is anyplace; it is temporary and it is moveable; it can be built, rebuilt, and carried in memory and by acts of imagination. Exiles locate themselves vis-à-vis their houses and homes synesthetically and synecdochically. Sometimes a small gesture or body posture, a particular gleam in the eye, or a smell, a sound, or a taste suddenly and directly sutures one to a former house or home and to cherished memories of childhood. [...] Sometimes a small, insignificant object taken into exile (such as a key to the house) becomes a powerful synecdoche for the lost house and the unreachable home, feeding the memories of the past and the narratives of exile. (Naficy, 1999: 5-6)

As already noted, the performance of "I'll Take You Home Kathleen" is prefaced or accompanied in both films by the caress of an object (a keg, a music box). Thus, the ballad-singing that is central to such films can be said to function synesthetically, triggering an emotive response, whereas the object functions synecdochically, reminding the viewer of the real, and of the absence of the real.

The use of Irish ballads in these and many other films of this period may thus be seen to provide a multiple address. To Irish immigrants they evoked Ireland as absent home, over the head, we might say, of the narrative, which carries on regardless. They also, as I have already mentioned, provided a bridge between those immigrant communities and other working-class cultures in cinema as did their predecessor, the music hall. In other words, they were central to what Peter Bailey has termed a "culture of consolation", part of a Utopian desire for escape (Bailey, 1986: xv). We might also consider that they linked Irish immigrant communities with the Irish who had remained in Ireland. Although the Irish ballad is not restricted to the type of sentimental content discussed here, embracing as it does local narratives and the expression of anti-colonial politics, ballad-singing was historically popular in Ireland and still retains a following, as the almost anthemic status of "The Fields of Athenry" testifies.

In the pre-war period, Count John McCormack's phenomenal international success embodied this linkage between the cultures of home and exile (and again proved the commercial appeal of the Irish tenor). McCormack appeared as himself in the Anglo-American production *Wings of the Morning* (1937), where he sang a medley of airs to the dinner guests at Clontarf Castle in a scene that has little to do with the film's main plot line (a fantastical tale of gypsy love across class and generation set in Killarney). Here, Ireland is visualised in concrete form but very much in the tradition of exilic representation. That this is an imagined space is underlined by a shot that introduces McCormack's rendition of "Killarney". The camera cuts to Sir Valentine's (Stewart Rome) blind wife Jenepher (Helen Haye), just as McCormack commences singing, and a dissolve is followed by a series of shots of Killarney's lakes and rustic villages. *Wings of the Morning* was made primarily as a vehicle for the new Technicolor process and this is put to full effect in these landscape shots, here presented as a blind woman's vision. The film's critical and commercial success may be attributed in large part to McCormack's singing and the views of Ireland, both of which were singled out for praise in Irish and overseas' reviews.

We might guess that indigenous Irish audiences could memorialise their departed family and neighbours through such songs, that they understood their exilic address at many levels, and that they connected to those absent members in the shared exilic space created by song. What distinguishes film from "live" entertainment is its replicative nature, so that audiences at home saw and heard exactly the same images and songs as viewers in Britain and America. Inevitably, such a line of argument calls to mind Benedict Anderson's concept of the "imagined community" in which members of a nation become aware of their commonality through the media (Anderson, 1983). Song, and especially ballads, foster this sense of commonality, inviting their audiences to join in the performance with other unseen spectators.

To return, by way of conclusion, to contemporary filmmakers' frequent interpolation of Irish ballads into their narratives, we could argue that these songs purvey an historical sense of loss that connects the films synaesthetically to a history of exile. Return to the "motherland" becomes an impossible dream only realisable after death. The reason why their performance should have passed from the traditional voice of the male tenor to that of the female performer may be attributed to commercial expediency as much as to diegetic signification. Certainly, the embrace of the female ballad-singer by popular culture is a recent phenomenon, signalled in particular by the compilations *A Woman's Heart* (1992) and *A Woman's Heart 2* (1994). There is, however, more to the ending of *Michael Collins* than this. We might read Sinéad O'Connor's rendition of "She Moved Thru' the Fair" — now "He Moved Thru' the Fair" — as the re-appropriation of the female lament from a male history of performance. It is common to critique Neil Jordan for his blindness to female characters and concerns, but in this instance he reverses many of the conventions of older modes of ballad-singing. As much as O'Connor's performance lends historical and contemporary resonances to a film that is concerned with the connections between past and present, it also retrieves the articulation of loss for female vocalisation. The moment passes, and in the final credits we hear Frank Patterson singing "Macushla" with full orchestral accompaniment, but it is a noteworthy moment for all that.

19

Navvy Narratives: Interactions between Autobiographical and Fictional Accounts of Irish Construction Workers in Britain

Tony Murray

Heated debates were generated in the Dáil over the plight of elderly Irish men in Britain in the wake of a documentary shown on RTÉ at the end of 2003.[1] Many of the men interviewed for the programme spent the best part of their working lives on the building sites of England. But due to major changes in the construction industry over the last fifteen years or so, and the insecure nature of their employment in the first place, they are now living out their final years in shockingly destitute conditions in the very towns and cities they helped build. They now effectively constitute an almost forgotten minority within what has become in recent decades a more visible Irish community in Britain (Hickman and Walter, 1997; McCool and McDonnell, 1997). Whilst historical studies of the Irish navvy in Britain exist (Coleman, 1965; Handley, 1970; Cowley, 2001), along with a growing body of criticism on autobiographical accounts (Canavan, 1994; Duffy, 1995), there are very few studies of fictional representa-

---

[1] *Prime Time*: Ireland's Forgotten Generation", RTÉ 1, 22 December 2003.

tions of this remarkably homogenous group of migrants.[2] By dig-
ging deep and wide (if you'll forgive the pun) for what Liam
Harte has described as "occluded narratives of migration" (Harte,
2003: 99), I wish to contribute to a fuller understanding of the history of the Irish navvy in Britain by exploring why a small but
significant number of Irish construction workers have chosen to
portray their experiences in a particular way. In this paper I propose to confine my comments to three recent novels, referring to
autobiography, oral memoir and other forms of textual narrative
where appropriate.

References to the fighting spirit and extraordinary strength of
Irish navvies have a pedigree as long as the history of this often
feared and denigrated sector of the working class (Brooke, 1983;
Sullivan, 1983). In his book on life in Camden Town, for example,
David Thomson refers to a major riot which took place at the
Roundhouse building site in August 1846 (Thomson, 1983: 168-
74). It took three police forces most of the day to quell the fighting
between English and Irish navvies, with seven constables being
required to carry one of the Irishmen to the nearby police station,
according to a report in *The Times*. The precise point at which fact
slips into fiction in such a story is difficult to discern, but whilst
historians would warn against mythologisation, something about
the epic nature of such stories nevertheless appeals to our imagi-
nations. The navvy narratives I am focusing on here exploit this
appeal, but mythical purchase cannot be secured unless we as
readers are prepared to reciprocate by suspending our disbelief.

Some theorists of narratology argue that a "grammar of myth"
underlies many forms of oral and written literature, and point to
the ubiquity of the figure of the hero in the genre of romantic epic.
Luisa Passarini, for example, explains how her subjects narrated
their life stories with a seemingly innate capacity to couch them in
an appropriate mythical genre, thereby vindicating the claims of
Lévi-Strauss and Barthes that literature, like all aspects of cultural

---

[2] The one notable exception is the navvy fiction of Patrick MacGill, which is usually read as *de facto* autobiography. See O'Sullivan (1991).

discourse, has a powerful mythical underpinning (Passarini, 1987). In the narratives under discussion here, the figure of Cúchulainn — the most iconic of Celtic heroes who had a magnetic attraction to the cultural nationalists of the Irish Literary Revival — crops up again and again, replete with immutable characteristics to serve as an aspirational figure for certain Irishmen on foreign soil.

The first novel I wish to discuss is John B. Keane's *The Contractors* (1993). Set in the 1950s, it contains a number of fight scenes, culminating in a meticulously staged brawl outside an Irish dancehall on St. Patrick's night. The intention behind such forward-planning by the novel's protagonist, Dan Murray, is to ensure that he and his gang of loyal workers would overthrow the corrupt contractors, the Reicey Brothers. The character of Dick Daly, or Crazy Horse as he is better known, has infamously "fought his way from one end of Kilburn to the other" (Keane, 1993: 170) and plays a crucial role in Dan's victory. He is chief bouncer at Dan's dancehall and like Cúchulainn, whose name translates as "the hound of Culann", Crazy Horse guards his master's property like his own. In the big set-piece battle of the novel, Crazy Horse faces Reicey's henchmen, the Morrican brothers. Their name is a clear reference to the shape-shifting figure of the Morrígan from *The Táin*, whom Cúchulainn meets on his way to the famous cattle raid of Cooley (Kinsella, 1970: 136-37). It was, we are told, "Crazy Horse's finest hour. He accepted everything that was offered. He never winced nor sacrificed a single fraction of an inch as the blows rained in on him from all sides. [...] Here indeed was a chieftain worth deposing" (Keane, 1993: 174).[3]

In his autobiography *Self Portrait* (1953) Keane recalls how as a child growing up in Listowel in the 1930s he was regularly regaled with semi-legendary stories about men of strength in the neighbourhood: "Wet nights were spent around the fire and there

---

[3] The imagery here is very reminiscent of that used by Walter Macken to describe a similar incident in his 1949 novel *I Am Alone*, where it borders on the homoerotic.

were stories about great men and great deeds. Men were remembered for their prowess with a slean or a spade or a shovel"
(Keane, 1953: 13). During the train journey to London at the beginning of *The Contractors*, Sylvester O'Doherty gives Dan Murray
some fatherly advice about the dangers of frequenting a notorious
Irish dancehall: "If you'll take my advice which you won't, you'll
give the Green Shillelagh a wide berth" (Keane, 1993: 10). This is
delivered in much the same tone that Keane himself employs in
his autobiography when addressing prospective young emigrants: "Avoid Irish pubs and notorious Irish dancehalls as you
would the plague" (Keane, 1953: 64). He had good reason to issue
this warning; on his first visit to such places he was embroiled in a
fight which led to his hospitalisation for two weeks, an experience
he later claimed was a turning point in his life.

Despite depicting himself as, for the most part, a "fish out of
water" in such company, he cannot resist the opportunity in *Self-
Portrait* to employ some of the purple prose that re-emerges years
later in his fiction:

> I hauled [him] off and hit the cup-smasher with a straight
> left on the most sensitive of organs, the nose. He recovered
> and I nailed him on the same spot again. (Keane, 1953: 60)

In *The Contractors*, however, Keane tempers the more gratuitously
violent scenes by ensuring that, like Horse Roche in *Children of the
Dead End* and Seamus in *I Am Alone*, his hero plays the chivalrous
"gentle giant" by rescuing one of the female protagonists from the
brutalising clutches of a malevolent suitor:

> Paddy Joe was well used to taking care of himself, but the
> size and the dogged lumbering gait of the oncoming giant
> sent him scurrying out of danger. Crazy Horse lifted the
> girl in his arms and brought her back to the Molly Malone
> [dancehall]. (Keane, 1993: 295)

Three years after *The Contractors*, another novel based on the
lives of Irish construction workers in Britain was published. Timo-
thy O'Grady's and Steve Pyke's *I Could Read the Sky* (1997) is a se-

ductive hybrid of oral history, fiction and visual imagery which features the voice of an old man commenting on his life, as if it were projected onto a cinema screen.[4] The man's recollections, which take on a hauntingly detached immediacy, are in fact a composite of material gathered from interviews with elderly men in London Irish community centres (Ottaway, 1999). Here again the borders between fact and fiction are transgressed as the story unfolds through a series of filmic sequences from the narrator's life, many of which relate to his time "on the buildings". Initially the Cúchulainn figure emerges intertextually in the shape of Horse McGurk (a figure from Dominic Behan's ballad "Building Up and Tearing England Down") whose moniker echoes the Celtic sagas, which have been referred to as a form of "dream-time" where the boundaries between humans and the rest of the natural world become unstable (Hilliers, 1994: 99). Such is the supernatural power of the horse, which carries sacred significance in Celtic mythology,[5] that it enters into the dreams of the narrator, who is haunted so much by the image of a particular horse from his youth that even burying it in his sleep proves troubling:

> To bury a horse you need a grave twice the length and twice the width of a man's. I hear then the sound of crying, a gagged and pitiful sound. I can't find it but I know it's coming from the ground. [...] A hoof breaks through, pawing at the air, a kind of caress [...] and then with a great heave the horse is finally up, wet and stained, blood still seeping from the wound in the side of the head where Da shot her. (O'Grady and Pike, 1997: 104-08)

---

[4] Publication of this book in 1995 under the title *Acts of Memory* by Chatto & Windus was aborted before Harvill took up the project. It was later adapted as a multimedia stage presentation including readings by O'Grady, back-projected photographs by Steve Pyke and musical accompaniment from Sinéad O'Connor, Martin Hayes and others. It was also adapted for the cinema, with Dermot Healy in the lead role.

[5] The corpses of Celtic chieftains and other notables were often buried with the trappings of their horses and in some cases horses themselves received ceremonial burials. See Delaney (1985).

Another character in the book, "The King", is based on the infamous ganger known as Elephant John who worked for the contractors Murphy, and is responsible for reinforcing one of the
abiding myths of Irish navvy folklore, the feat of lifting a bag of
cement with his teeth. "The King" responds to the sight of two
trainee bricklayers struggling to heave the said bag of cement over
a low wall.

> 'Will you look at them?' says the King. He leaves the
> cigarette on the ledge of the window and walks over. He
> tells the lads to stand aside. He leans over from the waist,
> grips the bag with his teeth and lifts it over the wall. He
> walks back to me then and takes up the cigarette. (O'Grady
> and Pike, 1997: 125)

It is probable that this story was told to O'Grady by one of his interviewees; it is certainly one that has done the rounds in different
forms down the years. It has, if you will, entered the bloodstream
of the navvy narrative and like the Cúchulainn myth has been
embellished and modified according to particular contexts. A
variation of this story features in Harry O'Brien's unpublished
memoir of the Irish in London during and shortly after the First
World War. O'Brien describes an incident in which a man known
simply as Sean Óg watched with bemusement as a group of Italian workers attempted to lift a large cornerstone onto the back of
a cart. After lifting the stone single-handedly himself, he looked at
the Italians with great disdain and said: "'And to think they make
Popes out of the likes of ye!'" (O'Brien, 1983). There is an intriguing parallel between this no doubt apocryphal story and a climac-
tic scene from the Ossian Cycle. Finn Mac Cool's son Oisín, on returning to Ireland from Tir na nÓg ("the land of the forever
young"), is stopped by a group of men who ask him to help them
lift a huge stone onto a wagon. Oisín responds to their request but
whilst stooping from his horse the reins snap and he falls to the
ground. The foretold consequence of this is that he ages instantly
by three hundred years (Heaney, 1994: 221). Clearly Sean Óg

hadn't read his Celtic mythology or he would never have attempted to play with fate in such a way!

Other recent fiction about the experience of Irish construction workers in Britain, such as J.M. O'Neill's *Open Cut* (1986), Dermot Healy's *Sudden Times* (1999) and Philip Casey's *The Water Star* (1999), rely on other narrative traditions for their impact.[6] But even as recently as 2003 another novel in the mould I am examining appeared. Peter Woods' *Hard Shoulder* is, like *Children of the Dead End*, an autobiography thinly veiled as fiction. The narrator, McBride, is clearly based on Woods who left Ireland in 1977 to work on the building sites of London.[7] While the economic changes precipitated by the oil crisis of the early seventies make for a very different narrative context to that of *The Contractors* and *I Could Read the Sky*, there are some significant similarities nonetheless. A ganger called Lonesome Tom, who appears briefly at the beginning of chapter four, is introduced by means of a familiar, Cúchulanoid myth:

> He'd spent most of his life digging tunnels underground and was, as I found out later, something of a legend. He was of that generation that elevated physical strength above most else and when it came to strength Tom had few parallels. I once saw him lift a bag of cement with his teeth. [...] The veins in his neck were bulging like canals systems seen from aloft. (Woods, 2003: 41)

---

[6] *Open Cut* is a neo-realist treatment of the semi-criminal underbelly of the London construction industry; *Sudden Times* is a darkly comic psychological thriller which follows the ill-fated fortunes of an Irishman on the periphery of this world; while *The Water Star* is a finely nuanced evocation of loss and exile in the lives of four London characters, one of whom is a navvy.

[7] Woods joined the Green Ink Writers Group whilst working in London in the early 1980s. The title of one of his short stories from this period, 'Running on the Hard Shoulder', reveals that the groundwork for his novel goes back at least twenty years. See Green Ink Writers Group (1985).

But Lonesome Tom is also a man who has helped to create his own personal mythology and intuitively understands the fictive mechanics of such narratives. As McBride recalls:

> When I first expressed doubts over something he'd told me, he smiled and muttered something about there being nothing wrong with the odd white lie. Something that was told to move the action on, if you like. (Woods, 2003: 42)

The fluidity between fact and fiction so redolent of Celtic mythology has here seemingly become part of a discrete oral tradition. Moreover, a degree of self-reflexivity, even irony, which is only hinted at in earlier works has also become integral to the telling of the tale. Other references in *Hard Shoulder* to gangers are less generous, including a pointed one to the ubiquitous Elephant John, who "would boot a young fella up the arse to see what his reaction would be" (Woods, 2003: 20). Throughout the novel there are indications of the physical and mental damage caused by the brutal demands of the building trade and in particular the exploitative role played by some sub-contractors. Whilst the "subbie" Dicey Reicey in *The Contractors* escapes conviction during a fraud squad bust, Sylvester his treasurer "takes the rap" and goes down for three years (Keane, 1993: 135). The incident is reminiscent of the inland revenue investigation into the contractors Murphy in 1976 when the company was fined £750,000 and two directors and the company secretary were jailed for three years (*Evening Standard Magazine*, 2004).

Novels such as *Hard Shoulder*, *I Could Read the Sky* and *The Contractors* afford us a unique insight into the lives and mindsets of a generation of men who, whilst familiar to many, still remain a largely hidden and somewhat mysterious sub-section of the Irish community in Britain. Within the textual landscapes of Irish migrant literature, these narratives stand out by virtue of their specificity, not only in terms of time and place but also by their pronounced link to Celtic mythology and the oral tradition. Admittedly, there is a tendency in some of these texts to glorify ritual violence, thereby reinforcing stereotypes of the "drunken brawling Paddy". But other accounts of Irish navvies in Britain provide an important corrective to this.[8]

Overall, there is a surprising paucity of accounts of Irish navvies in Britain given the legacy they left in bricks and mortar. But in the relatively few works that do exist, it is perhaps even more surprising how often the Cúchulainn motif is employed for dramatic effect. Through recurring references to feats of extraordinary physical prowess, these authors — whether consciously or not — draw on a deep well of oral tradition in Irish culture. It would appear, then, that the "land fit for heroes" envisaged by Eamon de Valera would, as a result of emigration in the middle decades of the twentieth century, have to be re-imagined on the building sites of England rather in the fields and mountains of Ireland.

---

[8] In *An Irish Navvy: The Diary of an Exile* (1964) Donall MacAmhlaigh, that most prolific chronicler of the migrant experience, tends to play down and even ridicule these supposedly heroic battles as nothing more than sordid scuffles. It is useful to compare his account of a dancehall fight in Northampton to Keane's account of a similar incident in the same town at roughly the same time.

Bibliography

Abbott, H.P. (1973), *The Fiction of Samuel Beckett: Form and Effect*, Berkeley: University of California Press.

Adorno, T.W. (1997) [1970], *Aesthetic Theory*, trans. R. Hullot-Kentor, London: Athlone Press.

Ahmad, A. (1992), *In Theory: Classes, Nations, Literatures*, London: Verso.

Anderson, B. (1983), *Imagined Communities*, London: Verso.

Andrews, J.H. (1970), "Baptista Boazio's map of Ireland", *Long Room*, vol. 1, 29-36.

Anonymous. (1717), *Part of a Letter to the Secretary of the Society in England for Propagating Christian Knowledge, from a Corresponding Member in Ireland*, Dublin: S. Powell.

Ashcroft, B., Griffiths, G. and Tiffin, H. (1998), *Key Concepts in Post-Colonial Studies*, London, Routledge.

Auden, W.H. (1977), *The English Auden*, ed. E. Mendelson, London: Faber and Faber.

Bailey, P. (ed.), (1986), *Music Hall: The Business of Pleasure*, Milton Keynes: Open University Press.

Bakhtin, M.M. (1984) [1981], *The Dialogic Imagination: Four Essays*, trans. C. Emerson and M. Holquist, Austin: University of Texas Press.

Barlow, J.M. (1998), "Fear and Loathing in Saint-Sylvestre: The Corrigan Murder Case 1855-58". Unpublished MA thesis, Simon Fraser University.

Barnard, T.C. (1975), *Cromwellian Ireland: English Government and Reform in Ireland 1649-60*, Oxford: Oxford University Press.

Barnard, T.C. (1993), "Protestants and the Irish language, c.1675–1725", *Journal of Ecclesiastical History*, vol. 44, no. 2, 243-72.

Barnard, T.C. (2001), "The Languages of Politeness and Sociability in Eighteenth-Century Ireland" in Boyce, D.G., Eccleshall, R. and Geoghegan, V. (eds.), *Political Discourse in Seventeenth- and Eighteenth-Century Ireland*, Basingstoke: Palgrave, 193-221.

Barnard, T.C. (2003), *A New Anatomy of Ireland: The Irish Protestants 1649-1770*, New Haven: Yale University Press.

Bartlett, T., Curtin, C., O'Dwyer, R. and O'Tuathaigh, G. (eds.) (1988), *Irish Studies: A General Introduction*, Dublin: Gill and Macmillan.

Barton, R. (2004), *Irish National Cinema*, London: Routledge.

Baxter, J.K. (1971), *The Sore-Footed Man and the Temptations of Oedipus*, New Zealand: Heinemann.

Beckett, S. (1958), *Nouvelles et Textes Pour Rien*, Paris: Les Éditions des Minuits.

Beckett, S. (1965), *Proust and Three Dialogues Samuel Beckett and Georges Duthuit*, London: John Calder.

Beckett, S. (1974), *First Love and Other Stories*, New York: Grove/Atlantic.

Beckett, S. (1980), *The Expelled and Other Novellas*, Harmondsworth: Penguin.

Beckett, S. (1983), *Disjecta. Miscellaneous Writings and a Dramatic Fragment*, ed. R. Cohn, London: John Calder.

Beckett, S. (1993) [1938], *Murphy*, London: Calder Publications.

Beckett, S. (1996), *Texts for Nothing (1-13)* in Gontarski, S.E. (ed.), *Samuel Beckett: The Complete Short Prose 1929-1989*, New York: Grove Press.

Beckett, S. (1999), *Collected Poems 1930-1978*, London: Calder.

Belfast Newsletter (2003), 24 September.

Bell, J.B. (1972), *The Secret Army: a History of the IRA, 1916-70*, London: Sphere.

Bell, T. (1829), *An Essay on the Origin and Progress of Gothic Architecture*, Dublin: William Frederick Wakeman.

Bély, L. (1990), *Espions et Ambassadeurs au Temps de Louis XIV*, Paris: Fayard.

Benjamin. W. (1992) [1969], *Illuminations*, ed. H. Arendt, trans. H. Zohn, London: Fontana Press.

Berkeley, G. (1901) [1735-37], *The Querist; Containing Several Queries Proposed to the Consideration of the Public* in Campbell Fraser, A. (ed.), *The Works of George Berkeley, D.D.; Formerly Bishop of Cloyne, Including his Posthumous Works, Volume IV: Miscellaneous Works, 1707–50*, Oxford: Clarendon Press.

Bhreathnach-Lynch, S. (1999), "Commemorating the Hero in Newly Independent Ireland: Expressions of Nationhood in Bronze and Stone" in McBride, L.W. (ed.), *Images, Icons and the Irish Nationalist Imagination*, Dublin: Four Courts Press, 148-65.

Bhreathnach-Lynch, S. and Stevens, J. (2005), "The Irish Artist: Crossing the Rubicon" in Cherry, D. and Halland, J. (eds.), *Studio, Space and Sociality*, Aldershot: Ashgate.

Blanchard, R. (1947), *Le Centre du Canada Francais*, Montreal, Librairie Beauchemin Ltee.

Bloomfield, K. (1998), *We Will Remember Them*, Belfast: The Stationery Office.

Bolger, D. (ed.) (1991), *Letters From The New Island*, Dublin: Raven Arts Press.

Bradley, J. (1998), *Sport, Culture, Politics and Scottish Society: Irish Immigration and the Gaelic Athletic Association*, Edinburgh: John Donald Publishers.

Bradley, J. (2004), *Celtic Minded: Essays on Religion, Politics, Society, Identity....and Football*, Argyll: Argyll Publishing.

Brah, A. (1996), *Cartographies of Diaspora: Contesting Identities*, London: Routledge.

Brooke, D. (1983), *The Railway Navvy: 'That Despicable Race of Men'*, London: David and Charles.

Brown, R.D. (2002), "'Your Thoughts Make Shape Like Snow': Louis MacNeice on Stephen Spender", *Twentieth-Century Literature*, vol. 48, no. 3, 292-323.

Brown, S. (1916), *Ireland in Fiction*, Dublin: Maunsel.

Brown, T. (1985), *Ireland. A Social and Cultural History 1922-1985*, London: Fontana Press.

Butler, J. (1993), *Bodies that Matter*, London: Routledge.

Canavan, B. (1994), "Story-tellers and Writers: Irish Identity in Emigrant Labourers' Autobiographies, 1870-1970" in O'Sullivan, P. (ed.), *The Irish Worldwide: History, Heritage, Identity: The Creative Migrant*, Leicester: Leicester University Press, 154-69.

Carlyle, T. (1842) [1837], *The French Revolution*, London: Chapman and Hall.

Carlyle, T. (1863a) [1834], *Sartor Resartus*, London: Chapman and Hall.

Carlyle, T. (1863b) [1841], *Lectures on Heroes*, London: Chapman and Hall.

Carlyle, T. (1893) [1843], *Past and Present*, London: Chapman and Hall.

Central Statistics Office (2003), *Ireland North and South: a Statistical Profile*, Dublin, Central Statistics Office.

Chippindale, C. (1983), "The Making of the First Ancient Monuments Act, 1882, and its Administration Under General Pitt-Rivers", *Journal of the British Archaeological Association*, vol. 86, 1-55.

Clifton, R. (1984), *The Last Popular Rebellion: the Western Rising of 1685*, London: Maurice Temple Smith.

Cochrane, R. (1892), "Notes on the Ancient Monuments Protection (Ireland) Act, 1892", *Journal of the Royal Society of Antiquaries of Ireland*, vol. 22, 411-29.

Cohn, R. (1973), *Back to Beckett*, Princeton: Princeton University Press.

Coleman, T. (1965), *The Railway Navvies*, London: Hutchinson.

Collis, M. (1970), *The Journey Up: Reminiscences 1934-1968*, London: Faber and Faber.

Colum, P. (1932), *Poems*, New York: Macmillan.

Connolly, S.J. (1992), *Religion, Law and Power: The Making of Protestant Ireland 1660–1760*, Oxford: Clarendon Press.

Connolly, S.J. (1998), "'Ag Déanamh *Commanding'*: Elite Responses to Popular Culture, 1650–1850" in Donnelly, J.S. and Miller, K.A. (eds.), *Irish Popular Culture 1650-1850*, Dublin: Irish Academic Press, 1-29.

Coogan, T.P. (1971), *The IRA*, London: Fontana.

Cowley, U. (2001), *The Men That Built Britain: A History of the Irish Navvy*, Dublin: Wolfhound Press.

Critchley, S. (1997), *Very Little . . . Almost Nothing: Death, Philosophy, Literature*, London: Routledge.

Croker, T.C. (1969) [1824], *Researches in the South of Ireland*, Shannon: Irish University Press.

Cross, D.S. (1969), "The Irish in Montreal, 1867-1896". Unpublished MA thesis, McGill University.

Culik, H. (1982), "Entropic Order: Beckett's Mercier and Camier", *Éire-Ireland*, vol. 17, no. 1, 91-106.

Damasio, A. (1994), *Descartes' Error: Emotion, Reason and the Human Brain*, New York: Avon Books.

Darwin, C. (1965) [1872], *The Expression of the Emotions in Man and Animals*, Chicago: University of Chicago Press.

Davidoff, L. (1974), "Mastered for Life: Servant and Wife in Victorian and Edwardian England", *Journal of Social History*, vol. 7, no. 4 , 406-59.

Davidoff, L. (1995), *Worlds Between: Historical Perspectives on Gender and Class*, Cambridge: Polity Press.

Davis, T. (1914), *Thomas Davis: Selections from his Prose and Poetry*, Rolleston, T., Graves, A.P., Magennis, W. and Hyde, D. (eds.), London: T. Fisher Unwin.

De Certeau, M. (1984), *The Practice of Everyday Life*, trans. S. Rendall, Berkeley: University of California Press.

De Paor, L. (1970), *Divided Ulster*, Harmondsworth: Penguin.

Deane, S. (1983), "Derry: City Besieged within the Siege", *Fortnight*, 18.

Deane, S. (1985), "Civilians and Barbarians" in Field Day Theatre Company, *Ireland's Field Day*, London: Hutchinson, 33-42.

DeBrou, A. (1991), "The Rose, The Shamrock and the Cabbage: The Battle for Irish Voters in Upper Town Quebec, 1827-1836", *Histoire Sociale/Social History*, vol. 24, 305-34.

Delaney, E. (2000), *Demography, State and Society: Irish Migration to Britain, 1921-71*, Liverpool: Liverpool University Press.

Delaney, F. (1985), *The Celts*, London: Guild Publishing.

Deleuze, G. and Guattari, F. (1983), *Anti-Oedipus: Capitalism and Schizophrenia*, London: Athlone Press.

Dennis, I. (1997), *Nationalism and Desire in Early Historical Fiction*, Basingstoke: Macmillan.

Devlin, B. (1969), *The Price of My Soul*, London: Pan.

Dickinson, P.L. (1929), *The Dublin of Yesterday*, London: Metheun.

Dillon, M. and Lehane, D. (1973), *Political Murder in Northern Ireland*, Harmondsworth: Penguin.

Donnelly, J.S. (2001), *The Great Irish Potato Famine*, Stroud, Gloucestershire: Sutton.

Doyle, T. (2004), *James Butler, Duke of Ormond and the Exclusion Crisis*. Unpublished M.Litt. thesis, NUI Maynooth.

Drew, T. (1900), *The National Cathedral of St. Patrick, Dublin*, Dublin: Church of Ireland Printing and Publishing.

Driver, T. (1979), "Beckett by the Madeleine" in Graver, L. and Federman, R. (eds.), *Samuel Beckett: The Critical Heritage*, London: Routledge, 217-23.

Dublin Penny Journal. (1834-5), vol. 3, no. 3, 51-2.

Duffy, C.G. (1968a) [1898], *My Life in Two Hemispheres*, vol. 1, Shannon: Irish University Press.

Duffy, C.G. (1968b) [1898], *My Life in Two Hemispheres*, vol. 2, Shannon: Irish University Press.

Duffy, P. (1995), "Literary Reflections on Irish Migration in the Nineteenth and Twentieth Centuries" in King, R., Connell, J. and White, P. (eds.), *Writing Across Worlds: Literature and Migration*, London: Routledge, 20-38.

Dunlop, R. (ed.) (1913), *Ireland Under the Commonwealth: Being a Selection of Documents Relating to the Government of Ireland from 1651 to 1659*, Manchester: Manchester University Press.

Dunmore, H. (1996), *A Spell of Winter*, Harmondsworth: Penguin.

Dunn S. and Dawson, H. (2000), *An Alphabetical Listing of Word, Name and Place in Northern Ireland and the Living Language of Conflict*, Lampeter: Edwin Mellen Press.

Earle, P. (1977), *Monmouth's Rebels: the Road to Sedgemoor 1685*, London: Weidenfeld and Nicolson.

Ellis Davidson, H.R. (1964), *Gods and Myths of Northern Europe*, London: Penguin.

Ellis, G. (ed.) (1829), *The Ellis Correspondence. Letters Written During the Years 1686, 1687, 1688 and Addressed to John Ellis esq . . . edited by Hon. George Agar Ellis*, London.

Engle, J. (1993), "A Modest Refusal: Yeats, MacNeice, and Irish Poetry" in Fleming, D. (ed.), *Learning the Trade: Essays on W. B. Yeats and Contemporary Poetry*, West Cornwall: Locust Hill, 71-88.

Evening Standard Magazine (2004), "Murphy's Law", 14 February.

Fabricant, C. (1986), *Swift's Landscape*, Baltimore: Johns Hopkins Press.

Fallow, T.M. (c.1894), *The Cathedral Churches of Ireland: Being Notes More Especially on the Smaller and Less Known of Those Churches*, London: Bemrose and Sons.

Fauske, C.J. (ed.), (2004), *Archbishop William King and the Anglican Irish Context, 1688-1729*, Dublin: Four Courts Press.

Fay, M.T., Morrissey, M. and Smyth, M. (1998), *Mapping Troubles-related Deaths in Northern Ireland 1969-1998*, Derry: Incore.

Fitzgerald, B. (1952), *The Anglo-Irish*, London: Staples Press.

Fitzpatrick, D. (1989a), "A Curious Middle Place: the Irish in Britain, 1871-1921" in Swift, R. and Gilley, S. (eds.), *The Irish in Britain, 1815-1939*, London: Pinter, 10-59.

Fitzpatrick, D. (1989b), "'A Peculiar Tramping People': The Irish in Britain, 1801-70" in Vaughan, W.E. (ed.), *A New History of Ireland. V. Ireland under the Union I, 1801-70*, Oxford: Clarendon Press, 623-60.

Fletcher, J. (1964), *The Novels of Samuel Beckett*, London: Chatto and Windus.

Forty, A. and Küchler, S. (eds.) (2001), *The Art of Forgetting*, Oxford: Berg.

Foster, R.F. (1988), *Modern Ireland: 1600-1972*, London: Penguin.

Foster, R.F. (2001a), *The Irish Story: Telling Tales and Making It Up in Ireland*, London: Allen Lane.

Foster, R.F. (2001b), "Remembering 1798" in McBride, I. (ed.), *History and Memory in Modern Ireland*, Cambridge: Cambridge University Press, 67-94.

Foster, R.F. (2003), *W.B. Yeats: A Life. II: The Arch-Poet 1915-1939*, Oxford: Oxford University Press.

Foucault, M. (1977), *Discipline and Punish: The Birth of the Prison*, London: Penguin.

Foucault, M. (1991), 'The Birth of the Asylum' in Rabinow, P. (ed.), *The Foucault Reader*, London: Penguin, 141-67.

Fussell, P. (1975), *The Great War and Modern Memory*, Oxford: Oxford University Press.

Gibbons, L. (2001), "Where Wolfe Tone's Statute Was Not" in McBride, I. (ed.), *History and Memory in Modern Ireland*, Cambridge: Cambridge University Press, 139-59.

Gifford, D. (1988), *Ulysses Annotated*, Berkeley: University of California Press.

Gladstone, W.E. (1869), *The Irish Church. A Speech Delivered in the House of Commons on Monday, March 1, 1869*, London: John Murray.

Goheen, P.G. (1999), "Honouring 'one of the great forces of the Dominion': The Canadian public mourns McGee", *Canadian Geographer*, vol. 41, no. 4, 350-62.

Graves, J. (1849-51), "Ancient Street Architecture in Kilkenny", *Journal of the Royal Society of Antiquaries*, vol. 1, 41-47.

Gray, J. (1868), *The Church Establishment in Ireland – The Freeman's Journal Church Commission*, Dublin: James Duffy.

Greaves, R.L. (1992), *Secrets of the Kingdom: British Radicals from the Popish Plot to the Revolution of 1688-1689*, Stanford: Stanford University Press.

Green Ink Writers Group (1985), *Over Here, Over There*, London: Green Ink Writers.

Greene, W.C. (1944), *Moira: Fate, Good and Evil in Greek Thought*, Cambridge: Harvard University Press.

Greer, A. (1993), *The Patriots and the People. The Rebellion of 1837 in Rural Lower Canada*, Toronto: University of Toronto Press.

Haddon, A.C. (1893), "A Batch of Irish Folk-Lore", *Folk-Lore*, vol. 4, 348-64.

Hamilton, E. (1963), *An Irish Childhood*, London: Chatto and Windus.

Handcock, W.G. (1989), *Soe Longe as There Comes Noe Women: Origins of English Settlement in Newfoundland*, St John's, Newfoundland: Breakwater Books.

Handley, J.E. (1970), *The Navvy in Scotland*, Cork: Cork University Press.

Hardinge, W.H. (1862), "On Manuscript Mapped and other Townland Surveys in Ireland of a Public Character, Embracing the Gross, Civil and Down Surveys, from 1640 to 1688", *Transactions of the Royal Irish Academy*, vol. 24.

Harrison, A. (1999), *The Dean's Friend: Anthony Raymond 1675-1726, Jonathan Swift and the Irish Language*, Dublin: Caisleán an Bhúrcaigh.

Hart, P. (1996), "The Protestant Experience of Revolution in Southern Ireland" in English, R. and Walker, G. (eds.), *Unionism in Modern Ireland: New Perspectives on Politics and Culture*, Basingstoke: Macmillan, 81-98.

Harte, L. (2003a), "Irish Im/migrant Autobiography: Towards an Interdisciplinary Hermeneutics" in Longley, E., Hughes, E. and O'Rawe, D. (eds.), *Ireland (Ulster) Scotland: Concepts, Contexts, Comparisons*, Belfast: Cló Ollscoil na Banríona, 99-106.

Harte, L. (2003b),"'Somewhere Beyond England and Ireland': Narratives of Home in Second-Generation Irish Autobiography", *Irish Studies Review*, vol. 11, no .3, 293-305.

Harte, L. and Whelan, Y. (eds.) (2006), *Ireland Beyond Boundaries: Mapping Irish Studies in the Twenty-First Century*, London: Pluto Press.

Hayes, R.F. (1949), *Biographical Dictionary of Irishmen in France*, Dublin: M.H. Gill.

Heaney, M. (1994), *Over Nine Waves: A Book of Irish Legends*, London: Faber and Faber.

Heaney, S. (1966), *Death of a Naturalist*, London, Faber and Faber.

Heaney, S. (1989), *The Government of the Tongue: the 1986 T.S. Eliot Memorial Lectures and Other Critical Writings*, London: Faber and Faber.

Heaney, S. (1990), *The Cure at Troy*, London, Faber and Faber.

Hewitt, J. (1991), *The Collected Poems of John Hewitt*, ed. F. Ormsby, Belfast: Blackstaff Press.

Hickman, M.J. and Walter, B. (1997), *Discrimination and the Irish Community in Britain*, London: Commission for Racial Equality.

Hickman, M.J. (1999), "The Religio-Ethnic Identities of Teenagers of Irish Descent" in Hornsby-Smith, M.P. (ed.), *Catholics in England, 1950-2000: Historical and Sociological Perspectives*, London: Cassell, 182-98.

Hickman, M.J., Morgan, S. and Walter, B. (2001), *Second-Generation Irish People in Britain: a Demographic, Socio-Economic and Health Profile*, London: University of North London Press.

Hickman, M., Morgan, S., Walter, B. and Bradley, J. (2005), "The limitations of whiteness and the boundaries of Englishness: second-generation Irish identifications and positionings in multiethnic Britain", *Ethnicities*, vol. 5, no. 2, 160-82.

Hill, J. (1998), *Irish Public Sculpture: A History*, Dublin: Four Courts Press.

Hill, L. (1990), *Beckett's Fiction*, Cambridge: Cambridge University Press.

Hilliers, B. (1994), "The Heroes of the Ulster Cycle" in Mallory, J.P. and Stockman, G. (eds.), *Ulidia: Proceedings of the First International Conference on the Ulster Cycle of Tales*, Belfast: December Publications.

Hooke, N. (1760), *A Secret History of Colonel Hooke's Negotiations in Scotland, in Favour of the Pretender; in 1707 ... written by himself*, London.

Howarth, W. (1999), "Imagined Territory: The Writing of Wetlands", *New Literary History: Ecocriticism*, vol. 30, no. 3, 509-39.

Hutcheon, L. (1988), *A Poetics of Postmodernism: History, Theory, Fiction*, London: Routledge.

Hylland Eriksen, T. (1993), "Do cultural islands exist?", *Social Anthropology*, no. 1, http://folk.uio.no/geirthe/Culturalislands.html.

Hynes, S. (1992) [1976], *The Auden Generation: Literature and Politics in England in the 1930s*, London: Pimlico.

Jameson, F. (1991), *Postmodernism, or the Cultural Logic of Capitalism*, London: Verso.

Jeffery, K. (2000), *Ireland and the Great War*, Cambridge: Cambridge University Press.

Johnston-Liik, E.M. (2002), *History of the Irish Parliament 1692-1800: Commons, Constituencies and Statutes*, vol. 5, Belfast: Ulster Historical Foundation.

Joyce, J. (1966), *Letters of James Joyce*, vol. 2, ed. R. Ellmann, London: Faber and Faber.

Joyce, J. (1992a) [1914], *Dubliners*, ed. T. Brown, London: Penguin.

Joyce, J. (1992b) [1922], *Ulysses*, ed. D. Kiberd, London: Penguin.

Junker, M. (1995), *Beckett: The Irish Dimension*, Dublin: Wolfhound Press.

Jupp, J. (ed.) (2001), *The Australian People: an Encyclopedia of the Nation, its People and their Origins*, Cambridge: Cambridge University Press.

Kaplan, F. (1984), *Thomas Carlyle: a Biography*, Cambridge: Cambridge University Press.

Keane, J.B. (1953), *Self-Portrait*, Cork: Mercier Press.

Keane, J.B. (1993), *The Contractors*, Cork: Mercier Press.

Kearney, R. (1988), *Transitions: Narratives in Modern Irish Culture*, Manchester: Manchester University Press.

Keatinge, B. (2004), "The Divided Self in *Murphy*". Paper delivered at the Dublin Beckett Forum, Trinity College Dublin.

Keep, G.R.C. (1948), "The Irish Migration to Montreal". Unpublished MA thesis, McGill University.

Keep, G.R.C. (1950), "The Irish Adjustment in Montreal", *Canadian Historical Review*, 31-46.

Kelleher, M. (1999), "Late Nineteenth-Century Women's Fiction and the Land Agitation: Gender and Dis/Union". Paper presented at the "Ireland and the Union: Questions of Identity" SSNCI Conference, Bath Spa University College, 9 April.

Kilmainham Jail Restoration Society. (1961), *Kilmainham*, Dublin: Aston Colour Press.

Kinahan, G.H., (1881), "Notes on Irish Folk-Lore", *Folk-Lore Record*, vol. 4, 96-125.

King, S. (1999), '*As Long as I Know, It'll be Quite Alright*': The Life Stories of Lucan and McShane, Blackpool: Lancastrian Transport Publications.

Kinsella, T. (1970), *The Táin*, Oxford: Oxford University Press.

Kinsella, T. (1996a), *Collected Poems 1956-1994*, Oxford: Oxford University Press.

Kinsella, T. (1996b), *The Pen Shop*, Dublin: Peppercanister Press.

Klein, B. (2001), *Maps and the Writing of Space in Early Modern England and Ireland*, Basingstoke: Palgrave.

Knowlson, J. (1996), *Damned to Fame: The Life of Samuel Beckett*, London: Bloomsbury.

Kristeva, J. (1989), *Black Sun: Depression and Melancholia*, New York: Columbia University Press.

Landry, D. and MacLean, G. (eds.) (1993), *Materialist Feminisms*, Oxford: Blackwell.

Lawless, E. (1881), "An Upland Bog", *Belgravia* , vol. xlv, 417-30.

Lawless, E. (1992) [1886], *Hurrish*, Belfast: Appletree Press.

Leerssen, J. (1996), *Remembrance and Imagination*, Cork: Cork University Press.

Leonard, J. (1997), *Memorials to the Casualties of Conflict*, Belfast: Community Relations Council.

Longley, E. (1988), "MacNeice and After", *Poetry Review*, vol. 78, no. 2, 6-10.

Longley, E. (1991), "Northern Ireland: Commemoration, Elegy, Forgetting" in Ní Dhonnchadha, M. and Dorgan, T. (eds.), *Revising the Rising*, Derry: Field Day, 29-49.

Longley, E. (1996) [1988], *Louis MacNeice: A Critical Study*, London: Faber and Faber.

Longley, M. (1997) "Say Not Soft Things" in Lucy, G. and McClure, E. (eds.), *Remembrance*, Lurgan: Ulster Society.

Loughlin, J. (2002), "Mobilising the Sacred Dead: Ulster Unionism, the Great War and the Politics of Remembrance" in Gregory A. and Paseta, S. (eds.), *Ireland and the Great War: A War to Unite Us All?* Manchester: Manchester University Press, 133-54.

Lyons, F.S.L. (1982), *Culture and Anarchy in Ireland 1890-1939*, Oxford: Oxford University Press.

MacCarthy, D.F. (ed.), (1874) [1846], *The Book of Irish Ballads*, Dublin: Duffy.

MacCurtin, H. (1717), *A Brief Discourse in Vindication of the Antiquity of Ireland*, Dublin: S. Powell.

MacCurtin, H. (1728), *The Elements of the Irish Language, Grammatically Explained in English*, Louvain: Martin van Overbeke.

MacDonagh, O. (1996), *The Sharing of the Green: a Modern Irish History for Australians*, Sydney: Allen and Unwin.

Maclean, C. and Phillips, J. (1990), *The Sorrow and the Pride: New Zealand War Memorials*, Wellington: Historical Branch, Department of Internal Affairs.

MacNeice, L. (1935), "Some Notes on Mr Yeats' Plays", *New Verse*, vol. 18, 7-9.

MacNeice, L. (1936), "*Dramatis Personae* by W. B. Yeats", *Criterion* vol. 16, no. 62, 120-22.

MacNeice, L. (1938), *Modern Poetry: A Personal Essay*, Oxford: Oxford University Press.

MacNeice, L. (1940), *The Last Ditch*, Dublin: Cuala Press.

MacNeice, L. (1941), *Plant and Phantom*, London: Faber and Faber.

MacNeice, L. (1944), *Springboard: Poems 1941-1944*, London: Faber and Faber.

MacNeice, L. (1949), *Collected Poems 1925-1948*, London: Faber and Faber.

MacNeice, L. (1965), *The Strings are False: An Unfinished Autobiography*, ed. E.R. Dodds, London: Faber and Faber.

MacNeice, L. (1967) [1941], *The Poetry of W. B. Yeats*, London: Faber and Faber.

MacNeice, L. (1979) [1966], *Collected Poems*, ed. E.R. Dodds, London: Faber and Faber.

Macray, W.D. (ed.) (1870), *Correspondence of Colonel Nathaniel Hooke, Agent from the Court of France to the Scottish Jacobites, in ... 1703-1707*, 2 vols, Edinburgh: Roxeburgh Club.

Magnusson, M. and Pálsson, H. (trans.) (1960), *Njal's Saga*, London: Penguin.

Malcolm, E.L. (2001), "Two million landed in Liverpool in seven years", *Táin*, vol. 15, 11.

Massey, D. (1994), *Space, Place and Gender*, Cambridge: Polity Press.

Masson, F. (ed.) (1884), *Journal Inédit de Jean-Baptiste Colbert, Marquis de Torcy ... Pendant les Années 1709, 1710 et 1711*, Paris, Ollendorff.

McCann, E. (1974), *War and an Irish Town*, Harmondsworth: Penguin, 1974.

McClintock, A. (1995), *Imperial Leather: Race, Gender and Sexuality in the Colonial Contest*, London: Routledge.

McCool, J. and McDonnell, A. (1997), *One Better Day: A Profile of the Irish Tenants of Arlington House*, London: Bridge Housing Association.

McDonald, P. (1991), *Louis MacNeice: the Poet in his Contexts*, Oxford: Clarendon Press.

McGee, T.D. (1865), *Speeches and Addresses Chiefly on the Subject of British-American Union*, London, Chapman and Hall.

McGee, T.D. (1869), *A Popular History of Ireland from the Earliest Period to the Emancipation of the Catholics*, New York: Sadlier.

McGinn, B. (2003), "The Irish in the Caribbean" in Lalor, B. (ed.), *The Encyclopaedia of Ireland*, Dublin: Gill and Macmillan, 157-58.

McGuckian, M. (2003), *Had I A Thousand Lives*, Loughcrew: Gallery Press.

McKittrick, D., Kelters, S., Feeney, B. and Thornton, C. (1999), *Lost Lives: The Stories of the Men, Women and Children Who Died as a Result of the Northern Ireland Troubles*, Edinburgh: Mainstream.

McMahon, S. (ed.) (2002), *The Derry Anthology*, Belfast: Blackstaff.

McMinn, J. (1998), "The Gardener in the Deanery" in Freiburg, R., Löffler, A. and Zach, W. (eds.), *Swift, The Enigmatic Dean: Festschrift for Hermann Josef Real*, Tübingen: Stauffenburg, 127-35.

Mease, J. (1849-51), "Notes on the Castles in the Freshford District", *Journal of the Royal Society of Antiquaries*, vol. 1, 462-69.

Meir, C. (1990) "A Review of Seamus Heaney's *The Cure at Troy*", *The Linen Hall Review*, 12.

Miller, J. (1984), "The Potential for Absolutism in Later Stuart England" *History*, vol. 69, 187-207.

Milne, K. (1997), *The Irish Charter Schools, 1730-1830*, Dublin: Four Courts Press.

Moi, T. (1985), *Sexual/Textual Politics: Feminist Literary Theory*, London: Methuen.

Moorjani, A. (1996), "Mourning, Schopenhauer, and Beckett's Art of Shadows" in Oppenhiem, L. and Buning, M. (eds.), *Beckett On and On*, Madison: Fairleigh Dickinson University Press, 83-101.

Moretti, F. (2004), "Graphs, Maps, Trees: Abstract Models for Literary History", *New Left Review*, vol. 26, 79-103.

Morrison, B. (2003), *Things My Mother Never Told Me*, London: Vintage.

Mosse, G. (1990), *Fallen Soldiers: Reshaping the Memory of the World Wars*, Oxford: Oxford University Press.

Mulligan, W.H. (2004), "Teaching the Irish Diaspora: Thoughts and Reflections". Paper presented at the Joint Annual Conference of the American Conference for Irish Studies and the British Association for Irish Studies, Liverpool.

Munnelly, T. (1996), "Narrative Songs in West Clare" in Shields, H. (ed.), *Ballad Research: The Stranger in Ballad Narrative and Other Topics*, Dublin: Folk Music Society of Ireland, 35-48.

Naficy, H. (1999), "Framing Exile" in Naficy, H. (ed.), *Home, Exile, Homeland: Film, Media and the Politics of Place*, London: Routledge, 3-13.

Naficy, H. (2001), *An Accented Cinema*, New Jersey: Princeton University Press.

Nash, C. (2002), "Genealogical Identities", *Environment and Planning D: Society and Space*, vol. 20, 27-52.

Naughton, N. (2003), "God and the Good People: Folk Belief in a Traditional Community", *Béaloideas*, vol. 71, 13-53.

Ní Chuilleanáin, E. (2001), *The Girl Who Married the Reindeer*, Loughcrew: Gallery Press.

Nicolson, W. (1724), *The Irish Historical Library*, Dublin: Aaron Rhames.

Nolan, E. (1995), *Joyce and Nationalism*, London: Routledge.

Nolte, W.M. (1975), "The Irish in Canada 1815-1867". Unpublished PhD thesis, University of Maryland.

Ó Broin, L. (1967), *Charles Gavan Duffy: Patriot and Statesman*, Dublin: James Duffy.

Ó Giolláin, D. (1991), "The Fairy Belief and Official Religion in Ireland" in Narváez, P. (ed.), *The Good People: New Fairylore Essays*, New York: Garland Publishing, 199-214.

Ó Giolláin, D. (1999), "The Pattern" in Donnelly, J.S. and Miller, K.A. (eds.), *Irish Popular Culture, 1650-1850*, Dublin: Irish Academic Press, 201-21.

O'Brien, C.C. (1972), *States of Ireland*, London: Hutchinson.

O'Brien, H.P. (1983), "Irishmen in London". Unpublished memoir, Archive of the Irish in Britain.

O'Brien, E. (1986), *The Beckett Country*, Dublin: Black Cat Press.

O'Brien, K. (2001), "The History Market in Eighteenth-Century England" in Rivers, I. (ed.), *Books and Their Readers in Eighteenth-Century England: New Essays*, London: Continuum, 105-33.

O'Boyle, S. (1976), *The Irish Song Tradition*, Dublin: Gilbert Dalton.

O'Callaghan, J.C. (1870), *History of the Irish Brigades in the Service of France from the Revolution in Great Britain and Ireland under James II to the Revolution in France under Louis XVI*, Glasgow, Cameron and Ferguson.

O'Connor, N. (1991), *Bringing it All Back Home*, London: BBC Books.

O'Flanagan, M. (ed.) (1927a), *Letters Containing Information Relative to the Antiquities of the County of Roscommon Collected During the Progress of the Ordnance Survey in 1837*, Bray: R.I.A. Typescript.

O'Flanagan, M. (ed.) (1927b), *Letters Containing Information Relative to the Antiquities of the County of Wexford Collected During the Progress of the Ordnance Survey in 1840*, Bray: N.L.I. Typescript.

O'Flanagan, M. (ed.) (1935), *Letters Containing Information Relative to the Antiquities of the County of Kerry Collected During the Progress of the Ordnance Survey in 1841*, Bray: R.I.A. Typescript.

O'Grady, T. and Pyke, S. (1997), *I Could Read the Sky*, London: Harvill Press.

O'Hanlon, J. (c.1875), *Lives of the Irish Saints*, Dublin: James Duffy and Sons.

O'Sullivan, P. (1991), "Patrick MacGill: the Making of a Writer" in Hutton, S. and Stewart. P. (eds.), *Ireland's Histories: Aspects of State, Society and Ideology*, London: Routledge, 203-22.

O'Sullivan, P. (2003), "Developing Irish Diaspora Studies: a Personal View", *New Hibernia Review*, vol. 7, no. 1, 130-48.

Ottaway, C. (1999), "Immigrants' Stories Tell of an Ireland Past", *Times Union*, 9 March.

Pascal, B. (1995) [1670] *Pensées and Other Writings*, trans. H. Levi, Oxford: Oxford University Press.

Passarini, L. (1987), *Fascism in Popular Memory*, Cambridge: Cambridge University Press.

Pearl, C. (1979), *The Three Lives of Gavan Duffy*, Sydney: New South Wales University Press.

Philips, J. (1985), "Distance, Absence and Nostalgia" in Ihde, D. and Silverman, H. (eds.), *Descriptions*, Albany: State of New York University Press, 64-75.

Philo, C. (2000), "The Birth of the Clinic: an Unknown Work of Medical Geography", *Area*, vol. 32, no. 1, 11-19.

Pieterse, J.N. (2001), "Hybridity, So What? The Anti-Hybridity Backlash and Riddles of Recognition", *Theory, Culture & Society*, vol. 18, nos. 2 and 3, 219-45.

Platt, l. (1998), *Joyce and the Anglo-Irish: A Study of Joyce and the Literary Revival*, Amsterdam: Rodopi.

Porter, J. (2001), *A Testimony to Courage: The Regimental History of the Ulster Defence Regiment*, Barnsley: Leo Cooper.

Reeves, W. (1859), *Memoir of the Church of St. Duilech, in the Diocese of Dublin*, Dublin: M. H. Gill.

Richardson, J. (1712), *A Short History of the Attempts that have been Made to Convert the Popish Natives of Ireland to the Establish'd Religion: with a Proposal for their Conversion*, London: Joseph Downing.

Rolston, B. (1991), *Politics and Painting: Murals and Conflict in Northern Ireland*, Cranbury, NJ: Associated University Presses.

Royle, S.A. (2001), *A Geography of Islands. Small Island Insularity*, London: Methuen.

Ryder, C. (1992), *The Ulster Defence Regiment: An Instrument of Peace?*, London: Mandarin.

Ryder, C. (2000), *The RUC: A Force Under Fire 1922-2000*, London: Arrow.

Said, E. (1991) [1978], *Orientalism*, London: Penguin.

Sands, B. (1983), *One Day in My Life*, Dublin: Mercier Press.

Sands, B. (1998), *Writings from Prison*, Cork: Mercier Press.

Sharkey, S. (1997), "A View of the Present State of Irish Studies" in Bassnett, S. (ed.), *Studying British Cultures: an Introduction*, London, Routledge.

Shaw, F. (1991) [1972], "The Canon of Irish History – A Challenge" in Deane, S. (ed.), *The Field Day Anthology of Irish Writing*, Derry: Field Day, vol.3, 590-95.

Smith, A.D. (1999), *Myths and Memories of Nation*, Oxford: Oxford University Press.

Smith, S. (1994), "Persuasions to Rejoice: Auden's Oedipal Dialogues with W.B. Yeats" in Bucknell, K. and Jenkins, N. (eds.), *W.H. Auden: 'The Language of Leaning and the Language of Love': Uncollected Writings, New Interpretations*, Oxford: Clarendon Press, 155-63.

Smith, S.B. (1979), *Sherca. After Sophocles' Philoctetes*, Newark, Delaware: Proscenium Press.

Smyth, G. (2001), *Space and the Irish Cultural Imagination*, Basingstoke: Palgrave.

Somerville, E. and Ross, M. (1891), *Naboth's Vineyard*, London: Spencer Blackett.

Somerville, E. and Ross, M. (1917), *Irish Memories*, London: Longmans.

Sophocles. (1998), *Sophocles' Philoctetes*, trans. D. Egan, Newbridge: Goldsmith Press.

Stallworthy, J. (1995) *Louis MacNeice*, London: Faber and Faber.

Stephen, L. and Lee, S. (eds.) (1885-1901), *Dictionary of National Biography*, 63 vols., London: Smith and Elder.

Stewart, A.T.Q. (1967), *The Ulster Crisis: Resistance to Home Rule, 1912-14*, London: Faber and Faber.

Sullivan, A. M. (1898) [1867], *Story of Ireland*, Dublin: Gill.

Sullivan, D. (1983), *Navvyman*, London: Coracle Books.

Sunday Times Insight Team. (1972), *Ulster*, Harmondsworth: Penguin.

Swift, J. (1965), *The Prose Works of Jonathan Swift XI*, ed. H. Davis, Oxford: Basil Blackwell.

Swift, J. (1968), *The Prose Works of Jonathan Swift IX*, ed. H. Davis, Oxford: Basil Blackwell.

Swift, J. (1971), *The Prose Works of Jonathan Swift XII*, ed. H. Davis, Oxford: Basil Blackwell.

Swift, J. (1973), *The Prose Works of Jonathan Swift IV*, ed. H. Davis, Oxford: Basil Blackwell.

Thomson, D. (1983), *In Camden Town*, London: Hutchinson.

Tóibín, C. (1996), "Playboys of the GPO", *London Review of Books*, 18 April, 14-16.

Tymoczko, M. (1994), *The Irish Ulysses*, Berkeley: University of California Press.

Wakeling, P. (1984), "Looking at Beckett – The Man and the Writer", *Irish University Review*, vol. 14, no. 1, 5-17.

Walker, J. (1948), "English Exiles in Holland During the Reigns of Charles II and James II", *Transactions of the Royal Historical Society*, 5th series, vol. 30, 111-25.

Walsh, J. (2000), *The Falling Angels: An Irish Romance*, London: Flamingo.

Walter, B. (1988), *Irish Women in London*, London: London Strategic Policy Unit.

Walter, B. (2001), *Outsiders Inside: Whiteness, Place and Irish Women*, London: Routledge.

Walter, B., Morgan, S., Hickman M.J. and Bradley, J. (2002), "Family Stories, Public Silence: Identity Construction Amongst the Second-Generation Irish in England", *Scottish Geographical Magazine*, vol. 118, 201-17.

Walter, B. (2004a), "Invisible Irishness: Second-Generation Identities in Britain", *AEMI Journal*, vol. 2, 185-93.

Walter, B. (2004b), "Irish Domestic Servants and English National Identity" in Fauve-Chamoux, A. and Sarti, R. (eds.), *Domestic Service and the Formation of European Identity: Understanding the Globalization of Domestic Work*, Bern: Peter Lang, 428-45.

Whelan, Y. (2003a), *Reinventing Modern Dublin: Streetscape, Iconography and the Politics of Identity*, Dublin: University College Dublin Press.

Whelan, Y. (2003b), "Decoding Symbolic Spaces of Dublin: A Photographic Essay", *Canadian Journal of Irish Studies*, vol. 28/29, no. 2/1, 46-73.

Williams, R. (1993), "Can Data on Scottish Catholics Tell Us About Descendents of the Irish in Scotland?", *New Community*, vol. 19, no. 2, 296-309.

Williams, W.H.A. (1996), *'Twas Only an Irishman's Dream*, Urbana: University of Illinois Press.

Wilson, D.A. (1925), *Carlyle on Cromwell and Others, 1837-48*, London: Kegan Paul.

Wilson, E. (1941), "The Wound and the Bow" in Wilson, E. (ed.), *The Wound and the Bow. Seven Studies in Literature*, Cambridge: Houghton Mifflin, 244-54.

Winter, J. (1995), *Sites of Memory, Sites of Mourning: The Great War in European Cultural History*, Cambridge, Cambridge University Press.

Woods, P. (2003), *Hard Shoulder*, Dublin: New Island.

Wyse Jackson, J. and Costello, P. (1997), *John Stanislaus Joyce: The Voluminous Life and Genius of James Joyce's Father*, London: Fourth Estate.

Yeats, W.B. (ed.) (1936), *The Oxford Book of Modern Verse*, Oxford: Clarendon Press.

Yeats, W.B. (1997), *The Major Works*, ed. E. Larrissy, Oxford: Oxford University Press.

Zeiger, M.F. (1997), *Beyond Consolation: Death, Sexuality, and the Changing Shapes of Elegy*, Ithaca: Cornell University Press.

Zook, M.S. (1999), *Radical Whigs and Conspiratorial Politics in Late Stuart England*, Pennsylvania: Pennsylvania University Press.

Index